Freud on Femininity and Faith

Freud

on Femininity and Faith

Judith Van Herik

University of California Press

Berkeley • Los Angeles • London

University of California Press
Berkeley and Los Angeles, California

University of California Press, Ltd.
London, England

BF
173
.F85
V26
1982

Library of Congress Cataloging in Publication Data

Van Herik, Judith.
　Freud on femininity and faith.

　Bibliography p.
　Includes index.
　1. Freud, Sigmund, 1856-1939.　2. Religion and
psychoanalysis.　3. Femininity (Psychology)
4. Masculinity (Psychology)　5. Self-realization.
6. Renunciation (Philosophy)　I. Title.
BF173.F85V26　　　　155.3'33'0924　81-3413
ISBN 0-520-04368-5　　　　　　AACR2

to

Gary T. Alexander

and

Caroline Walker Bynum

Contents

Acknowledgments

Treatment of a body of work as complex and open to multiple interpretations as is Freud's risks inappropriate emphasis. One risk is that of stressing the interpreter's themes to the detriment of the rich detail of Freud's texts. Another is burial of these themes in the contextual particulars that give them their meaning. In sketching inner relationships among three aspects of Freud's thought—gender, religion, and criticism—my choice has been to stroke thick, dark lines, to place in sharp relief their patterning. I have accented figure but not, I hope, to the unwarranted muting of ground.

Several institutions and many persons have helped me during the stages of research, pondering, writing, and preparation for publication. In 1974–1975, when I was beginning to formulate my questions, the Harvard Divinity School gave me the opportunity, as a Research/Resource Associate in Women's Studies, to teach a course related to them. In 1978, the Women's Caucus and Divinity School of the University of Chicago provided an occasion for me to present and discuss my theses with a group of vital and informed critics. The Pennsylvania State University Institute for the Arts and Humanistic Studies awarded me a research fellowship which released me from teaching a course, allowing me to begin revisions for publication. The Pennsylvania State University Liberal Arts Research Office, through Thomas F. Magner, provided funds for typing and for some permissions fees. The Department of Religious Studies at Penn State was generous with the competent clerical support of Cathy Thompson and Sandi Lucas. The institution to which I owe most is the University of Chicago, and particularly the Divinity School, for the intellectual guidance which made possible the earliest draft of this work.

In Chicago and Pennsylvania, friends and colleagues have contributed advice, information, and challenging comments. Anne E. Carr, Donald N. Levine, Isabel Knight, Kathryn Hume, and Judith Milhous read the whole and made valuable suggestions; Don Levine also introduced me to Georg Simmel's writings on what is now called "gender." Margaret Allen Peters, Beth Glazier-McDonald, and Ernest B. Lowrie called my attention to passages that became epigraphs. Marylee C. Taylor alerted me to methodological unclarity. Over the years, John L. Cella has identified and provided me with numerous relevant books. Nancy Wilkinson has twice been an exceptional proofreader. Carol Brown and Debra Greene have done excellent typing. Sheila Levine at the University of California Press has been a pleasure to work with in transforming this from manuscript to book.

Peter Homans, who taught me to read Freud, often took time away from his own work to consider mine, particularly in its early stages. So have Gary T. Alexander and Caroline Walker Bynum who, through their friendship and their scholarship, have given me so much that I dedicate this to them.

It is true, as is often said, that none of those who has helped me is responsible for the problems that remain.

Permissions Acknowledgments

Passages from *The Standard Edition of the Complete Psychological Works of Sigmund Freud*, translated and edited by James Strachey, are reprinted by permission from Sigmund Freud Copyrights Limited, the Institute of Psycho-Analysis, and the Hogarth Press Limited.

Passages from *Thomas Woodrow Wilson: Twenty-Eighth President of the United States*, by Sigmund Freud and William C. Bullitt, copyright © 1966 by Sigmund Freud Copyrights Limited and William C. Bullitt, are reprinted by permission of the publisher, Houghton Mifflin Company, and Sigmund Freud Copyrights Limited.

Passages from *The Future of an Illusion* by Sigmund Freud, translated by James Strachey, are reprinted by permission of W. W. Norton & Company, Inc. Copyright © 1961 by James Strachey.

Passages from *New Introductory Lectures on Psychoanalysis*, translated and edited by James Strachey, are reprinted by permission of W. W. Norton & Company, Inc. Copyright © 1965, 1964 by James Strachey. Copyright 1933 by Sigmund Freud. Copyright renewed 1961 by W. J. H. Sprott.

Passages from *An Outline of Psycho-Analysis* by Sigmund Freud, translated and edited by James Strachey, are reprinted by permission of W. W. Norton & Company, Inc. Copyright 1949 by W. W. Norton & Company, Inc. Copyright © 1969 by the Institute of Psycho-Analysis and Alix Strachey.

Passages from *Moses and Monotheism* by Sigmund Freud, copyright © 1939 by Sigmund Freud, are reprinted by permission of Alfred A. Knopf, Inc.

Passages from essays in *Philosophische Kultur* by Georg Simmel as translated in "The Flight from Womanhood: The Masculinity-Complex in Women as Viewed by Men and Women" by Karen Horney, in her *Feminine Psychology*, edited by Harold Kelman, copyright © 1967, are reprinted by permission from W. W. Norton & Company.

Poem no. 745, "Renunciation—is a piercing Virtue—" by Emily Dickinson, copyright © 1929 by Martha Dickinson Bianchi, copyright © 1957 by Mary L. Hampson, is reprinted by permission of the publishers and the trustees of Amherst College from *The Complete Poems of Emily Dickinson*, edited by Thomas H. Johnson, Cambridge, Mass.: The Belknap Press of Harvard University Press, copyright © 1951, 1955, 1979 by the President and Fellows of Harvard College; and by permission of Little, Brown and Company.

Diagrams from "On Freud and the Distinction Between the Sexes" by Juliet Mitchell in *Women and Analysis: Dialogues on Psychoanalytic Views of Femininity*, edited by Jean Strouse, copyright © 1974, are reprinted by permission of Viking Penguin Inc.

Note on Abbreviations

References to books and papers in *The Standard Edition of the Complete Psychological Works of Sigmund Freud*, translated and edited by James Strachey in collaboration with Anna Freud, assisted by Alix Strachey and Alan Tyson, 24 vols. (London: The Hogarth Press and the Institute of Psycho-Analysis, 1953-1974), are given by title and date of publication, followed by *SE*, volume, and page number(s).

Introduction

"As a woman, for God's sake, Frances, . . . surely you object?"

"Well, sort of," said Frances. The problem with Hugh was that he really was quite well aware of the feminist arguments against Freudian faith. . . . And she herself was also rather confused about Freud's view of women. While not quite able to accept the theory of penis envy, she was more and more convinced that . . . the only possibility of happiness and harmlessness on earth were to be found where Freud would have us find them, and that there was no point in being reasonable, life wasn't reasonable, motives weren't very mixed, they were horribly pure, appallingly unmixed, life wasn't at all complex, it was truly of an unfair, terrifying, rigid, irreducible, wicked, amoral simplicity. One just couldn't accept the simplicity. It was almost improper to accept it. She could see Hugh's point. . . . "It's like religion. I object but I believe," she said. "Because that's how it is."
—MARGARET DRABBLE, *The Realms of Gold*

This study argues that Freud's theories of gender (mental femininity and masculinity) and of religion are internally related. It examines the nature of the relationship and suggests some of its implications. It is an interpretation of Freud's thought through his texts.

Several kinds of studies could conceivably examine this relationship, so it is wise to be straightforward at the outset about the purpose of this one. It is not to discredit either of these parts of Freud's thought, both of which have been widely criticized. Nor is it to repeat these criticisms, although I refer to them when relevant. Neither do I read the clinical portions of Freud's writings as a clinician would, for I am not a clinician. I do examine Freud's views on how religiosity and gender "identity" are psychologically or culturally valuable, but I make no claims in these domains myself.

In ways that will become clear, I find Freud's thought intellectually valuable; my concern is with its challenges when read as a theory of culture more than with its clinical utility. Because Freudianism, if not Freud, has been so influential in America, it is important to continue to return to his writings. My interest is in the theoretical texture of his texts. My purpose is to understand the critical direction of his thought about religion as it is revealed by examination of internal links between his theories of religion and gender. It is methodologically interesting to read Freud's theory of religion through his theory of gender because these two parts of his thought have often been set aside as erroneous, offensive, or both, without study of their consistency with each other or with the critical direction of his psychoanalytic texts as a whole. But this direction is clearly visible in these two frequently discarded Freudian inquiries. I intend to show that Freud's theory of gender is inseparable from the critical claims of the whole of his thought and from his critique of religion in particular. I argue, in terms explained in Chapter 2, that if Freud's is a gender-asymmetrical theory, this asymmetrical structure is also basic to his understanding of the value of religion as part of culture.

It is substantively interesting to read Freud's theory of religion through his theory of gender because doing so reveals previously unnoticed critical components of the theory of religion, particularly of *Moses and Monotheism*, which, in this reading, emerges as an implicit defense of Judaism. By relating gender and criticism in Freud's thought, one can discover ways in which Freud discerned similar mental structures in (a) femininity and Christian "illusion"; (b) masculinity and Jewish renunciation of wish; and (c) the human ideal (which is the masculine ideal) and the postreligious, psychoanalytic "scientific attitude." One can see that these three groups constitute a critical hierarchy so that, for Freud, Christianity and femininity are least valuable psychologically and culturally and the scientific attitude of ideal masculinity is the most valuable.

Because this book is an interpretive inquiry into the structure of Freud's thought, insofar as it offers grounds for criticizing this structure or for constructing a revised version, these grounds are what Freud called "secondary gains." The intention of this interpretation is to show how diverse parts of Freud's writings fit together into a message about the related inner meanings of patricentric culture, psychological gender, and religious belief.

The guiding questions with which I read Freud include the following. What difference does Freud's diagnosis of femininity as less valuable than masculinity make in the rest of his theory? How are patricentrality and criticism related in the Freudian texts? How does his theory of the asymmetrical genders inform his psychoanalytic criticism of an issue that at first glance appears to be irrelevant to gender distinction, that is, mental relationships to God? My primary interest, then, is not in what is correct or incorrect in Freud's views of femininity and masculinity but in the critical weight these views have.

This interest was encouraged by a passage in Philip Rieff's monumental *Freud: The Mind of the Moralist*, which reads, in part:

> A denial of the Freudian psychology of women cannot depend on historical reductions of Freud's own psychology. It is not enough to say that Freud himself reproduced the "masculine protest" characteristic of his time and place. His misogyny, like that of his predecessors, is more than prejudice; it has a vital intellectual function in his system. In the nineteenth century strong links, the forging of which has not yet been closely studied, existed between irrationalist philosophy and misogyny. . . . [A]ctually the pejorative image of women serves as a measure of the general critical component in Western philosophies.[1]

This study is about the intellectual functions of Freud's misogyny. It examines how Freud's theory of gender difference *is* a measure of the critical component of his general theory and of his theory of religion in particular. The measure of misogyny has two poles: the negative qualities of femininity and the positive qualities of masculinity. Specifically, I relate femininity and masculinity to two crucial categories in Freud's thought: fulfillment and renunciation of wish.

The question of how gender asymmetry measures criticism within a theory is informed by feminist questions and scholarship, scholarship both on gender as distinguished from sex and on gender asymmetry in psyche and society. My conclusions, however, are not particularly feminist or antifemin-

---

1. Philip Rieff, *Freud: The Mind of the Moralist* (1961), pp. 200-201 (all page references are to the 1961 edition). Discussions abound which limit themselves to attributing Freud's views on women to personal or cultural bias without recognizing their critical function. For example, see Erich Fromm, *Sigmund Freud's Mission: An Analysis of His Personality and Influence* (1959). See Karen Horney, "The Flight from Womanhood" (1967), for her discussion of cultural bias in Freud's psychology of women. Those who still either excuse or indict Freud for inserting the passive Victorian woman, supposedly the only type he encountered, directly into his theories, might examine two descriptions of the character of his mother, Amalie Freud. Writing about his grandmother (Sigmund's mother), Martin Freud commented that she had "great vitality," much impatience, a great "hunger for life," an "indomitable spirit." "Nobody," writes Martin, "envied Aunt Dolfi, whose destiny it was to dedicate her life to the care of an old mother who was a tornado"; *Glory Reflected: Sigmund Freud, Man and Father* (1957), p. 11. One of Freud's nieces, Judith Bernays Heller, describes her maternal grandmother as volatile and strong-willed. "She was charming and smiling when strangers were about, but I, at least, always felt that with familiars she was a tyrant, and a selfish one. Quite definitely, she had a strong personality and knew what she wanted . . ."; "Freud's Mother and Father: A Memoir" (1956), p. 420.

ist; they are claims about the critical structure of Freud's thought rather than about desirable or just situations for women.

This inquiry is related to a large and elusive question, which is whether and how particular categories of thought by which religious and psychological phenomena are understood are implicitly or explicitly rooted in, or reflective of, evaluative understandings of gender difference. Several trends in the sociology of knowledge and in feminist scholarship converge on one principle of interpretation: that "existential factors," such as class and, for our purposes, gender, influence thought. How they do so and how one can show that they do so are far from settled questions even for a particular instance. But from a feminist viewpoint, it is important to undertake studies that bear on the question of whether women's experiences and points of view, if they are different from men's, have been simply omitted from an otherwise gender-neutral cultural tradition. If this is the case, the increased presence of women in previously male domains, and of men in previously female domains, would solve the problem of the equality of the sexes. But if a graver hypothesis gains support, the hypothesis that gender differentiation is so deeply rooted in culture that social differentiation of supposedly sex-appropriate activities is dialectically related to androcentry in our very categories of thought, then a feminist position must call for a transformation of the mental bases of culture and not just a redistribution of functions, or it must see a redistribution of functions as but part of a transformation of the mental bases of culture. One precondition for addressing this question on the level of theory is to study a theorist who, like Freud, distinguishes sex and gender, who has a theory of gender difference, and who also has a theory of the mental bases of culture in order to see whether the latter is separable from the former. One must see clearly whether and how an androcentric bias (gender asymmetry) spreads throughout the categories of a theory before one goes about constructing either a gender-symmetrical or a "femininely" weighted theory. The present study is this prior kind of undertaking. Its conclusions, as I have said, are not feminist in the political sense of calling for alternatives to gender asymmetry in psyches, in society, or in theory. They are related claims about the relationships between Freud's asymmetrical theory of the genders, the patricentrality of his theory of culture, his critical principle (which I call the renunciation of illusion), and his psychologies of Christianity and Judaism. I understand this inquiry methodologically as a contribution to feminist scholarship, but substantively it is intended to contribute to Freud scholarship in general and to scholarship on his psychoanalytic theory of religion in particular. These, of course, are not mutually exclusive.

The argument takes place in the following steps. First, I show how in Freud's theory as a whole, renunciations of wishes are seen as the source of higher (later and more valuable) mental and cultural achievements. Reality principle thinking, a moral sense, a cultural achievement, and the scientific attitude are traced to renunciations. Conversely, Freud sees fulfillments of wishes as mitigating against such achievements. Second, I show that in Freud's theory the development of mental masculinity occurs through a series of renunciations of attachments, particularly of attachments to fathers and their representatives or functional equivalents, whereas the development of femininity entails achieving a mental position from which fulfillments are received from paternal figures. The figure of the father is Freud's referent for masculine renunciation and feminine fulfillment. Third, I trace the way Freud draws on his views of wish-fulfilling and renunciatory processes to define and evaluate religious belief psychoanalytically, particularly in *The Future of an Illusion*, in which religion is criticized as wish fulfillment, and in *Moses and Monotheism*, in which the Mosaic tradition is presented as renunciatory. I argue, then, that Freud's theory of gender difference measures thoroughgoing evaluative themes within his psychoanalytic thought as a whole: renunciation and fulfillment of wish. I further argue that Freud's criticism of religion can better be understood in terms of the theoretical relationships between masculinity and renunciation, on the one hand, and femininity and fulfillment, on the other, as these relationships were already implicitly drawn within Freud's writings.

Part 1 sets the scholarly and conceptual context for this reading of Freud. Chapter 1 locates my questions within previous scholarship that views Freud's texts as offering a theory of culture; introduces the key terms, "renunciation," "fulfillment," "masculinity," and "femininity"; and briefly examines how selected scholars have treated the renunciation-fulfillment ambiguity in Freud's theory of religion. Chapter 2 explains the two major external categories that I bring to this reading of Freud, criticism and gender asymmetry. Chapter 3 is about what kind of theory Freud's psychoanalysis is; it presents Freud's and others' views on the subject and methods of psychoanalysis in terms of the domains of biology, psychology, and culture.

Part 2 addresses the internal relationships between masculinity and renunciation in Freud's thought. Chapter 4 presents Freud's "moral economy," that is, his economic claims about wish and reality, primary and secondary processes and narcissism and object love which constitute a critical claim about the mental value of renunciation over against fulfillment. Chapter 5 shows how this moral economy works in Freud's discussions of the superiority of science to religion, the stages of cultural development, and the moral and the healthy character. Chapter 6 examines how Freud understands the development of masculinity as a renunciatory process, so that the masculine, cultural, and psychological "ideal types" coincide.

Part 3 discusses relationships between femininity and fulfillment within Freudian theory. Chapter 7 examines ways in which femininity is bound to fulfillment in Freud's view. It then discusses the distinction between sex and gender in general and in Freud, arguing that Freud developed a theory of gender, not sex, difference. Chapter 8 presents the contents of Freud's theory of femininity as it is asymmetrical to masculinity and explains how this theory may be understood as a critique of femininity.

Part 4 applies the categories of renunciation and masculinity and fulfillment and femininity to Freud's theory of religion in a rereading of *The Future of an Illusion* and *Moses and Monotheism*. Chapter 9 discusses Freud's psychology of religion in general and the place of these two books within it. Chapter 10 reads *The Future of an Illusion* in terms of femininity and fulfillment; Chapter 11 reads *Moses and Monotheism* in terms of masculinity and renunciation.

Chapter 12 integrates the relationships that have been traced between Freud's critical principle, his theory of the asymmetrical genders, and his claims about mental relationships to God. In it, I summarize my argument and suggest its implications.

PART ONE

Body, Mind, and Culture

Chapter 1

The Problem and Its Context

[Freud] said, "My discoveries are not primarily a heal-all. My discoveries are a basis for a very grave philosophy. There are very few who understand this; there are very few who are capable of understanding this."
—HD, *Tribute to Freud*

Freud as a Critical Theorist of Culture

Freud said this in 1933 or 1934. Since then, many have spelled out their views of the contents and adequacy of the grave philosophy which they find based in his texts. Yet Freud by no means considered himself a philosopher, nor did he respect what he understood philosophy to do. It clings to the "illusion of being able to present a picture of the universe which is without gaps and coherent. . . . It goes astray . . . by over-estimating the epistemological value of our logical operations, . . ." he charged.[1] Freud saw himself, in contrast, as a careful observer of mental phenomena, an empirical discoverer of the unconscious and its laws. The unconscious is a piece of nature, so he named psychoanalysis a natural science. He was fond of castigating the "majority of philosophers" for treating as a contradiction in terms his psychoanalytic discovery that the psychical is itself unconscious. "Whereas the psychology of consciousness never went beyond the broken sequences which were obviously dependent on something else, the other view, which held that the psychical is unconscious in itself, enabled psychology to take its place as a natural science like any other," he claimed.[2] Is psychoanalysis best understood as a natural science, a social science, an ersatz philosophy, a theory of culture? There are precedents for reading his texts as a theory of culture, and interpretive gains in doing so.

1. "The Question of a *Weltanschauung*," Lecture 35 of *New Introductory Lectures on Psycho-Analysis* (1933), SE 22:160-161.
2. *An Outline of Psycho-Analysis* (1940), SE 23:158.

9

Many responsible expositions of the contents of Freud's writings exist and this study does not provide another summary of the whole.[3] But critical studies and interpretations diverge widely, both in the parts of Freud's theories that they emphasize and in the implications that they draw from them. Arguments have been made that Freud's thought is politically conservative, liberal, or radical; innocent of sociology or profoundly sociological in its basic concepts; valid only for late Victorian Viennese or universally applicable; expressive of a mechanistic or scientistic world view or profoundly humanistic in its major intentions. Freud has been seen as an Enlightenment rationalist, a romantic, a cryptomystic, a cryptobiologist, a dualist, a dialectical thinker, an apologist for the status quo, an "unmasker" in the tradition of Marx and Nietzsche.[4]

Although this work addresses Freud's texts rather than those of his critics, followers, or interpreters, its treatment of these texts has been guided by some of their major interpreters. In particular, interpretations by Philip Rieff, Paul Ricoeur, Peter Homans, Norman O. Brown, Herbert Marcuse, and Octave Mannoni (who draws heavily on the thought of Jacques Lacan) have drawn attention away from arguments about whether and to what degree Freud was a mechanistic or a humanistic theorist of personality by showing that the Freudian texts advance a psychoanalytic theory of culture.[5]

3. For example, Ernest Jones, *The Life and Work of Sigmund Freud* (1953-1957); Henri Ellenberger, *The Discovery of the Unconscious: The History and Evolution of Dynamic Psychiatry* (New York: Basic Books, 1970), Chap. 7; Marthe Robert, *The Psychoanalytic Revolution: Sigmund Freud's Life and Achievement*, trans. Kenneth Morgan (London: George Allen & Unwin, 1966; New York: Avon Books, Discus edition, 1968); Max Schur, *Freud: Living and Dying* (New York: International Universities Press, 1972); David Stafford-Clark, *What Freud Really Said* (New York: Schocken Books, 1971); Robert Waelder, *Basic Theory of Psychoanalysis* (New York: International Universities Press, 1960); Dieter Wyss, *Depth Psychology: A Critical History: Development, Problems, Crises*, trans. Gerald Onn (New York: Norton, 1966). Of course, expositors also interpret; Jones, Ellenberger and Robert clearly do so.

4. For a discussion of these and other strains in and sources of Freud's thought, see Ellenberger, *Discovery of the Unconscious*, pp. 534-546; also Paul A. Robinson, *The Freudian Left* (1969), pp. 1-7.

5. Philip Rieff, *Freud: The Mind of the Moralist* (1961) and his *The Triumph of the Therapeutic: Uses of Faith After Freud* (New York: Harper & Row, 1966; Torchbook edition, 1968); Paul Ricoeur, *Freud and Philosophy* (1970); Peter Homans, *Theology After Freud* (1970); Norman O. Brown, *Life Against Death* (1959); Herbert Marcuse, *Eros and Civilization* (1962); O[ctave] Mannoni, *Freud* (1971); Jacques Lacan, *The Language of the Self* (1968) and his *The Four Fundamental Concepts of Psycho-Analysis* (1978). For a discussion of mechanistic and humanistic images of the person in Freud's thought, see Robert Holt, "On Reading Freud," Introduction to *Abstracts of the Standard Edition of the Complete Psychological Works of Sigmund Freud*, ed. Carrie Lee Rothgeb (New York: Jason Aronson, 1973). The argument between mechanistic

Despite great variety in the uses which these interpreters find for Freudian theory, all would probably agree with the characterization of the core of Freud's theory of culture as summarized by Jack Jones:

> the most important contribution of Freudianism has been and remains its para-artistic but "scientific" insight into the past and continuing *contradiction* between natural and cultural reality. In the last, in the acculturated consciousness, there is always the factor of *repression*: there must be excluded some aspect or degree of natural-biopsychology. The idea of repression, Freud himself insisted, was "the most essential part" of psychoanalysis. Almost as important . . . is Freud's belief that the contradiction between nature and culture has steadily worsened in the course of cultural evolution.[6]

Jones's view is that these two theses, contradiction between nature and culture and a progressive increase in contradiction, are those in the Freudian corpus that are still valid. Whatever one's position on their validity, they make Freudian thought a theory of culture. Further, Freud's emphasis on contradiction between nature and culture situates him as a critic of culture but one who emphasizes the necessity of both terms.

Rieff contrasts Freud with Dewey to argue that Freud locates his critical principle in human nature whereas Dewey locates his in society: "by their very existence, the [Freudian] instincts serve notice of the inadequacies of all social arrangements," he writes.[7] Rieff insists that Freud's psychological theory, his natural science, is simultaneously a social science. "To have a psychology at all requires, I believe, an understanding of the mind in terms of social and moral behavior," he writes.[8] He argues that because Freud "treated the psyche . . . largely as the theater for conflicts taking place in the external, social world—in character development and family relations," Freud's theory separates psychology from natural science.[9] Freud's idea of the self is that it is a moral agent, which is "the subject of a struggle be-

---

and humanistic readings has been recast in terms of Freud as biologist or psychologist by Frank J. Sulloway in *Freud: Biologist of the Mind* (1979), in which Sulloway presents Freud as a "cryptobiologist." Freud's biological point of view is primarily evolutionist rather than physiological, in Sulloway's reading.

6. Jack Jones, "Five Versions of 'Psychological Man': A Critical Analysis" (1975), p. 58. The quoted phrase is from Freud's *On the History of the Psycho-Analytic Movement* (1914), *SE* 14:16.

7. Rieff, *Freud: The Mind of the Moralist*, p. 34.

8. Ibid., p. 29.   9. Ibid., p. 18

tween two objective forces—unregenerate instincts and overbearing culture. Between these two forces there may be compromise but no resolution."[10] Rieff emphasizes the critical weight of Freud's key concepts—the drives, unconsciousness and consciousness, repression, symptoms, ego, id and superego, sexuality, the father—to present Freud as having made "the greatest single contribution to the understanding of civilization—not merely to the understanding of our own."[11]

Paul Ricoeur places himself in the company of Rieff (as well as Herbert Marcuse and J. C. Flugel) in his viewpoint on Freud as a critical theorist of the self and culture. Ricoeur explains that, unlike Flugel, he does not believe that Freud's work "may be confined to the exploration of the less human elements in man" (the mechanistic, reductive reading). Ricoeur's study of Freud "stems from the opposite conviction: Psychoanalysis conflicts with every other global interpretation of the phenomenon of man because it is an interpretation of culture."[12] Peter Homans defines and demonstrates a "third reading" of Freud, which can be contrasted with the opposed mechanistic and humanistic readings. He names the third reading "iconic" and argues that "Freud's psychology is fundamentally about images, symbol, and myth, about interpretations that presuppose levels of meaning, and about culture rather than therapy."[13] Herbert Marcuse begins his interpretation with Freud's proposition that "civilization is based on the permanent subjugation of the human instincts" and with his own proposition that Freud's theory is "in its very substance" sociological.[14] Norman O. Brown's interpretation relies on the Freudian perspective for which "the essence of society is repression of the individual, and the essence of the individual is repression of himself."[15]

Freud has been read both as defending the claims of the individual against those of society and as championing the social order against amoral drives. He does both. When one reads his work as a whole, one sees him not choosing sides but making increasingly more complex his delineation of the uneasy relations between them. In this study, emphasis is placed on the ways Freud attributes value to culture itself and to mental processes which are "cultural achievements," but it is seldom unambiguously clear that these at-

10. Ibid., p. 29.   11. Ibid., p. 373.
12. Ricoeur, *Freud and Philosophy*, p. xii. J.C. Flugel's study is *Man, Morals, and Society: A Psycho-Analytical Study* (New York: International Universities Press, 1945).
13. Homans, *Theology After Freud*, p. 14.
14. Marcuse, *Eros and Civilization*, Vintage edition, pp. 3, 5.
15. Brown, *Life Against Death* (1970), p. 3.

tributions are meant as statements of personal respect. Often they are presented as descriptive: what is culturally valuable is what culture values. Freud wrote to Romain Rolland:

> our terms such as *regression, narcissism, pleasure principle* are of a purely descriptive nature and don't carry within themselves any valuation. The mental processes may change direction or combine forces with one another; for instance, even reflecting is a regressive process without losing any of its dignity or importance in being so. Finally, psychoanalysis also has its scale of values, but its sole aim is the enhanced harmony of the ego, which is expected successfully to mediate . . . between inner and outer reality.[16]

By claiming that his terms are descriptive, Freud maintained an explicit, perhaps disingenuous, critical nonalignment, which reinforced his claim to be engaged in natural science. And he wrote in *Civilization and Its Discontents* that "it is very far from my intention to express an opinion upon the value of human civilization. I have endeavoured to guard myself against the enthusiastic prejudice which holds that our civilization is the most precious thing that we possess. . . ."[17] Despite such claims, many scholars have found in Freud's texts a critically aligned theory of culture, which is neither identical to nor separable from his psychoanalytic terminology. The present study shows where one finds bridges between description and criticism but does not provide a critique of Freud's handling of this issue. It also documents how the apparently descriptive question of appropriate mediation between inner and outer reality is especially visible in Freud's theories of gender and religion, where it reveals its ties with his critical theory of culture.

When the English text reads "civilization" or "culture," Freud's term was *Kultur*, in which he included material, economic, social, and mental factors. "The word [*Kultur*] describes the whole sum of the achievements and the regulations which distinguish our lives from those of our animal ancestors and which serve two purposes—namely to protect men against nature and to adjust their mutual relations," he wrote.[18] When he referred to current European social conditions, he considered them a subset of *Kultur*. Though he did not always equate society with culture, neither did he distinguish rigorously between them.

16. Letter to Romain Rolland, January 19, 1930, in Ernst L. Freud, ed., *The Letters of Sigmund Freud* (Harper, Colophon, 1960), p. 393.
17. *Civilization and Its Discontents* (1930), SE 21:144.
18. Ibid., p. 89.

So the reading of Freud as a theorist of culture is now well established.[19] Both religion and gender are central aspects of culture in his thought; seeing them as such makes my question about the critical weight of his theory of gender possible. There are inner links between these two parts of Freud's theory of culture—gender and religion—which scholars of Freud have not looked at together, links which become visible when gender asymmetry is explicitly treated as one of Freud's basic claims about culture. My understanding of the relationships between the theory of gender, as found throughout Freud's texts but particularly in several papers on the Oedipus complex in girls and boys, and his theory of religion, as found primarily in *The Future of an Illusion* and *Moses and Monotheism*, is indebted both to Rieff's study of Freud's moralizing mind and to Juliet Mitchell's study of his analysis of femininity. Rieff examines Freud's misogyny to explain that "the pejorative image of woman serves as a measure of the general critical component" in Freud's mix of romantic and rationalist presuppositions.[20]

Rieff refers to Freud's "misogyny," but the term often connotes personal animosity of the disposable sort rather than a critical principle. Herein, references are, instead, to the "asymmetrical positions" of the genders in Freud's oedipal theory and to the "asymmetrical evaluations" of masculinity and femininity in Freud's thought in general. The notion of sexual, or gender, asymmetry is current in cultural anthropology of a structuralist bent.[21] I prefer to speak of gender rather than sexual asymmetry because, as I will argue, there is an implicit but important distinction between sex and gender in Freud's texts. Juliet Mitchell's *Psychoanalysis and Feminism* focuses on the asymmetrical relationships of the sexes to each other and to the father figure in Freud's theories. Mitchell treats this asymmetry as an endorsement for

19. Nonetheless, the discussion about to what extent Freud's writings contain a mechanistic or a humanistic image of the human continues. For example, see George S. Klein, "Freud's Two Theories of Sexuality" (1976), p. 15, in which Klein distinguishes between the "clinical" theory, which "centers . . . upon the values and meanings associated with sensual experiences in the motivational history of a person," and the "drive-discharge theory," which "translates this psychological conception into the quasi-physiological terms of a model of energic forces that 'seeks' discharge." See also Roy Schafer's *A New Language for Psychoanalysis* (1976).

20. Rieff, *Freud: The Mind of the Moralist*, p. 200. On the romantic-rationalist combination, see p. 202: "How significant that Freud combined his rationalist creed with a Romantic mythology of women. To the same degree as he respected intellect, he made the ordinary *Hausfrau* whom he had elevated into a mystery, a 'problem,' the scapegoat of his rationalism."

21. For example, see Michelle Z. Rosaldo and Louise Lamphere, eds., *Woman, Culture, and Society* (1974).

the accuracy of Freud's analysis, over against theories which presuppose a complementarity between the genders which does not in fact exist in society. She explains: "if we live in a patriarchal society in which, from whatever your political standpoint, the sexes are treated at least differently, . . . then is it not highly unlikely that the psychological development of the sexes should be one of parity? Psychology must reflect the social *at least* as much as the biological background. . . ."[22] In her reading, Freud's theories of oedipal development are analyses of how "the human animal with a bisexual psychological disposition becomes the sexed social creature—the man or the woman."[23] For Mitchell, Freud, in discovering the laws of the unconscious, discovered "how ideology functions, how we acquire and live the ideas and laws within which we must exist." She writes that if the unconscious is a "concept of mankind's transmission and inheritance of his social (cultural) laws, . . . a primary aspect of the law is that we live according to our sexed identity, our ever imperfect 'masculinity' or 'femininity.'"[24] On the basis of this understanding of the unconscious as cultural, Mitchell agrees with the Freudian view of masculinity and femininity as asymmetrical and attributes it to their concrete asymmetrical positions in culture. (She also obviously reads Freud as a theorist of culture.)

In Mitchell's view, a disparaging view of women which functions critically does so not in Freud's theory alone, or in theory alone, but in actual unconscious individual and cultural processes. Mitchell is more willing than Rieff to accept this frequently disavowed part of Freud's thought, his psychology of women, as descriptive truth; Rieff limits himself to claiming its consistency with Freud's critical message and with the messages of other nineteenth-century irrationalist thinkers. The irony that a feminist scholar should take Mitchell's position is only apparent, for the severe critique of femininity which one finds in Freud agrees in its severity with the feminist diagnosis of the sociohistorical situation which has been imposed on and accepted by women.[25] But Rieff, too, is attracted by the severity of Freud's diagnoses. He emphasizes that Freud's critique of religion is part of a critique of paternal authority. Mitchell reads Freud's critique of femininity for its usefulness in her critique of patriarchy. In very different ways, both are interested in the problem of legitimate authority and, therefore, in Freud's

22. Juliet Mitchell, "On Freud and the Distinction Between the Sexes" (1974), p. 30.

23. Juliet Mitchell, *Psychoanalysis and Feminism* (1974), p. 402.

24. Ibid., p. 403.

25. By "feminist," I simply mean one who views gender asymmetry that is prejudicial to women as undesirable.

view of authority as necessarily paternal. In fact, for Rieff, the nature of authority is Freud's basic question. "Marxists assume—wrongly, . . . that Freud did not start 'from the examination of the social relationships of the individual as the ultimate source of his consciousness.' The Marxists fail to comprehend Freud's fundamental inquiry: into the nature of authority; this is, for example, the real question of the Oedipus complex," he observes.[26] In Rieff's view, Freud's understanding of authorities—superegos, rulers, and gods—as father figures is not descriptive but critical. "Freud does not concentrate on the father-figure as such, but rather on the manner in which parental models persist and continue to influence public conduct," he writes.[27]

It is obvious, then, that the problems of gender and religion might be related within a theory of culture which defines civilization as patriarchal. The key to the relationship is that Freud understands both religious belief and psychical gender as mental relationships to fathers and their substitutes. Whether one should locate consistencies between Freud's critiques of gender and religion in his accuracy about the deep structure of mental life in culture or in Freud's own critical consistency is not an issue which this study decides. It remains internal to Freud's writings, carving passages between many parts of his texts in order to arrive at a formulation of Freud's gender theory in which his notions of femininity and masculinity are visible as measures of psychical and sociocultural value.

The Problem

Rieff's study raises a question about Freud's psychoanalytic studies of religion that a prior examination of his theory of gender allows us to address in a new way. Rieff charges that Freud misunderstands religion itself as social. "All sociology, and now psychology as well, has been repeating Kant's mistake in regarding religion as the apprehension of our moral duties as divine commands."[28] He then traces a second Freudian error to his view of religion as social authority. This is Freud's claim that religious belief always functions as consolation so that the proper psychological alternative to religious belief is resignation to harsh, parentless reality. The historical alternative, for

26. Philip Rieff, "Freud's Contribution to Political Philosophy" (1954), p. 104; quoted phrase from Albert Starr, "Psychoanalysis and the Fiction of the Unconscious," *Science and Society* 15 (1951):129.

27. Rieff, *Freud: The Mind of the Moralist*, p. 263.

28. Ibid., p. 325.

Rieff, is adherence to a faith that criticizes socially approved consolations. Rieff's second criticism is valid, however, only for *The Future of an Illusion*, but not for *Moses and Monotheism*, wherein Freud portrays Moses as an imposer of renunciations on an unwilling populace and the Mosaic tradition as a bulwark against premature consolation. Freud called *Moses and Monotheism* "an investigation based on analytical assumptions of the origin of religion, specifically Jewish monotheism," which "can be called an attack on religion only in so far as any scientific investigation of religious belief presupposes disbelief."[29] He further commented that his personal disbelief was no secret. Such disbelief in no way precluded admiration for the cultural results of the Mosaic religion, and Freud's admiration is evident in *Moses and Monotheism*.

Thus, although Freud did understand religion as a cultural system, in the sense that religion was part of the psychoanalytically explicable history of human civilization, he did not consider its function to be only consolatory. Ricoeur writes: "it has been said that Freud does not speak of God, but of god and the gods of men; what is involved is not the truth of the foundation of religious ideas but their function in balancing the renunciations and satisfactions through which man tries to make his harsh life tolerable."[30] The psychoanalytic question Freud asks about religion—and about other aspects of culture—is how it functions in relation to the drives, how it balances instinctual renunciations and gratifications.[31] Fulfillment is not the only Freudian function of religion; renunciation is another. The different mental consequences which Freud attributes to religion (intellectual restriction in the case of Christianity as it is discussed in *The Future of an Illusion*; intellectual advance in the case of Judaism in *Moses and Monotheism*) can be understood in terms of these psychical functions of religion. In the first case, wishes are fulfilled; in the second, they are renounced. This critical distinction in Freud's theory of religion recapitulates Freud's critical understanding of gender distinction.

Freud's critical themes of wish fulfillment, or illusion, and instinctual renunciation guide his psychoanalytic studies of religion and correspond to

29. Letter to Charles Singer, October 31, 1938, in Ernst L. Freud, ed., *The Letters of Sigmund Freud*, p. 453.
30. Ricoeur, *Freud and Philosophy*, p. 235. "It has been said" refers to Ludwig Marcuse, *Sigmund Freud* (Rowohlts Deutsche Encyklopädie, 1956), p. 63.
31. It is often pointed out that Strachey's translation of *Trieb* ("drive") as "instinct" is misleading. Freud rarely used *Instinkt* ("instinct"). Sulloway notes that in German-speaking countries prior to Darwin, "the words *Instinkt* and *Trieb* were carefully reserved for animals and man, respectively"; *Freud: Biologist of the Mind*, p. 250.

his evaluative understandings of femininity and masculinity as asymmetrical in structure. ("Evaluative" means simply that Freud considers masculinity and femininity to be of uneven value both as psychical attitudes and as positions in culture.) But Freud did not deliberately look at religion through the categorial lenses that he developed in his studies of masculinity and femininity. Rather, the relationship betwen gender and religion is mediated by his critical themes of illusion and renunciation. Renunciation *of* illusion is Freud's consistent critical principle; it grounds both his critique of femininity within the theory of gender and of illusion within the theory of religion. In these terms, the specific values which Freud awards masculinity measure the valuable in general. The specific failures in value which he attributes to femininity measure such failure in general.

In *The Future of an Illusion*, Freud defined illusions as "fulfilments of the oldest, strongest, and most urgent wishes of mankind. . . . we call a belief an illusion when a wish-fulfilment is a prominent factor in its motivation, and in doing so we disregard its relations to reality, just as the illusion itself sets no store by verification."[32] The wish to which Freud traces religious belief is the wish for paternal protection and consolation, so the illusion is of the existence of the paternal god. Thus, in *The Future of an Illusion*, fulfillment refers to the wish for the father's care and not, as one might immediately assume, the sexual wish for the mother. The wish for the mother has no *cultural* significance in Freud's system; it is "natural" and must be superseded; it is contradicted by patriarchal culture.

"Instinctual renunciation" is the usual translation of *Triebverzicht*, which is itself an abbreviation for "renouncing the satisfaction of an urge derived from an instinct."[33] It is not a technical psychoanalytic term and cannot be unequivocally defined in terms of the psychical dynamics that underlie it. Renunciation may connote repression, suppression, or sublimation of wishes derived from a drive. It may be a conscious or an unconscious process.[34]

32. *The Future of an Illusion* (1927), *SE* 21:30 and 31.
33. Translator's note to *Moses and Monotheism*, trans. Katherine Jones (New York: Random House, Vintage edition, n.d.), p. 144.
34. The meanings of these terms and Freud's view of what differentiates them from one another were not altogether constant over the years. But, in general, repression is "an operation whereby the subject attempts to repel, or to confine to the unconscious, representations (thoughts, images, memories) which are bound to an instinct." It occurs when to satisfy the instinct—though pleasurable in itself—would "incur risk of provoking unpleasure because of other requirements"; J. Laplanche and J.-B. Pontalis, *The Language of Psycho-Analysis* (1973), p. 390. Suppression, when it is not a broad category of which repression is a specific instance, is the conscious elimination of distressing representations, so that they are banished to pre-

As early as 1897, Freud wrote that "civilization consists in a progressive renunciation of [incest]."[35] This renunciation is imposed by the primal, and each individual, father. Freud presents its cultural results in masculine oedipal theory in general and, for the history of religions, in *Totem and Taboo* (1913). Renunciation is both the foundation of culture, religion and ethics, and the occasion of each individual male's entry into culture. An act of renunciation is synonymous with Freud's notion of a "cultural achievement."[36]

My focus on Freud's psychology of femininity in tandem with his oedipal theory of masculinity transforms what is generally understood as oedipal theory, that is, the masculine model, into a theory of gender, that is, the oedipal differentiation of masculinity and femininity in the mental lives of both boys and girls. Freud's *definitions* of the Oedipus complex usually treat . the boy's situation, his desire for his mother and rivalry with his father, as the prototype and merely add that the girl's situation is its symmetrical opposite. In this vein, he described the Oedipus complex as "an emotional attachment of the child to the parent of the opposite sex accompanied by an attitude of rivalry to the parent of the same sex."[37] But, by 1925, when this definition was written, Freud had discovered that girls as well as boys passed through a "masculine" stage, in which they take their mothers as love objects. Therefore, a girl's feminine oedipal attachment to the father was a secondary position, a psychological reversal rather than an original or natural attitude. With this discovery came Freud's realization that the Oedipus complexes were not symmetrical for the two sexes. A feminist interpretation of this revision might be that Freud found that the feminine position taken by an oedipal girl is a retreat from her prior masculinity, a retreat which serves to situate her as feminine in a patricentric world.

---

consciousness and not, as in repression, to unconsciousness. Or, in the case of an affect, suppression may refer to its inhibition or abolition rather than its transposition to the unconscious; ibid., p. 438. Sublimation is the most problematic of the three. In general, it refers to a process by which the energy of a sexual drive is diverted toward achieving a new, nonsexual aim, the objects of which are socially valued (usually, artistic creation and intellectual inquiry); ibid., p. 431. Thus, it is not a renunciation of the satisfaction of an urge derived from a drive—satisfaction does occur—but of its original aim, which is renounced and replaced. On the problems in Freud's writings on sublimation, which Ricoeur describes as "both fundamental and episodic," see ibid., pp. 432-433, and Ricoeur, *Freud and Philosophy*, pp. 483-493; quoted phrase from p. 484.

35. Draft N, in Marie Bonaparte et al., eds., *The Origins of Psycho-Analysis* (1954), p. 210.
36. See *Beyond the Pleasure Principle* (1920), *SE* 18:14-16.
37. "The Resistances to Psycho-Analysis" (1925), *SE* 19:220.

The definitions of "masculinity" and "femininity" for psychoanalysis were a problem for Freud. Although by 1915 he had called for a clear distinction among psychological, sociological, and biological meanings of the terms, he continued to use them as conventional adjectival designations without always specifying which use he had in mind.[38] In Freud's conventional usage, femininity was associated with passivity, with the lack of a penis, with narcissism, and with the traits of modesty, vanity, inclination to envy and jealousy, lack of social conscience or sense of social justice, a generally weaker moral sense (a weaker superego), inferior capacity for sublimation, greater disposition to neuroses, particularly to hysteria, a weaker sex urge, masochistic tendencies, earlier arrest of psychological development (rigidity), and an antagonistic attitude towards civilization as the enemy of family and sexual life.[39]

Masculinity was associated with activity, possession of a penis, and with the psychical strengths and cultural capacities which femininity lacks in the above list. However, in strict psychoanalytic usage, "the difference between the sexes can lay claim to no special psychical characterization," Freud wrote. "What we speak of in ordinary life as 'masculine' or 'feminine' reduces itself from the point of view of psychology to the qualities of 'activity' and 'passivity'—that is, to qualities determined not by the instincts themselves but by their aims. The regular association of these 'active' and 'passive' instincts in mental life reflects the bisexuality of individuals."[40] Because psychoanalysis postulates original mental bisexuality, masculinity and femininity are seen as (oedipally) differentiated in the process of psychical development. In Freud's theory they are not qualities which naturally accompany sex difference from the beginning. This is the basis of the distinction of his theory of gender difference from a theory of sex difference.

Rieff has pointed out that Freud's misogyny is of the "Russo-German" variety whereby women are considered deficient in intellect and "of a lower ethical ambition and cultural caliber" than men. "In the strife between sensuality and culture, women represent the senses. . . . Women express what is primal and static as contrasted with masculine dynamism. Because symbols of origins and arrestment are feminine, the element of misogyny in Freud's doctrine may be linked directly to his idea of nature as developmental,"

---

38. For the threefold distinction, see the note added in 1915 to *Three Essays on the Theory of Sexuality* (1905), *SE* 7:219-220, quoted on p. 123 below.

39. Summarized by Viola Klein in her *The Feminine Character* (1971), p. 165.

40. "The Claims of Psycho-Analysis to Scientific Interest" (1913), *SE* 13:182.

Rieff writes.[41] For Freud, individual and collective development requires renunciation of wishes for consolation, for dependence, and for omnipotence
in favor of the "reality principle." Femininity represents such wishes; "the
feminine is passive and proper to the constraints a person may suffer
through the persistence of certain primal forms."[42] As Marcuse puts it, gratification "is represented by the woman who, as mother, has once, for the first
and last time," provided it.[43] For members of both sexes, the mother is the
image of fulfillment; hence the frequent assimilation of womanhood to sexuality itself. But for men, the feminine person who is allowed to be dependent on a father figure may also represent the recipient of fulfillments.
Freud seems to have seen it this way. He views masculinity as an achievement of obedience to the reality principle which entails renunciation of
femininity. In Ricoeur's words, the reality principle is "an essentially critical
theme directed against archaic objects and illusions."[44] The mother is an
"archaic object"; feminine dependence on paternal strength is like an illusion. When Rieff examines Freud's theory of religion, he mentions the critical function of Freud's rhetoric when he compares religious believers to
women; Freud wants to emphasize that belief betrays a passive, dependent,
and compliant longing for paternal consolation.[45]

In *Freud and Philosophy*, Ricoeur discusses the complementary Freudian
theme of renunciation of instinct, which in *The Future of an Illusion* appears
as the "cure" for religious illusion. Ricoeur correctly understands Freud's
recommendation of *Logos* and *Ananke*, the postillusory "gods," as a recommendation which is based in Freud's notion of the "dissolution of the Oedipus complex." The "dissolution of the Oedipus complex," the title of a 1924
paper, entails renunciation of submission to fathers. For Freud, it is the
"ideal" outcome of masculine development. Given the ideal outcome, reality is "stripped of any paternal coefficient."[46] Freud develops the theme of renunciation in *Moses and Monotheism*. In this last of his studies of religion, he
treats stringent renunciations of wishes as the source of the Mosaic tradition

41. Rieff, *Freud: The Mind of the Moralist*, p. 201. Rieff names the other variety of misogyny
"Franco-British"; for it, women are sexually deficient: "women are considered more delicate
emotionally and more cultivated . . ." (ibid.).
42. Ibid.
43. Marcuse, *Eros and Civilization*, p. 61.
44. Ricoeur, *Freud and Philosophy*, p. 337.
45. Rieff, *Freud: The Mind of the Moralist*, p. 293.
46. Ricoeur, *Freud and Philosophy*, p. 327. Freud's association of ideal masculinity with the
dissolution of the Oedipus complex is found in "Some Psychical Consequences of the Anatomical Distinction Between the Sexes" (1925), *SE* 19:257. See pp. 99, 133 below.

and the basis of its continuation, and he associates grandeur and sublimity, intellectual, ethical, and spiritual achievements, as well as the "victory of patriarchy," with such renunciation.[47]

When *The Future of an Illusion* and *Moses and Monotheism* are read against the background of Freud's theory of gender, the critical intent of a central ambiguity in Freud's theory of religion is revealed. This ambiguity is that, on the one hand, he charges religion with offering illusory consolation that only a wish fulfillment can provide, and, on the other, he sees the stringent renunciations enforced by Judaism as, if anything, too demanding for the psychical economy. He treats the second situation as mentally and culturally valuable just as masculinity is valuable, while he denies such value to femininity and to Christian illusion. Different gender models undergird these different evaluations. Whatever extratheoretical reasons may be suggested for Freud's use of different models, they were developed and available in his own oedipal theory of gender.[48]

Although this argument is based on internal conceptual comparisons and contrasts, there is historical warrant for its plausibility. It is well known that Freud's studies of religion originated less in any independent investigation of religious phenomena than in his continuing theoretical interest in the subterfuges of "civilized" sexuality. The psychological differences between the sexes was a problem which already preoccupied him by 1897, in his letters to Wilhelm Fliess, and references to research on such differences occur throughout his work.[49] In contrast, his highly selective interest in contempo-

47. *Moses and Monotheism* (1939), *SE* 23:111-122; quoted phrase on p. 113.

48. Freud's Jewish "identity" has most often been referred to in order to explain his more positive attitude toward religion when the religion of Moses was his topic. Freud's Jewishness is discussed by Rieff, *Freud: The Mind of the Moralist*, pp. 282-287; Reuben M. Rainey, *Freud as Student of Religion* (1975), pp. 61-79; Earl A. Grollman, *Judaism in Sigmund Freud's World* (New York: Bloch, 1965); and Ronald W. Clark, *Freud: The Man and the Cause* (1980), pp. 11-13, 520-521. More interpretive, even speculative, discussions of this issue are found in David Bakan's *Sigmund Freud and the Jewish Mystical Tradition* (New York: Schocken Books, 1965); John Murray Cuddihy's *The Ordeal of Civility* (1974); and Marthe Robert's *From Oedipus to Moses* (1976). My intention is not to argue that Freud's view of Judaism was unimportant to his thought but to suggest the importance of another influence from within his own theories. These two issues, the influence of Freud's understanding of Judaism (versus Christianity) and his understanding of masculinity (versus femininity) are mutually reinforcing. The impact of Freud's attitudes toward Judaism on his thought has been studied; the impact of his theory of gender difference has not.

49. In May 1897, Freud enclosed a draft (Draft M) in a letter to Fliess, which contains the following suggestion: "It is to be suspected that the essential repressed element is always femininity. This is confirmed by the fact that women no less than men admit more easily to

rary theories about religion is noteworthy. For example, he never referred to William James's *The Varieties of Religious Experience* (1902) or Rudolf Otto's *The Idea of the Holy* (1917) although both were widely read and influential.[50] Freud's theory of religious phenomena has been repeatedly criticized for being inadequate to the complexity and variety of the topics he considered.[51]

---

experiences with women than with men. What men essentially repress is their paederistic element"; Marie Bonaparte et al., eds., *The Origins of Psycho-Analysis*, pp. 203-204. The editors comment that "the idea alluded to here . . . occupied Freud throughout his life" (p. 204, n. 1). In a letter written in November of the same year, Freud commented: "I have also given up the idea of explaining libido as the masculine factor and repression as the feminine one"; ibid., p. 234. Sulloway explains these ideas as they related to Fliess's theory of sexual periodicity; *Freud: Biologist of the Mind*, pp. 179-184. Yet Freud seems not to have given up this *kind* of hypothesis because in 1910 he is reported to have commented:

> it is true that in the woman one does find in neurosis repressed masculinity, but in the man one finds only the repression of "masculine" impulses and not of "feminine" ones. Neurosis always has a "feminine" character. But the concepts of "masculine" and "feminine" are of no use in psychology and we do better . . . to employ the concepts of libido and repression. Whatever is of the libido has a masculine character, and whatever is of repression is of a feminine character. Psychologically, we can present only the character of activity and passivity. (Herman Nunberg and Ernst Federn, eds., *Minutes of the Vienna Psychoanalytic Society, Vol. II: 1908-1910* [1967], minutes of meeting of February 23, 1910, p. 432)

These comments were in criticism of a presentation by Alfred Adler. Perhaps because of his growing opposition to Adler's ideas, Freud seems to have refrained from theorizing about "masculinity" and "femininity" until the 1920s. Adler left the Psychoanalytic Society in 1911; for Freud's arguments against him, see Freud, *On the History of the Psycho-Analytic Movement* (1914), *SE* 14:48-61. In his last written fragments, produced when he was approaching death in 1938, Freud was still worried about femininity. He wrote: "As a substitute for penis-envy, identification with the clitoris: neatest expression of inferiority, source of all inhibitions. At the same time [in Case X] disavowal of the discovery that other women too are without a penis"; "Findings, Ideas, Problems" (1941), *SE* 23:299. In between these chronological extremes of 1897 and 1938, he wrote the papers on gender difference.

50. See Rainey, *Freud as Student of Religion*, p. 120. Rainey's point is not that Freud was ignorant about religion; in fact, he was far better read in the area than is usually supposed. However, his questions and methods came not from contemporary religious studies but from his own psychoanalytic theory.

51. Rieff's study criticizes Freud's theories on many counts, *Freud: The Mind of the Moralist*, pp. 281-328, as do Ricoeur's *Freud and Philosophy*, pp. 531-551, and Paul Roazen's *Freud: Political and Social Thought* (New York: Knopf, 1963), pp. 125-192. Ernest Jones summarizes several major objections to Freud's writings on religious topics; *The Life and Work of Sigmund Freud*, 3:358-362. So does Leszek Kolakowski in the course of a critical discussion of the theory of culture, "The Psychoanalytic Theory of Culture," in Robert Boyers, ed., *Psychological Man* (1975), p. 28. Anthropologists have focused on *Totem and Taboo* to provide criticisms, many of which also may be applied to his later works; for example, Bronislaw

He viewed his writings on religion as applications of his psychoanalytic method and insights rather than comprehensive studies; they were contributions made from one viewpoint.[52] He offered no formal definition of religion and he selected his data and organized his discussions according to prior theoretical concerns.[53] As Freud wrote on many occasions, his constant interests were in the topics which defined psychoanalysis for him: the unconscious, infantile sexuality and its oedipal formation, repression, and the resistances.[54] Freud's oedipal theory of development was the basis of his theory of gender and his theory of religion.

Freud's papers on femininity and masculinity and his major books on religion were written during the same time period. His explicit attention to feminine development as asymmetrical to masculine development took form in a paper published in 1925.[55] Excepting *Totem and Taboo* (1913), Freud's major works on religion were written thereafter: *The Future of an Illusion* in 1927, *Civilization and Its Discontents* in 1929, and *Moses and Monotheism* between 1934 and 1938. The papers on femininity appeared in 1925, 1931, and 1933.[56] During these years a debate in psychoanalytic circles was taking place on the problem of the psychology of women. This debate is

Malinowski, *Sex and Repression in Savage Society* (London: Routledge, 1953); Alfred L. Kroeber, "Totem and Taboo: An Ethnologic Psychoanalysis" (1920) and "Totem and Taboo in Retrospect" (1939) in his *The Nature of Culture* (Chicago: University of Chicago Press, 1952), pp. 301-305, 306-309; Derek Freeman, "Totem and Taboo: A Reappraisal," in Warner Muensterberger, ed., *Man and His Culture: Psychoanalytic Anthropology After Totem and Taboo* (New York: Taplinger, 1969), pp. 53-78. H.L. Philp, in *Freud and Religious Belief* (London: Rockliff, 1956), drew on the work of anthropologists and historians to provide a comprehensive (nonpsychoanalytic) critical discussion of Freud's psychology of religion. Hans Küng's *Freud and the Problem of God* (1979), Chap. 3, is the most recent, if seldom original, Christian theological critique. Psychoanalytically oriented critics have differed not so much on method as on results; several have argued that from a psychoanalytic viewpoint, it is possible to take a more faithful stance. For example, see Karl Stern, *The Third Revolution: A Study of Psychiatry and Religion* (Garden City, N.Y.: Doubleday, Image Books, 1961); Gregory Zilboorg, *Psychoanalysis and Religion* (New York: Farrar, Straus and Giroux, 1962); and Erich Fromm, *Psychoanalysis and Religion* (1950).

52. For example, see *The Future of an Illusion* (1927), SE 21:35.

53. The absence of formal definition has been noted by Paul Pruyser, "Sigmund Freud and His Legacy" (1973), p. 258; and by Rainey, *Freud as Student of Religion*, p. 130.

54. For example, *On the History of the Psycho-Analytic Movement* (1914), SE 14:15; *An Autobiographical Study* (1925), SE 20:34-35.

55. "Some Psychical Consequences of the Anatomical Distinction Between the Sexes" (1925), SE 19:248-258.

56. Ibid.; "Female Sexuality" (1931), SE 21:225-243; and "Femininity," Lecture 33 of *New Introductory Lectures on Psycho-Analysis* (1933), SE 22:112-135.

now being reconstructed, but its place in the history of Freud's thought has not yet been addressed in any of the major scholarly discussions of the development of his ideas.[57] Scholarship on the influence of Freud's views of femininity on his thought as a whole has not been undertaken. Historical considerations will remain on the periphery of the present argument; I will be content to add the theory of gender to those parts of Freud's theories which scholars consider important for understanding him.

57. For discussions of this debate, often called the Jones-Freud debate (but not mentioned by Jones in his biography of Freud), see Gregory Zilboorg, "Masculine and Feminine: Some Biological and Cultural Aspects," *Psychiatry* 7 (1944):257-296; Zenia O. Fliegel, "Feminine Psychosexual Development in Freudian Theory: A Historical Reconstruction," *Psychoanalytic Quarterly* 42 (1973):385-408; Robert J. Stoller, *Sex and Gender*, vol. 1: *The Development of Masculinity and Femininity* (1968), pp. 50-55; Mitchell, *Psychoanalysis and Feminism*, pp. 121-131; Moustapha Safouan, *La sexualité féminine dans la doctrine freudienne*, Le champ freudien: collection dirigée par Jacques Lacan (Paris: Editions du Seuil, 1976), pp. 11-61; and Nancy Chodorow, *The Reproduction of Mothering* (1978), pp. 114-117.

Chapter 2

Excursus on Method

The centuries have a way of being male.
—WALLACE STEVENS, *"The Figure of the Youth as Virile Poet"*

Criticism

In the main, this study is faithful to the terminology Freud himself used. Two exceptions are the terms "criticism" and "gender asymmetry." Because these terms are the foundation of my interpretation, it is wise to clarify, in a preliminary way, both what I understand by them and how I see them functioning in Freud's thought.

In everyday English usage, to be critical means to give adverse or unfavorable judgment. It may also mean to exercise careful judgment or observation: to be exact, accurate, precise. Consistently, "critique" refers to a critical action, essay, or article. A recent study of theories of literary criticism defines its concern, criticism, as "an inquiry into the nature and function of literature, because to be so concerned is to face fundamental questions prior to or at least intertwined with the problem of value."[1] In both of these basic senses, Freud's treatment of religious illusion and of femininity is critical. He renders unfavorable judgment about their mental and cultural value, but he also carefully observes the nature and the function of the objects of analysis. Such "careful observation" also characterizes his examination of masculinity and religious renunciation, but his judgment of them is not altogether unfavorable. In *The Future of an Illusion*, the nature of religion is "illusion"; its function is to fulfill a wish.[2] As such, religion is understood as a human psychical product. Freud would agree with Kant's criterion for illusion: "all illusion consists in holding the subjective ground of

1. Hazard Adams, *The Interests of Criticism: An Introduction to Literary Theory* (New York: Harcourt, Brace and World, 1969), p. 3.
2. There are, of course, other psychical functions that Freud assigns to religious phenomena. For example, religion can be understood as defense in general and as particular defenses, such as projection. For a catalogue, see Paul W. Pruyser, "Sigmund Freud and His Legacy" (1973), pp. 258-277.

our judgments to be objective."[3] Freud is specific about the content of the subjective wish: for paternal protection and consolation. In the Kantian sense of "critical" too, Freud engaged in a critical analysis of religion, for Kantian criticism is speculation following a prior examination of the scope and limits of knowledge.[4] For Freud, psychoanalytic theory of mind provides this prior examination. When the results of this examination were applied to religion, Freud's project was to assess the psychical determinants of religious ideas and to use such determinants to explain the function of the ideas and their contents.

In his theory of gender too, Freud assessed the psychical determinants of both masculinity and femininity. However, when I refer to Freud's critique of femininity I mean something more than that Freud was judgmental of, and that he explored the psychical bases of, femininity. A summary of parts of a recent discussion of the history of the idea of critique will help clarify this additional meaning. The idea of a critique may be traced to the Enlightenment idea of the function of reason, an idea which in turn had adopted and transformed the notion of critique which was employed by the humanists and reformers "to describe the art of informed judgment appropriate to the study of ancient texts, whether the Classics or the Bible."[5] Critical methods at this stage were largely philological. In the argument between church tradition and scriptural authority, "the appeal to critique gradually displaced the criterion of truth from revelation towards clear and rational, or 'critical,' thought. . . . 'Critique' came to be seen no longer as simply a symptom of the sharpening opposition between reason and revelation. It was viewed as itself the activity which separated the two spheres. It was the essential activity of reason." Gradually, the reference of the term was extended from textual criticism to include criticism of political and religious institutions. So, for the Enlightenment, "critique" connoted "oppositional thinking, . . . an activity of unveiling, or debunking."[6]

The purpose of this historical discussion, which is Paul Connerton's, is to

---

3. Immanuel Kant, *Prolegomena to Any Future Metaphysics*, ed. Lewis White Beck, Library of the Liberal Arts (Indianapolis: Bobbs-Merrill, 1950), p. 76.

4. Ibid., editor's Introduction, p. ix, n. 1.

5. Paul Connerton, Introduction to *Critical Sociology* (1976), p. 15. Trent Schroyer traces "the reflective critique of socially unnecessary constraints of human freedom" to the classical Greek concept of *nous*: "Plato mythically depicts Socrates' 'inner voice' (the symbol for reason) as always saying no, and while this does not exhaust the concept of reason it is clearly its major function"; *The Critique of Domination* (1973), p. 15.

6. Connerton, Introduction to *Critical Sociology*, pp. 16-17.

clarify the meaning of "criticism" for members of the Frankfurt school of critical theory. In the writings of Horkheimer, Adorno, Marcuse, Habermas, and others, Connerton identifies two meanings of critique which are not always distinguished from each other. Both of these meanings are found in Freud's texts as well. According to Connerton, they originated respectively in the works of Kant and Hegel and were drawn from but surpass the Enlightenment idea of "unveiling." The first meaning "denotes reflection on the *conditions* of possible knowledge: on the potential abilities of human beings possessing the faculties of knowing, speaking, and acting." This is the Kantian meaning. The second meaning, which is exemplified, in Connerton's view, both by the Frankfurt school and by Freudian psychoanalysis as it is understood by critical theorists, is "reflection on a system of *constraints* which are humanly produced: distorting pressures to which individuals, or a group of individuals, or the human race as a whole, succumb in their process of self-formation."[7] Further, this critique of constraints is grounded in a specific sociopolitical experience, "which is set down in Freud's psychoanalysis, in Hegel's *Phenomenology of Mind*, and in Marx's critique of ideology: the experience of an emancipation by means of critical insight into relationships of power, the strength of which lies, at least in part, in the fact that these relationships have not been seen through."[8]

In this sense of critique, as reflection on humanly produced constraints from which reflection, or understanding, can provide liberation, Freud can be understood as having produced a "critique of unreason," for the psychoanalytic cure lies in liberation from the power of the unconscious forces which are the source of "unreasonable" psychical constraints.[9] It is in this sense of "critical" that Freud's unifying critical motif is the renunciation of illusion. By attributing religious belief to psychical wish and seeing it as illusion, from which humankind would best be emancipated (through science), Freud contributed to the development of a critique of religion as humanly produced constraint. It is clear from his own statements that such was his intention. On one occasion, he wrote: "Of the three powers which may dispute the basic position of science, religion alone is to be taken seriously as an enemy." The others are art and philosophy.[10]

7. Ibid., pp. 17-18.   8. Ibid., p. 19.
9. In the context of a comparison of Freud and Kant as "great enlighteners," Walter Kaufman calls Freud's contribution his "critique of unreason"; *Critique of Religion and Philosophy* (Garden City, N.Y.: Doubleday, Anchor edition, 1961), p. 413.
10. "The Question of a *Weltanschauung*," Lecture 35 of *New Introductory Lectures on Psycho-Analysis* (1933), *SE* 22:160.

Far from claiming that he intended to provide a critique of femininity as a constraint that should be overcome, Freud accepted femininity (and masculinity) as practically inevitable, even though both were undoubtedly "humanly produced." The psychical consequences of sex difference were, for Freud, one more limiting constituent of mental life, and although he saw them as constraints and although he wrote that "in our civilization the relations between the sexes are disturbed by an erotic illusion, . . ."[11] he showed little practical interest in strategies for overcoming the illusion that culturally loaded notions of masculinity and femininity are inevitable concomitants of sex difference. Nonetheless, his own theory questions this view. Therefore, while viewing Freud's critique of religion as a critique of constraint follows his own intentions, viewing his critique of femininity as such is consistent in principle with his intention to criticize illusion, but not with his practice. I read Freud's theory of gender as carrying on a critique of femininity, in particular, as a constraint, a constraint that has the same psychical structure as religious attachment to the father. But, as far as we can tell, Freud did not view it this way.

Gender Asymmetry

Distinction of gender from sex difference allows gender to be understood as a humanly produced constraint. In much current usage, "gender" refers to psychosocial elaborations of sex difference. If male and female are terms appropriate to describe bioanatomical differences, masculinity and femininity connote gender differentiation. The distinction between sex and gender in Freud's thought is discussed at length in Chapter 7; here it will help to outline three related functions which the concept of gender serves in this study.

First, gender refers to qualities which are considered to be psychosocial elaborations of, or results of, sex difference. Many of these are shared assumptions or prejudices about sex-appropriate characteristics. Conceptually, psychosocial "gender" links biological sex difference and cultural understandings and uses of such difference. Therefore, second, gender refers to an interpretation of the meaning of sex difference. Freud's psychoanalytic explanations of the development of masculinity and femininity can be understood as explanations of how children and, therefore, adults interpret sex

11. *The Future of an Illusion* (1927), SE 21:34.

difference. Such interpretations are by no means primarily conscious. The meanings assigned to masculinity and femininity may then be understood as "humanly produced" definitions or limitations, whether the process of their production is located in mental lives in culture, which is where Freud locates it, or in society seen as somehow more external, which is where some learning theory locates it.[12] According to Freud's theory of gender development, the interpretations arrived at in the process of girls' and boys' libidinal development place masculinity and femininity in a relationship of uneven value to one another; at some point, one's own femininity is "repudiated" whether consciously or unconsciously. This idea of the shared repudiation of femininity provides the content of the Freudian critique of femininity, in the sense that femininity is explained in terms of its psychical origins and receives primarily negative valuation, not only for Freud but, in Freud's view, for children and thereby for adults of both sexes.

A third function of the idea of gender is as a methodological principle by which one may reread Freud's theories about religion. Here, gender *asymmetry* is the crucial issue. A reviewer of Jacques Derrida's *Of Grammatology* (1974) comments: "since a structural opposition—life/death, speech/writing, or whatever—is never perfectly balanced but always values one of its elements over the other, an inversion of the values will not simply turn things around but will displace the whole system."[13] Implicit in this observation is the hypothesis that such structural oppositions define and maintain the whole system, whatever the system might be. The way in which this is true for Freud's critical theory of religion is the topic of this study; the structural opposition which I see as defining the system is that of the uneven value of masculinity and femininity, understood as renunciation and fulfillment.

One should look first at the idea of asymmetrical genders in general before looking at it in Freud's thought because Freud's theory of gender is unique insofar as it is psychoanalytic but certainly not insofar as it is asymmetrical. Freud's is a gender-asymmetrical theory, *and* it is a psychoanalytic theory of gender asymmetry. That is, it is an asymmetrical theory which also examines the psychical sources of the asymmetrical meaning and value of the genders. The sort of gender asymmetry which characterizes Freud's theory, and the sort which his theory also accounts for, has three related char-

12. See Nancy Chodorow's discussion of where different theories locate the "source" of women's being mothers in *The Reproduction of Mothering* (1978), Part 1.
13. Michael Wood, "Deconstructing Derrida," *New York Review of Books* 24, no. 3 (March 3, 1977):28.

acteristics. First, masculinity is treated as the general human norm, femininity as a special case or deviation. Second, the point of view taken, which is presumed to be that of the general human subject, is masculine. A passage from William James illustrates these two characteristics: "This enchantment . . . is either there or not for us and there are persons who can no more become possessed by it than they can fall in love with a given woman by mere word of command. Religious feeling is thus an absolute addition to the Subject's range of life."[14] Here, "us," "persons," and the "Subject" are, if not male, those who fall in love with women. The third characteristic of Freud's variety of gender asymmetry is that the masculine, as the human norm and the point of view taken, is presumably of greater value. Because it considers itself the "general human" point from which to evaluate the feminine, it easily (but not inevitably) appears superior. Related to this is the asymmetrical assumption that only masculinity has the potentiality to realize the *human* ideal, understood both as ideal type and as best. One can see that these characteristics construct a circular system and that a reversal of the terms would displace it.

In 1911, Georg Simmel raised the question of the influence of cultural and psychological asymmetry on thought.[15] From a description of the uneven weighting of masculinity and femininity in all realms of life, including theory, Simmel arrived at an explanation for this unevenness, which differed from the explanation that was then predominant in Germany, that is, that women *were* inferior. Rather, Simmel linked this differentiation in value to the power position of men and to the resulting fact that even apparently neutral products of culture were mediated by men's energy to become integrated into culture.[16] Law is one example; although law "in itself," that is, in the abstract, is neither masculine nor feminine, its specific historical form is masculine. In Simmel's words:

> the requirements of art, patriotism, morality in general and social ideas in particular, correctness in practical judgment and objectivity in theoretical knowledge, the energy and the profundity of life—all these are categories which belong as it were in their form and their claims to humanity in general, but in their actual historical configuration they are masculine throughout.

14. William James, *The Varieties of Religious Experience* (1958), p. 54.
15. Georg Simmel, "Das Relative und das Absolute im Geschlechter-Problem" (1911), pp. 67-100.
16. Georg Simmel, "Weibliche Kultur" (1911), p. 281.

In sum, he suggested that if "we describe these things, viewed as absolute ideas, by the single word 'objective,' we then find that in the history of our race the equation objective = masculine is a valid one."[17] But this equation, he has already explained, is one of many instances in which one term of a duality expands to include its other pole so that symmetrical alternatives, originally relative to each other, experience the "fate" by which one term becomes absolute and the other is encompassed by it.[18]

Because Simmel's viewpoint is not well known, I will quote at length a passage in which he explains how he thinks masculinity has become the human norm, the point of view taken, and presumably more valuable:

> To take from two opposite notions, which derive their meaning and value from each other, one, and to raise this one to embrace and dominate once more the whole game of give and take and of balance, this time in an absolute sense, is a thoroughly human tendency, presumably of deep metaphysical origin, which has found an historic paradigm in the fundamental sexual relation of man.
>
> The fact that the male sex is not only considered relatively superior to the female, but that it is taken as the universal human norm, applied equally to the phenomena of the individual masculine and of the individual feminine—this fact is, in many different ways, based on the power position of the male. If we express the historic relation between the sexes crudely in terms of master and slave, it is part of the master's privileges not to have to think continuously of the fact that he is the master, while the position of the slave carries with it the constant reminder of his being a slave. It cannot be overlooked that the woman forgets far less often the fact of being a woman than the man of being a man. . . . Because masculinity, as a differential factor, in phantasies and principles, in achievements and emotional complexes, escapes the consciousness of its protagonists more easily than is the case with femininity in the corresponding situation (for within the sphere of his activities man's interest in his relation to the Feminine is not as vital as woman's interest in her relation to the Masculine) expressions of masculinity are easily elevated for us to the realm of a supra-specific, neutral, objectivity and validity (to which their specifically masculine

17. Georg Simmel, "Das Relative und das Absolute," trans. in Karen Horney, "The Flight from Womanhood" (1967), pp. 55-56.
18. Simmel, "Das Relative und das Absolute," paraphrased from p. 67.

connotation, if noticed at all, is subordinated as something individual and casual).[19]

In this way, Simmel argues, a social relation has been turned into a logical one, and what could be understood as particularly masculine is instead seen consensually as absolute, universal, normative, objective. Simmel writes:

> Domination based on subjective unilateral power has from time immemorial had the tendency to clothe itself in a mantle of objective justification: might is transformed in[to] right. . . . Insofar as the will of the pater familias through which he dominates the household is perceived as "authority," it appears no longer to be arbitrary use of power, but the expression of an objective moral law which aims at the general superpersonal interest of the family as a whole. In such a way, and in this connection, the psychological superiority granted male behavior through the domination of man over woman, is transformed into a logical superiority; this state of affairs is given normative significance and claims a transsexual validity as the yardstick of truth and justice for both men and women.[20]

Because this transformation has occurred within our very categories of thought, the standards by which masculinity and femininity are evaluated are "not neutral, arising out of the differences of the sexes, but in themselves essentially masculine . . .":

> We do not believe in a purely "human" civilization, into which the question of sex does not enter, for the very reason that prevents any such civilization from in fact existing, namely, the (so to speak) naive identification of the concept "human being" [Mensch] and the concept "man" [Mann], which in many languages even causes the same word to be used for the two concepts. . . . this is the reason why, in the most varying fields, inadequate achievements are contemptuously called "feminine," while distinguished achievements on the part of women are called "masculine" as an expression of praise.[21]

19. Georg Simmel, "Das Relative und das Absolute," trans. in Viola Klein, The Feminine Character (1971), pp. 82-83.
20. Georg Simmel, "Das Relative und das Absolute," trans. in Lewis A. Coser, "Georg Simmel's Neglected Contribution to the Sociology of Women," Signs 2, no. 4 (1977):872-873.
21. Simmel, "Das Relative und das Absolute," trans. in Horney, "The Flight from Womanhood," p. 56.

Both Karen Horney and Viola Klein, whose translations I have used, relied on Simmel's thought to criticize Freud's views of women's psychology. Neither, however, addressed the deeper question which Simmel raises: how has Freud's asymmetrical view of the genders informed the concepts with which he understands mind and civilization in general, and religion as part of them. Freud's theories can be seen to exemplify this process of assimilating masculinity, objectivity, culture itself, and value.

The characteristics of gender asymmetry have been rediscovered by numerous thinkers (many of them women) who have applied themselves to the "woman problem," as the topic was asymmetrically named in Germany and Austria in Simmel's and Freud's day. In her preface to *The Second Sex*, Simone de Beauvoir observed:

> The terms *masculine* and *feminine* are used symmetrically only as a matter of form, as on legal papers. In actuality the relation of the two sexes is not quite like that of two electrical poles, for man represents both the positive and the neutral, as is indicated by the common use of *man* to designate human beings in general; whereas woman represents only the negative, defined by limiting criteria, without reciprocity. . . . It amounts to this: just as for the ancients there was an absolute vertical with reference to which the oblique was defined, so there is an absolute human type, the masculine. . . . She [woman] is defined and differentiated with reference to man and not he with reference to her; she is the incidental, the inessential as opposed to the essential. He is the Subject, he is the Absolute—she is the Other.[22]

Dorothy Sayers discussed the issue in an essay appropriately entitled "The Human-Not-Quite-Human," which begins, "*Vir* is male and *Femina* is female: but *Homo* is male and female." She continues:

> This is the equality claimed and the fact that is persistently evaded and denied. No matter what arguments are used, the discussion is vitiated from the start, because Man is always dealt with as both *Homo* and *Vir*, but Woman only as *Femina*.
>
> I have seen it solemnly stated in a newspaper that the seats on the near side of a bus are always filled before those on the off side, because, "men find them more comfortable on account of the camber of the road, and women find they get a better view of the shop windows." As though the camber of the road did not affect male and fe-

22. Simone de Beauvoir, *The Second Sex* (1953), pp. xv-xvi.

male bodies equally. Men, you observe, are given a *Homo* reason; but Women, a *Femina* reason, because they are not fully human.[23]

In asymmetrical theory, as soon as the human norm and the human subject are assimilated to the masculine, the image of the human ideal easily becomes masculine. Mary Ellman, in an erudite and witty criticism of a wide range of literature in terms of its gender stereotypes, discovered that women seem to attain their ideal condition by rising above themselves as women whereas men attain theirs by *"becoming* and (with luck) remaining, simply men."[24] This asymmetry holds in contemporary clinicians' concepts of maturity and mental health. According to one study, their concepts of mentally healthy, mature adults and men largely coincide, but those of healthy, mature adults and women do not.[25]

Klein, following Simmel, provides a succinct description of how asymmetric assumptions become misogynistic. "The adoption of masculine standards as the absolute norm applicable to mankind as a whole has two equally harmful results for the judgment of women. . . . ; a mystifying overestimation of woman by virtue of those qualities which cannot be explained by male criteria . . . [and] contempt for human beings who fail to live up to the norm," she observes.[26] Rieff identified both these trends in Freud's thought. He understands Freud's "mystifying over-estimation" of women as an index of his romanticism and his "contempt" as an index of his rationalism. Rieff writes:

> How significant that Freud combined his rationalist creed with a Romantic mythology of women. . . . It is in his Romantic typology of the sexes [wherein the feminine represents primal, sensual, untamed vitality] that Freud's rationalist inclination most clearly emerges. In explaining how "women have but little sense of justice," how "their social interests are weaker than those of men," how "their capacity for the sublimation of their instincts is less," Freud places a strong positive accent upon the sense of justice, upon social interests, upon the capacity for instinctual sublimation. In his polite and profound misogyny, the rationalist Freud is confirmed: men must come to terms with the sexual and overcome it.[27]

23. Dorothy L. Sayers, in her *Unpopular Opinions* (1946), pp. 116-117.
24. Mary Ellman, *Thinking About Women* (1968), pp. 67-68.
25. Inge K. Broverman et al., "Sex-Role Stereotypes and Clinical Judgments of Mental Health" (1970), pp. 1-7.
26. Klein, *The Feminine Character*, p. 84.
27. Philip Rieff, *Freud: The Mind of the Moralist* (1961), pp. 202-203; quoted phrases from

Femininity represents a particular which masculinity, as humanity, encompasses and surpasses.

Freud's is undoubtedly as close to a pure culture of asymmetrical theory as one could wish to come. A few of his statements will illustrate the identification of the masculine with the human and with the point of view taken. In a eulogy for Lou Andreas-Salomé, he wrote that "those who were closer to her had the strongest impression of the genuineness and harmony of her nature and could discover with astonishment that all feminine frailties, and perhaps most human frailties, were foreign to her or had been conquered by her in the course of her life."[28] While this is not necessarily a misogynous statement, Freud has quite easily distinguished two classes of frailties: feminine and human. Discussing a story by Stefan Zweig, which "ostensibly sets out only to show what an irresponsible creature woman is," Freud perhaps catches himself in his asymmetry but lets it stand. He comments that a psychoanalytic interpretation of the story reveals that it represents something "quite different, something universally human, or rather something masculine."[29] This "something" is a son's oedipal fantasy about his mother.[30] In both these examples, gender categories are grouped asymmetrically: the human and the masculine are interchangeable, but the feminine is peculiar and apart. In another passing comment, Freud is describing the unconscious reasons for a (male) fetishist's ambivalent disavowal and affirmation of a maternal penis: "If females, like other living creatures, possess a penis, there is no need to tremble for the continued possession of one's own penis," he writes.[31] Once again, females are peculiarly set apart, not only from the subject but also from "other living creatures."

In this example, though, we must note that Freud is speaking for a man's unconscious and not necessarily for himself. When he claims to discover what I call asymmetry in the formulations of unconscious processes, he is contributing to a theory of gender asymmetry. Let us look at one of Freud's constructions, which is basic to his theory of asymmetrical gender differentiation. He writes that an analysis of the development of the child's formulation of ideas of maleness and femaleness out of three mental polarities that

Freud, "Femininity," Lecture 33 of *New Introductory Lectures on Psycho-Analysis* (1933), *SE* 22:172-173.

28. "Lou Andreas-Salomé" (1937), *SE* 23:297.

29. "Dostoevsky and Parricide" (1928), *SE* 21:191.

30. Ibid., pp. 193-194.

31. *An Outline of Psycho-Analysis* (1940), *SE* 23:203.

the child has already experienced—subject and object, activity and passivity, and phallic versus castrated—reveals that "maleness combines [the factors of] subject, activity and possession of the penis; femaleness takes over [those of] object and passivity."[32] Prior to this developmental meeting of the sets of polarities, neither masculinity nor femininity was found to exist in the child's mental life. Freud's differential oedipal theories of the development of gender were worked out to explain how the polarities by which "our mental life as a whole is governed" are differently related for boys and girls. The three polarities are activity and passivity, subject and object (ego and external world), and pleasure and unpleasure.[33] As soon as activity, ego and the subject are assimilated to masculinity, the genders are asymmetrically conceived. Femininity takes on the mental meaning of passive object. This situation is Freud's conceptualization of the asymmetrical situation described by Simmel and de Beauvoir; he claims that everyone's unconscious construes the genders thus.

In psychoanalytic genetic (developmental) terms, Freud's understanding of gender difference as it is lived mentally turns on the pivot of the father's function in mental life, so he gives the formal conceptual asymmetry of the genders historical, cultural, and psychological concreteness. Mitchell's study of Freud emphasized this fourth and specifically Freudian characteristic of asymmetry between the genders: the *father's*, not just the male's, privileged position. She would argue that, for an explanation of how cultural asymmetry produces mental asymmetry, as well as how mental asymmetry produces cultural asymmetry (the first in the ontogenetic oedipal situation; the second in the phylogenetic reconstruction of this situation, the primal horde), one must read Freud. The "asymmetrical specific of a *father-dominated* social structure" is the Freudian contribution to an explanation of gender asymmetry, in Mitchell's view. "Freud's analysis of the psychology of women [and of men] takes place within a concept that is neither socially not biologically dualistic," she writes. "It takes place within an analysis of patriarchy."[34] So Freud specifies Simmel's "power position of the male" to focus on paternal power. The Oedipus complex, with its emphasis on the predominance of the father figure in the psychical lives of both daughters and sons is, Mitchell writes:

32. "The Infantile Genital Organization (An Interpolation into the Theory of Sexuality)" (1923), *SE* 19:145.
33. "Instincts and Their Vicissitudes" (1915), *SE* 14:133.
34. Juliet Mitchell, *Psychoanalysis and Feminism*, p. 402.

a patriarchal myth and, though he never said so, the importance of this fact was doubtless behind Freud's repudiation of a parallel myth for women—a so-called Electra complex. Freud always opposed any idea of symmetry in the cultural "making" of men and women. A myth for women would have to bear most dominantly the marks of the Oedipus complex because it is a man's world into which a woman enters; complementarity or parallelism are out of the question.[35]

Mitchell's topic is the cultural and psychical creation of the feminine woman; mine is Freud's theory of religion in its relation to his theory of gender. But it should by now be apparent that the Freudian theme of familial, psychical, social, and religious authority as paternal is the point of contact not only between his theories of gender and religion but also between his analyses of individual and collective psychical dynamics. Perhaps Freud's relative lack of care in distinguishing among society, culture, and civilization results from his equation of the father complex with the hidden dynamics of all shared institutions and ideas so that groups of any size and any historical period are analyzed in terms of the oedipal relations to fathers.[36] In Freud's

35. Ibid., pp. 403-404. As is discussed in Chapter 8, the child's oedipal relations to the father and the castration complexes explain how activity, the subject, and masculinity join forces in the mind.

36. In contrast to Mitchell's agreement with Freud that civilization equals patriarchy and that, therefore, different societies are not all that different when paternal predominance is one's criterion (an agreement which is influenced both by Marxian and structuralist anthropological views), several sociologists have attempted to understand Freud's thought as expressive of a more specific social situation. Peter Berger proposes a dialectical relationship (a) between social structure and psychological reality and (b) between psychological reality and any prevailing psychological model; "Towards a Sociological Understanding of Psychoanalysis" (1965), p. 33. Berger suggests that the plausibility of psychoanalysis rests on the postindustrial separation of economic and political (public) from family (private) institutions. Fred Weinstein and Gerald Platt draw on the postindustrial differentiation of private life from public work to suggest that Freud's discovery of sons' oedipal rivalry expresses a change in family structure attendant upon this larger societal change. They argue that sons came to resent fathers' claims to authority as fathers withdrew from nurturant roles and mothers came to specialize in them. The Oedipus complex is the son's way of renouncing emotional ties to the mother, who now represents gratification, in order to enter the paternal world of restraint, self-denial, and abstract, public achievement; The Wish To Be Free (1969). John Murray Cuddihy's sociological explanation of the origin of oedipal theory relies on similar categories of modern versus traditional personality, family, and social structure, according to which public and private spheres are newly separated in modernity, but it assimilates Jewish personality to traditional society and Gentile civil personality to modernity. For Cuddihy, Freud's theory translates the Jewish entry into civil society after the Emancipation into psychical terms; The

view, but in Mitchell's words, the repressed father complex is "the mental representation of the reality of society."[37] And culture itself results from this mental complex.

Ordeal of Civility (1974). For a sociological view that sees the oedipal situation as universal *because* of the universal sociocultural authority of fathers, see Talcott Parsons, "The Father Symbol," in his *Social Structure and Personality* (London: Collier-Macmillan, Glencoe, Ill.: Free Press, 1964), esp. p. 38; and his "The Contribution of Psychoanalysis to Social Science," in Jules Masserman, ed., *Psychoanalysis and Social Process*, Science and Psychoanalysis (New York: Grune and Stratton, 1961), 4:32-35. For field reports and theory in cultural anthropology which relate sexual asymmetry to the "universal opposition between 'domestic' and 'public' roles," see the papers in Michelle Z. Rosaldo and Louise Lamphere, eds., *Woman, Culture, and Society* (1974); quoted phrase from p. 8. See also Rosaldo's recent criticism of the domestic/public framework of analysis in her "The Use and Abuse of Anthropology: Reflections on Feminism and Cross-Cultural Understanding," *Signs* 5, no. 3 (1980):389-417.

37. Mitchell, *Psychoanalysis and Feminism*, p. 406.

Chapter 3

Biology, Psychology, and Culture in Psychoanalysis

Psychoanalytical research is . . . led to an explanation of man, not in terms of his sexual substructure, but to a discovery in sexuality of relations and attitudes which had previously been held to reside in consciousness. *Thus the significance of psychoanalysis is less to make psychology biological than to discover a dialectical process in functions thought of as "purely bodily," and to reintegrate sexuality into the human being.*
—MAURICE MERLEAU-PONTY,
Phenomenology of Perception

Mitchell's statement, that the unconscious father complex is the mental representation of social reality and its converse, that social reality results from the repressed mental complex, requires explanation. What kind of theory of culture does Freud offer? In what sense is Freud's *not* a circular theory? And how does a focus on gender asymmetry as the root of his theory of culture help us understand that the theory is not circular? We can address these questions by examining Freud's understanding of how body, mind, and culture are related for psychoanalysis. The Oedipus complex is the point where their relationships are most visible.

The oedipal situation consists in paternal authority, maternal submission, and proscribed filial desire. As a mental complex that arises within the context of the family, it renders the psychoanalytic theory of neuroses a social psychology. Then, when the psychoanalytic "discovery" of the hidden oedipal structure of mind in individuals (the object observed) is employed as the principle of investigation (the method) when the subject of study is religion and culture, this application of a psychoanalytic hypothesis to problems of cultural history makes psychoanalysis an explicit theory of culture. And Freud's psychoanalysis is also an implicit theory of culture when it postulates that the civilizing of each individual is based on culturally directed re-

40

nunciations which are communicated by the mental presence of the castrating, oedipal father. Mental asymmetry between the parental figures, therefore, grounds the Oedipus complex (the nucleus of the neuroses). Simultaneously, the son's psychical response to the father complex has generated religion and culture "originally" and continues to do so ever anew. As Norman O. Brown puts it, "the link between the theory of neurosis and the theory of history is the theory of religion, as is made perfectly clear in *Totem and Taboo* and *Moses and Monotheism*,"[1] for religion is treated as the collective and institutionalized psychical response to the "original" father complex; it has the structure of a symptom which betrays the origin of civilization.

In order to clarify how biological, psychological, and cultural considerations are both conceptually distinguished and dynamically interrelated in Freudian theory, let us examine some of Freud's and other scholars' observations about its foci and method. Doing this will also allow us to see that gender asymmetry is both the methodological and postulated historical beginning and the individual and cultural result in the Freudian theory of mind. In one sense, Freud's entire theory is about gender asymmetry.

Biology and Psychology

Freud's psychoanalysis postulates psychical, not chemical or physiological, processes, insofar as it is psychoanalysis. Once the main concepts of psychoanalytic theory are understood to be about psychology and not about biology, it is also the case that they must be about human nature in culture rather than outside or prior to it. The explicit location of psychoanalysis as a psychology is particularly important in a discussion which focuses on gender. This is because the widespread opinion that sex difference is, for Freud, merely a matter of his misinterpretation of biological difference in the form of thinking that women are castrated, has obscured the importance of psychical gender, as distinguished from sex, in his thought.

Several French interpreters of Freud's thought have emphasized that his theories, particularly of the Oedipus complex, but also of the instincts, sexuality, and repression, are not about what is biological or natural per se but about contradiction in the encounter between "nature" and "culture." Drawing on the thought of Claude Lévi-Strauss and Jacques Lacan in this

---

1. Norman O. Brown, *Life Against Death* (1970), p. 12.

regard, interpreters such as Ricoeur and Mannoni have stressed that Freud's concepts refer to mental or psychical reality and that as soon as mental life enters the oedipal situation, the resulting structure is peculiarly human and already "encultured." Biological sex difference is psychoanalytically important when it functions in the mind in relation to the cultural oedipal structure.

An influential German reading of Freud, put forth by members of the Frankfurt school of social research and those influenced by it, also insists that Freud, unlike many neo-Freudians, was concerned to comprehend a provisionally independent psychical reality, but they claim that at its deepest level this reality expresses psychical transformations that are necessitated by social reality. For them, Freud's analysis is of mind, which already "contains" society within it. Thus, they consider Freud's theories to be both more socially critical and potentially more radical than those of his revisers.

In America until relatively recently, emphasis has been placed on Freud's "biologism," "mechanism," or "scientism" often in order to prepare for humanistic criticism of these reductive perspectives. (Or it has been placed on his speculativeness in order to prepare for empiricist criticism.) Many Americans have found Freud's critical pessimism unpalatable and have attributed this pessimism to his failure to recognize sociocultural diversity.[2] Lionel Trilling nicely summarized the reading that emphasizes Freud's "biologism":

> The place of biology in Freud's system of thought has often been commented on, and generally adversely. It is often spoken of as if it represents a reactionary part of Freud's thought. The argument takes this form: if we think of a man as being conditioned not so much by biology as by culture, we can the more easily envisage a beneficent manipulation of his condition; if we keep our eyes fixed upon the wide differences among cultures which may be observed, and if we repudiate Freud's naive belief that there is a human *given* in all persons and all cultures, then we are indeed encouraged to think that we can do what we wish with ourselves, with mankind. . . .

Trilling's purpose is not to quarrel with this estimate of Freud's emphasis but to reverse its implications:

2. For an account of a sustained argument with Freud on the issue of his supposed sociological innocence, an account which fails to grasp that the intrapsychic economy of the individual was Freud's first focus, see Joseph Wortis, *Fragments of an Analysis with Freud* (New York: Simon & Schuster, 1954).

I think we must stop to consider whether this emphasis on biology, whether correct or incorrect, is not so far from being a reactionary idea that it is actually a liberating idea. It proposes to us that culture is not all-powerful. It suggests that there is a residue of human quality beyond the reach of cultural control, and that this residue of human quality, elemental as it may be, serves to bring culture itself under criticism and keeps it from being absolute.[3]

Perhaps because he was contesting a prevailing American view in the fifties, Trilling does not distinguish in this passage between biology and mind or between biology and "nature" understood more broadly.[4]

Freud distinguished methodologically between biology and psychology, but what was "natural" was not only biological. The psychical is also "natural" for him. Ludwig Binswanger defined Freud's image of *homo natura* as including: bodily instinct, gaining of pleasure by sacrificing a lesser for a greater gain, inhibition because of compulsion from society (the prototype being the family), "a developmental history in the sense of ontogenetic and phylogenetic transformations of outer into inner compulsions, and the inheritance of these transformations."[5] The ideas of socially induced inhibition and transformation of outer into inner compulsions (that is, humans repress themselves) are clearly questions neither of biology nor of nature when the latter is understood as somehow outside culture. Freud's "natural" psyche is not necessarily pre- or acultural.

In 1922, Freud defined psychoanalysis as:

The name (1) of a procedure for the investigation of mental processes which are almost inaccessible in any other way, (2) of a method (based

3. Lionel Trilling, *Freud and the Crisis of Our Culture* (1955), pp. 47-48. Trilling's statement is based on Freud's argument in *Civilization and Its Discontents* and, if the drives are considered biological, it adequately locates Freud's view of the critical component in his thought, as well as his main criticism of a socialist theory of human nature. However, it is doubtful whether Freud could have imagined the drives as a "liberating idea." For him, they were instead a "limiting idea" among other limiting ideas although Marcuse and others have found warrant in Freud's texts for treating them as liberating.

4. Trilling later emphasized mind rather than biology as Freud's critical principle: "Freud, in insisting upon the essential immitigability of the human condition as determined by the nature of the mind, had the intention of sustaining the authenticity of human existence that formerly had been ratified by God. It was his purpose to keep all things from becoming 'weightless'"; *Sincerity and Authenticity* (1971), p. 156.

5. Ludwig Binswanger, "Freud's Conception of Man in Light of Anthropology" (Torchbook edition, 1963), p. 153.

upon that investigation) for the treatment of neurotic disorders and (3) of a collection of psychological information obtained along those lines, which is gradually being accumulated into a new scientific discipline.[6]

The reference to inaccessible processes is to the hypothesis of the unconscious. In *An Outline of Psycho-Analysis*, Freud repeated his frequent assertion that the psychoanalytic hypothesis that "the psychical is unconscious in itself" has "enabled psychology to take its place as a natural science like any other. The processes with which it is concerned are in themselves just as unknowable as those dealt with by other sciences, by chemistry or physics, for example; but it is possible to establish the laws which they obey and to follow their mutual relations and interdependences. . . ."[7] Psychoanalytic concepts "can lay claim to the same value as approximations that belongs to the corresponding intellectual scaffolding found in other natural sciences, . . ."[8] but, beyond this, "reality will always remain 'unknowable.'"[9]

Lacan, among others, has insisted on the psychical focus of Freud's concepts. Lacan's translator and commentator, Anthony Wilden, has expanded upon Freud's statements which were just quoted:

> it is worth digressing slightly with a view to establishing Freud's own position in respect of the "intellectual scaffolding" . . . which he constructed around psychic *relationships*, a scaffolding which has so often been taken in two persistent misreadings of his text: that he was describing anything other than psychic reality, or a psychical system which is not in itself psychic, by these metaphors, and that he was describing "substances" rather than the interrelation of parts of a structure whose real nature is beyond definition or grasp.[10]

Even when it is understood that the processes postulated by psychoanalysis—repression, resistances, the drives, and the Oedipus complex—are psychical, that the psychical is unconscious,[11] and that consciousness is simply a *quality* of the psychical, it must be further understood that a psychical process is not analyzed into components that are other than psychical them-

6. "Two Encyclopaedia Articles" (1923), *SE* 18:235.
7. *An Outline of Psycho-Analysis* (1940), *SE* 23:158.
8. Ibid., p. 159.   9. Ibid., p. 196.
10. Anthony Wilden, "Lacan and the Discourse of the Other" (1968), p. 197.
11. The processes listed are taken from "Two Encyclopaedia Articles" (1923), *SE* 18:247, where Freud calls them the principal subject matter and theoretical foundations of psychoanalysis.

selves (that is, which are biological or sociological). In 1913 Freud warned: "not every analysis of psychological phenomena deserves the name of psycho-analysis. The latter implies more than the mere analysis of composite phenomena into simpler ones. It consists in tracing back one psychical structure to another which preceded it in time and out of which it developed."[12] By limiting the domain of psychoanalysis to the psychical so that its principles of explanation referred to unconscious psychical reality, Freud distinguished its perspective from those of other natural sciences, from sociology, and from philosophy. In a letter written in 1917, Freud made one of his many statements restricting the domain of his science and insisting on a multiplicity of viewpoints, among which psychoanalysis was but one. The statement is a cautioning plea to Georg Groddeck:

> Your experiences, after all, don't reach beyond the realization that the psychological factors play an unexpectedly important role also in the origin of organic diseases. But are these psychological factors *alone* responsible for the diseases, and do they call the difference between the psychic and the physical into question? To me it seems just as arbitrary to endow the whole of nature with a psyche as radically to deny that it has one at all. Let us grant to nature her infinite variety which rises from the inanimate to the organically animated, from the just physically alive to the spiritual. No doubt the UCS is the right mediator between the physical and mental. . . . But just because we have recognized this at last, is that any reason for refusing to see anything else?[13]

In a similar vein, Freud wrote to an endocrinologist, who had expressed an interest in psychoanalysis, that he was "very pleased to see from your letter that you are not among those who place psychoanalysis in opposition to endocrinology, as though psychic processes could be explained directly by glandular functions, or as though the understanding of psychic mechanism could replace the knowledge of the underlying chemical process."[14] Freud's reference to the "underlying" process is consistent with his expectation that psychoanalytic concepts would eventually meet those of biochemistry, when both disciplines were sufficiently advanced that such a meeting could

---

12. "The Claims of Psycho-Analysis to Scientific Interest" (1913), *SE* 13:182-183.
13. Letter to Georg Groddeck of June 5, 1917, in Ernst L. Freud, ed., *The Letters of Sigmund Freud* (1960), p. 318.
14. Letter to Alexander Lipschutz of August 12, 1931; ibid., p. 406.

be arranged.[15] Often, when faced with something which seemed psychoanalytically inexplicable, he invoked "biological factors" as the speculative fringe of his thought.

In my view, the most interesting interpretations of Freud's thought have been advanced by those who accept his treatment of the psychical as provisionally independent. Among others, Ricoeur and Mitchell have properly insisted that even the Freudian concept that is apparently the most biological, that of the instincts (more precisely, "drives," from *Triebe*), is to be understood as psychical in Freud's usage. Ricoeur claims that Freud's hypothesis that "instincts themselves represent or express the body to the mind" is perhaps "the most fundamental hypothesis of psychoanalysis, the one that qualifies it as *psycho*analysis."[16] These psychical representatives are concepts not for a biology but for a psychology. For Ricoeur, "psychoanalysis never confronts one with bare forces, but always with forces in search of meaning; this link between force and meaning makes instinct a psychical reality, or, more exactly, the limit concept at the frontier between the organic and the psychical."[17] Mitchell makes a similar observation about Freud's understanding of sexuality. "Freud's theory of sexuality as a complex unity involved also a redefinition of what sexuality 'itself' is," she writes. "Prior to Freud it was conceived of as one of the 'instincts,' and therefore, as with instincts in animals, it implied a preadaptation to reality. Freud humanized it, seeing that because of its ideational mental character, as it manifested itself, it existed only within the context of human culture."[18] "Freud's achievement," Mitchell continues, "was to transform the biological theory of instincts into the notion of the human drive, then to trace its possible expressions and to relegate them to their place within the person's history of

15. See "The Claims of Psycho-Analysis to Scientific Interest" (1913), *SE* 13:181-182: "We have found it necessary to hold aloof from biological considerations during our psycho-analytic work and to refrain from using them for heuristic purposes, so that we may not be misled in our impartial judgement of the psycho-analytic facts before us. But after we have completed our psycho-analytic work we shall have to find a point of contact with biology. . . ."

16. Paul Ricoeur, *Freud and Philosophy* (1970), p. 137. The reference is to "Instincts and Their Vicissitudes" (1915), where Freud writes that from a biological point of view "an 'instinct' appears to us as a concept on the frontier between the mental and the somatic, as the psychical representative of the stimuli originating from within the organism and reaching the mind . . ."; *SE* 14:121-122.

17. Ricoeur, *Freud and Philosophy*, p. 151.

18. Juliet Mitchell, *Psychoanalysis and Feminism* (1974), p. 21. It is not clear that Mitchell is historically correct in making Freud the first to "humanize" sexuality, but she is correct about Freud's view of his achievement.

subjectivity."[19] Precisely the same point can be made about gender differ-ence; gender is a psychological structure with a history that occurs within the context of human culture. Within this context, the difference in genders is internal to each psyche. From this perspective, structure and dynamics of mind are not simply reflections of biological givens, but neither are they un-related to these.

The intrapsychic "realm" consists in processes and relationships that are explicable only in relation to unconsciousness, both ontogenetic and phylo-genetic. Mannoni describes Freud's view of the human as psychically split. He writes that an analysis "reveals profoundly . . . a kind of original fracture in the way man is constituted, a split that opposes him to himself (and not to reality or to society) and exposes him to the attacks of his unconscious."[20] For Freud, insofar as "reality," "society," or "biology" contributes to this split, it is already psychical, that is, already in some way transformed. It is not mentally identical to the ego's view of it or to the biologist's or sociolo-gist's view. The unconscious is incapable of reality testing, and unconscious *ideas*, rather than biological, social, or even biographical facts by them-selves, produce other psychical events. "What lie behind the sense of guilt of neurotics are always *psychical* realities and never *factual* ones," Freud wrote.[21]

Psychology and Culture

If Freud's major concepts refer to psychical processes which transform and interpret the organic, and if clinical psychoanalysis encounters a biological "factor" when and because it is already psychical, it is likewise the case that a "cultural factor" meets a psychoanalytic clinical investigator only when it is already translated into the psychical life of the subject. The "real event," in its presumed pristine objectivity, is not understood as explanatory from a psychoanalytic point of view. The explicit attention which Freud paid to the influence of social "factors" on the mental lives of individuals was less than many neo-Freudians have paid. Even so, social life is part of psychoanalytic theory at least because of the importance of the mental Oedipus complex as a psychical structure. As H. Stuart Hughes observed, Freud had been from the start a special kind of social theorist. "Although he began only late in

19. Ibid., p. 27.
20. O[ctave] Mannoni, *Freud* (1974), pp. 192-193.
21. *Totem and Taboo* (1913), SE 13:159.

life to apply to the world of human communities the insights that he had earlier derived from the study of individuals, in one sense he had all along been writing about society. For he had written of individuals *in families. . . ."*[22]

As we have seen, there is significant critical agreement that the Freudian psyche is not "natural" in the sense of presocial or asocial once it has met with the oedipal situation. Freud's writings have taught social theorists how concretely the family is "the inner indwelling principle of sociality operating in an unconscious way. . . ."[23] That the oedipal father had social as well as psychical functions was, of course, clear to Freud from the earliest days of his psychoanalytic career. In 1899 he noted that "a Prince is known as the father of his country; the father is the oldest, first, and for children only authority, and from his autocratic power the other social authorities have developed in the course of the history of human civilization. . . ."[24] Because of a child's emotional relationship to the father, which is based in the erotic dilemma of the oedipal triangle, and because of the father's social position, psychoanalysis "could not avoid dealing with the emotional basis of the relation of the individual to society." Freud wrote: "it has been found that the social feelings invariably contain an erotic element. . . ."[25] Thus, his *Group Psychology and the Analysis of the Ego*, as well as *Totem and Taboo* and his later books on religion, examine social institutions in terms of their origins in, and functions for, the erotic difficulty of the repressed father complex. The relationship between psyche and society also obtains in the other direction; erotic life is shaped by social forces which are paternally defined. But they are not simply defined by a particular father in an individual case; the cultural unconscious subtends the individual's history. In Freud's words:

> psycho-analysis has fully demonstrated the part played by social conditions and requirements in the causation of neurosis. The forces which, operating from the ego, bring about the restriction and repression of instinct owe their origin essentially to compliance with the demands of civilization. . . . Young people are brought into contact with the demands of civilization by upbringing and example; and if instinctual repression occurs independently of these two factors, it is a plausible hypothesis to suppose that a primaeval and prehistoric demand has at

22. H. Stuart Hughes, *Consciousness and Society* (Vintage edition, 1958), p. 144.

23. G. W. F. Hegel, *The Phenomenology of Mind*, trans. J. B. Baillie (New York: Harper Torchbooks/Academy Library, 1967), p. 468.

24. *The Interpretation of Dreams* (1900), SE 4:217, n. 1.

25. "The Claims of Psycho-Analysis to Scientific Interest" (1913), SE 13:188.

last become part of the organized and inherited endowment of mankind. A child who produces instinctual repressions spontaneously is thus merely repeating a part of the history of civilization. What is today an act of internal restraint was once an external one, imposed, perhaps, by the necessities of the moment; and, in the same way, what is now brought to bear upon every growing individual as an external demand of civilization may some day become an internal disposition to repression.[26]

So, if the psychoanalytic method traces psychical events back to prior psychical events when it reconstructs the history of the individual, it presumes an external restraint at the origin of these now internalized structures, an external restraint which must have occurred in the history of civilization and which began the endless chain of causal psychical events. For Freud, this presumption authorizes his claim for the historicity of the terrible primal father. Furthermore, although presumably any number of external restraints could by now be internalized, the only external restraint which Freud repeatedly hypothesized was the primal father's restraint of all the sons (and possession of all the women). His conclusion to *Totem and Taboo* is that

> its outcome shows that the beginnings of religion, morals, society and art converge in the Oedipus complex. This is in complete agreement with the psycho-analytic finding that the same complex constitutes the nucleus of all neuroses, so far as our present knowledge goes. It seems to me a most surprising discovery that the problems of social psychology, too, should prove soluble on the basis of one single concrete point—man's relation to his father.[27]

Freudian theory of culture, then, turns on the concrete sociological and historical postulate of paternal authority as it operates mentally. This concrete postulate is the cultural and mental asymmetry of fathers' and mothers' relative positions.

On the basis of Freud's hypothesis about the internalization of external restraints so that, in effect, oppression is transformed into repression, members of the Frankfurt school have read Freud's works as sociological in their depth dimension and as critical of the culture that has necessitated "surplus" instinctual repressions.[28] Although there are differences in the views of

26. Ibid., pp. 188-189.
27. *Totem and Taboo* (1913), *SE* 13:156-157.
28. See Martin Jay, *The Dialectical Imagination: A History of the Frankfurt School and the Institute of Social Research, 1923-1950* (Boston: Little Brown, 1973), pp. 86-112; Paul A. Robin-

members of this school, the shared claim has been that Freud, in his "stubborn pursuit of the genesis and structure of the individual psyche, [has] testified to the power of society in and over the individual. . . . psychoanalysis rediscovers society in the individual monad." They note that Freud's psychology, "by its own logic, turns into sociology and history."[29] This sociology and history is reconstructed by being read through the psyche which distorts it. Marcuse argues:

> Freud's "biologism" is social theory in a depth dimension that has been consistently flattened out by the Neo-Freudian schools. In shifting the emphasis from the unconscious to conscious, from the biological to the cultural factors, they cut off the roots of society in the instincts and instead take society at the level on which it confronts the individual as his ready-made "environment," without questioning its origin and legitimacy. . . . Moreover, we believe that the most concrete insights into the historical structure of civilization are contained precisely in the concepts that the revisionists reject. Almost the entire Freudian metapsychology, his later theory of the instincts [Eros and death], his reconstruction of the prehistory of mankind belong to these concepts.[30]

On this basis, the primal horde theory may be read as Freud's reconstruction of what historically and socially must have been the case in order for the instinctual dynamics discovered by psychoanalysis to be as they are. With his "scientific myth" or "Just-So-Story" of the primal horde, "Freud himself in his metatheory— . . . derived the instinctual biology from a prehistory of violence and force."[31] The sons' responses to the primal father's threats of castration have become part of instinctual structure itself, according to this view. In Marcuse's words, "the repressive transformation of the instincts becomes the biological constitution of the organism: history rules even in the instinctual structure; culture becomes nature as soon as the individual learns to affirm and to reproduce the reality principle from within himself, through

son, *The Freudian Left* (1969), esp. pp. 1-7, 147-244; H. Stuart Hughes, *The Sea Change: The Migration of Social Thought, 1930-1965* (New York: Harper & Row, 1975), pp. 189-201; Trent Schroyer, *The Critique of Domination* (1973), pp. 149-155; Russell Jacoby, *Social Amnesia* (1975), pp. 19-45; Phil Slater, *Origin and Significance of the Frankfurt School: A Marxist Perspective*, International Library of Sociology, ed. John Rex (London: Routledge & Kegan Paul, 1977), pp. 94-118.

29. Jacoby, *Social Amnesia*, p. 79.

30. Herbert Marcuse, *Eros and Civilization* (Vintage edition, 1962), pp. 5-6.

31. Jacoby, *Social Amnesia*, p. 31.

his instincts."[32] The social dimension of the father complex is not properly understood, then, as a reflection of particular or even currently typical familial politics. It is a component of *Kultur* itself, understood by Freud to be universal.

Whether one reads French structuralists, who speak of "culture," or German social theorists, who speak of "society," the point made is the same: sociocultural reality is contained in Freud's concepts and, in particular, in the idea of the Oedipus complex. This "universal" reality is discovered within individual psychical structures, and then it is treated as the principle by which history and culture are interpreted. "Here, the doctrine is method," as Ricoeur has commented in a different context.[33] The overarching Freudian notion—in the (ontogenetic and phylogenetic) beginning is paternal domination—means, as Mitchell has asserted, that his psychology is about patriarchal culture and, therefore, about mental expression and reproduction of gender asymmetry. When Freud expands individual psychology into a theory of culture, the Oedipus complex, the nucleus of individual psychology, is already the basis of the psychological concepts that Freud *applies* to culture in order to provide his psychoanalytic interpretation of it.

Such an application, which has been frequently criticized, is not merely circular reasoning. It is the result of Freud's analogy between psychical processes discovered within a current, individual context that is characterized by gender asymmetry and psychical processes within an original, collective context that he assumed to have been similarly characterized. By means of this analogy, "civilization" and "patriarchy" are equated. Because the son must respond to paternal restraints in oedipal development, and sometimes does so disproportionately to the "real" threat, Freud postulated that the beginning of all civilizational development was likewise a response to paternal restriction. But, as he wrote in *Totem and Taboo*: "Our assertion that taboo originated in a primaeval prohibition imposed at one time or other by some external authority is obviously incapable of demonstration."[34] So, Freud's psychoanalysis becomes a theory of culture by positing a psychological analogy between the collective and the individual. For example, in explaining taboo, Freud drew upon the similarity of "emotional ambivalence." Because the original paternal prohibition was not demonstrable, Freud wrote:

32. Herbert Marcuse, "Freedom and Freud's Theory of Instincts" (1970), p. 11. Although Freud never mentioned this implication, the daughters' and mothers' mental responses to threats of incestuous rape must also be part of the structure of drive, according to his logic.
33. Ricoeur, *Freud and Philosophy*, p. 433.
34. *Totem and Taboo* (1913), *SE* 13:35.

What we shall rather endeavour to confirm, therefore, are the psychological determinants of taboo, which we have learnt to know from obsessional neurosis. . . . If, now, we could succeed in demonstrating that ambivalence, that is, the dominance of opposing trends, is also to be found in the observances of taboo, or if we could point to some of them which, like obsessional acts, give simultaneous expression to both currents, we should have established the psychological agreement between taboo and obsessional neurosis in what is perhaps their most important feature.[35]

The analogy is drawn, not directly between the two substantives (taboo and obsessional neurosis) but rather between the relationships between ambivalance and obsessions, on the one hand, and ambivalence and taboo, on the other. Ambivalence is in turn traced to the son's psychical attitudes to the father.

Freud's psychology is primarily about the socialized son and secondarily about the socialized daughter in a situation where father-son dynamics are primary. It delineates masculine and feminine psychical attitudes toward the father figure. His theory of culture is what an application of this psychology suggests about the mental origins and processes of culture. His theory of religion is about the psychical renunciations and fulfillments possible under these cultural conditions. Freud's economic hypothesis, that "the whole course of the history of civilization is no more than an account of the various methods adopted by mankind for 'binding' their unsatisfied wishes, which, according to changing conditions (modified, moreover, by technological advances) have been met by reality sometimes with favour and sometimes with frustration,"[36] is the topic of the next section.

35. Ibid., pp. 35-36.
36. "The Claims of Psycho-Analysis to Scientific Interest" (1913), *SE* 13:186.

PART TWO

Renunciation and Masculinity

Chapter 4

The Value of Renunciation: Freud's Moral Economy

Analysts . . . cannot repudiate their descent from exact science and their community with its representatives. Moved by an extreme distrust of the power of human wishes and of the temptations of the pleasure principle, they are ready, for the sake of attaining some fragment of objective certainty, to sacrifice everything. . . .
—FREUD, *"Psycho-Analysis and Telepathy"*

Because Freud's psychology is about the paternally socialized son, a complete understanding of his psychology of masculinity requires prior explanation of his entire theory. For reasons which Simmel has made clear, an explanation of Freud's psychology of femininity is possible simply by contrasting it to his psychology of masculinity, that is, to his apparently "general" oedipal psychology. Here I focus on Freudian texts that treat masculine development as human development to see how renunciation, masculinity, and the human ideal coincide in Freud's estimation. I outline the ethical meanings of several polar Freudian concepts that can be seen as a series of structurally analogous counterpoints. Within each polarity, the second term is the result of development; it follows the first term chronologically and surpasses it in mental, cultural, and moral value. The chronological and evaluative development is in each instance traceable to renunciation of wish.

As the quotation opening this chapter shows, for Freud the pleasure principle and wish fulfillment must be sacrificed to reality. In Freud's view, the sacrificial advance toward reality is achieved by science, by analysis as part of science, and by prescientific historical changes that were steps on the way to the "conquest" of wishes by the reality principle. It is also achieved in a psychoanalytic cure.

This chapter and the two that follow it trace the theme that fulfilled wish signifies stasis or regression whereas renounced wish represents progression or development. The relationship between wish and reality whereby higher development issues from reality-directed renunciation of wish is the dynamic core of Freud's economic and genetic viewpoints. The genetic viewpoint asks questions of origin and development. The economic viewpoint takes into account quantities of mental energy in relation to pleasure and unpleasure.[1] The way Freud associates mental and cultural value with development through renunciation of pleasure may be called his "moral economy." In this chapter, the moral economy will be outlined as it occurs in Freud's theoretical discussions of primary and secondary processes, pleasure and reality principles, narcissism and object relations, and the specialized topographical "regions" (unconscious, preconscious) and mental structures (id, ego, and superego). In Chapter 5, the themes of wish and reality are traced in some of Freud's many statements about the relative positions of religion (and other wish-fulfilling illusions) and science within the psychological schema of renunciation and fulfillment. His related views about stages of cultural development and the renunciatory bases of individual and collective cure are also discussed.

Freud's genetic explanation of the development of (male) individuals relies on the ideas of the father as castrator, of the (male) Oedipus and castration complexes, and of the overcoming of these complexes as the key to psychical maturity. The discussion in Chapter 6 of these ideas will establish the Freudian relationships between masculinity, the primacy of the intellect, the paternal superego, and the ethical and cultural value of renunciation.

Wish and Reality

Freud's earliest descriptions of the "mental apparatus" (a term which he later replaced with "psychical system") attribute to it an "original trend to inertia." The aim of the apparatus is to keep its level of energetic excitation as low as possible, or at least constant.[2] In the draft which Freud mailed to Wilhelm Fliess, in 1895, which was published in 1950 as the *Project for a Scientific Psychology*, Freud wrote that "since we have a certain knowledge of a trend in psychical life towards *avoiding unpleasure*, we are tempted to identify that trend with the primary trend towards inertia."[3] In later years, this unpleasure principle was revised and related to the constancy principle, the

1. *Beyond the Pleasure Principle* (1920), SE 18:7.
2. *Project for a Scientific Psychology* (1950), SE 1:296-297. For a discussion of unresolved problems in Freud's formulations of the tendency to inertia, the principle of constancy, and the Nirvana principle, see J. Laplanche and J.-B. Pontalis, *The Language of Psycho-Analysis* (1973), pp. 342-347.
3. *Project for a Scientific Psychology* (1950), SE 1:312.

pleasure principle, and, in 1920, the Nirvana principle. Although Freud distinguished among them,[4] for our purposes it is sufficient to note what all these principles have in common: the assumption of an original and immortal psychical trend toward satisfaction, which is attained by *reducing* the level of energy within the psychical system. The economic hypothesis that underlay all these conceptions was that wish fulfillment entails discharge of energy so that an increase of energy in the psychical system, which results in psychical development, is traceable to the unpleasure of an unsatisfied wish or, in stricter economic terms, of undischarged energy. "Wishful states," which are unpleasurable because the wish is maintained without being satisfied, entail increased intrapsychical tension.[5] "Unpleasure remains the only means of education," Freud wrote in 1895.[6] So Freud proposes an inverse relationship between education, or mental advance, and wish fulfillment. He proposes a direct relationship between renunciation of the satisfaction of a wish, which raises the energic level, and an advance in mental level.[7]

In a letter to Fliess, Freud wrote: "Reality—wish-fulfilment: it is from this contrasting pair that our mental life springs."[8] If reality did not prevent immediate fulfillment, no mental development would be necessary. Conversely, the dynamics of repression, sublimation, and other defenses, which underlie the highest mental achievements, are detours from satisfactions of instinctual wishes, the fulfillment of which has been outlawed by material or cultural reality. Repression is described as a process that "turns a possibility of pleasure into a source of unpleasure."[9] Reality opposes the fulfillment of wishes; it makes their fulfillment threatening to the civilized censor. At the same time, the continued pressure of wishes may falsify perception of reality. "Illusions of memory arise in the mind with a compelling force which they draw from real sources; but they turn psychical reality into material reality," Freud commented in the course of explaining an experience of telepathy.[10] A wish gives rise to illusion when what is wished for (a psychical reality) is experienced as external reality.

4. See "The Economic Problem of Masochism" (1924), SE 19:160.

5. *Project for a Scientific Psychology* (1950), SE 1:322.

6. Ibid., p. 370.

7. See Freud's "The Case of Lucy R.," in Josef Breuer and Freud, *Studies on Hysteria* (1893-1895), SE 2:118-121, for an early discussion of an illness precipitated by an unconscious, unfulfillable wish and its cure by a (conscious) renunciation of the wish.

8. Letter to Wilhelm Fliess of February 19, 1899, in Marie Bonaparte et al., eds., *The Origins of Psycho-Analysis* (1954), p. 277.

9. *Beyond the Pleasure Principle* (1920), SE 18:11.

10. "Dreams and Telepathy" (1922), SE 18:217.

In 1911, Freud explained that his "gloomy prognosis" that the claims of sexuality and the demands of civilization will never be reconciled was based on his "conjecture" that "the non-satisfaction that goes with civilization is the necessary consequence of certain peculiarities which the sexual instinct has assumed under the pressure of culture." But his gloom is ambiguous because

> the very incapacity of the sexual instinct to yield complete satisfaction as soon as it submits to the first demands of civilization becomes the source . . . of the noblest cultural achievements. . . . For what motive would men have for putting sexual instinctual forces to other uses if, by any distribution of those forces, they could obtain fully satisfying pleasure? They would never abandon that pleasure and they would never make any further progress.[11]

The reality that opposes wishes includes both cultural and material reality. Demands made by civilization for renunciation result from demands made by external natural conditions on human life: "the main motive force towards the cultural development of man has been real external exigency, which has withheld from him the easy satisfaction of his natural needs. . . . This external frustration drove him into a struggle with reality. . . ." In this struggle, renunciations are inevitable. Freud concludes this passage with the judgment that "every individual on his journey from childhood to maturity has in his own person to recapitulate this development of humanity to a state of judicious resignation."[12] This affective resignation or detachment— renunciation—is the psychical source of culture itself, of morality, and of scientific objectivity.

Wish and reality are the poles of mental life. Hysterical symptoms and dreams were at first explained psychoanalytically as results of conflict between an unconscious wish and its opponent, the preconscious, reality-oriented, and "civilized" censor. In a metaphor from Greek myth, Freud described the two parties to this conflict: "These wishes in our unconscious, ever on the alert and, so to say, immortal, remind one of the legendary Titans, weighed down since primaeval ages by the massive bulk of the mountains which were once hurled upon them by the victorious gods and which are still shaken from time to time by the convulsion of their limbs."[13] Here

11. "On the Universal Tendency to Debasement in the Sphere of Love (Contributions to the Psychology of Love II)" (1912), SE 11:190.
12. "A Short Account of Psycho-Analysis" (1924), SE 19:207.
13. *The Interpretation of Dreams* (1900), SE 5:553.

the "victorious gods" are reality, the mountains are repressions, and the Titan wishes, struggling for release, move the world. In a better-known simile, Freud compared the function of wishes in dreams to that of a capitalist in the economic system.[14] In these comparisons, Freud claims that wishes are the prime movers of the mind; "nothing but a wish can set our mental apparatus at work."[15] Unconscious wishful impulses are "the core of our being."[16]

In Freud's famous formula, distorted dreams are disguised fulfillments of repressed wishes, infantile dreams are open fulfillments of permitted wishes, and anxiety dreams, which awaken the dreamer, are open fulfillments of repressed wishes.[17] Dream formation is at once fulfilling and regressive. Dreams, which served as Freud's model for the analytic interpretation of symptoms, myth, and religion, are inexpedient for gaining satisfaction in the world of waking reality. If this kind of fulfillment were an adequate strategy for survival, the mental apparatus and human civilization with it would never have developed. But note the "moral" which Freud draws from the continued viability of the suppressed Titans, the wishes. In his view, the shared fulfillments of wishes that create illusions play a continuing part in individual and cultural life. He identified and criticized many such illusions—religious, political, philosophical, and occult—and contrasted them with the realism of the psychoanalytic viewpoint. Indeed, Freud frequently attributed resistance to psychoanalytic findings to their disillusioning, and therefore unpleasurable, implications. As one audience was warned, "When you reject something that is disagreeable to you, what you are doing is *repeating* the mechanism of constructing dreams rather than understanding it and surmounting it."[18] This Freudian ethic associates acquiescence to unpleasure through renunciation with recognition of reality and truth, and the pleasure of fulfillment with retaining an illusory wish.

The direction of development from pleasure to reality principle functioning is simultaneously *progressive* and based on renunciation whereas the opposite is simultaneously *regressive* and based on fulfillment. In an early discussion of regression, Freud associates it with the sensory as opposed to

14. Ibid., p. 561.

15. Ibid., p. 567.

16. Ibid., p. 603. A wish was defined in energic terms as a "current . . . in the apparatus, starting from unpleasure and aiming at pleasure . . ."; ibid., p. 598.

17. "Wish-Fulfilment," Lecture 16 of *Introductory Lectures on Psycho-Analysis* (1916-1917), *SE* 15:217.

18. "The Censorship of Dreams," Lecture 9 of *Introductory Lectures on Psycho-Analysis* (1916-1917), *SE* 15:145-146.

the rational; fulfillment has ties with the body, renunciation with the mind. In *The Interpretation of Dreams*, Freud visualized mental activity occurring on a continuum between sensory and motor "ends" of the mental apparatus. The sensory end received stimuli and the motor end, through movement, discharged the excitations created by stimuli.[19] It was a pleasure-attaining apparatus. However, a "critical agency" was located somewhere close to the motor end of the apparatus.[20] Because of its criticism, not all stimuli could enter consciousness and proceed to discharge; the critical agency renounced some activities of discharge that were incompatible with reality by keeping the mental presentations of the stimuli (wishes) out of consciousness (repression). Thinking processes belong near the motor end; they are considered to be calculations about the advisability of action. Given this apparatus on a continuum, the direction of psychical activity could proceed either from the sensory to the motor end or from the motor to the sensory end. Psychical activity that began with a perception of a stimulus and moved toward activity in the external world (motor discharge) was considered progressive whether it achieved discharge or not. Psychical activity was considered regressive when excitation moved "backward" toward becoming a sensory (perceptual) image rather than forward toward discharge.[21] The regressive direction was taken in the formation of dreams, hallucinations, and illusions. Regressions are "thoughts transformed into images."[22] This dynamic model of the mind thereby associated instinctual wishes and their fulfillment with sensory receptivity and with images based in sensation. It associated thought, criticism, and activity in the external world with psychical developments which were later, and more highly developed, than sensory perception. "What is older in time is more primitive in form and in psychical topography lies nearer to the perceptual end," Freud wrote.[23] What was later was more advanced and had also been subjected to criticism; what was prior was more primitive and had eluded criticism.

With this model, it was no great step to view materials discovered in dreams and neuroses as encoded messages about mental origins and history, both individual and shared. "Dreams and neuroses seem to have preserved more mental antiquities than we could have imagined possible; so that psycho-analysis may claim a high place among the sciences which are concerned with the reconstruction of the earliest and most obscure periods of the beginnings of the human race," Freud commented.[24] The mental deriva-

19. *The Interpretation of Dreams* (1900), SE 5:537.
20. Ibid., p. 540.   21. Ibid., p. 542.   22. Ibid., p. 544.
23. Ibid., p. 548.   24. Ibid., p. 549.

tives of wish fulfillment, which takes place through regressive psychical action, are considered to be simultaneously earlier in mental chronology and lower in mental hierarchy; wish is both prior to and "beneath" development. Freud's fondness for the metaphor of archeology for his science reveals this double conception of his discoveries: the archeologist unearths the buried past. In 1900, when Freud's topographical concepts consisted in the unconscious and preconscious mental regions, he wrote that "even where psychical health is perfect, the subjugation of the *Ucs.* by the *Pcs.* is not complete; the measure of suppression indicates the degree of our psychical normality."[25] Intrapsychic *activity* is required for development toward normality, and this activity is a suppression or a renunciation, which issues from a criticism. This normality is not a statistical norm; it is not a frequent achievement but is rather the ideal which is approached.

Primary and Secondary Processes

It is unnecessary to chronicle the complicated history of Freud's three instinct theories to emphasize that his late (1920) description of the two irreducible drives (Eros, or life, and death) maintained, like his previous descriptions, that the drives themselves strive to reduce the quantity of stimulation in the mental apparatus.[26] "*An instinct is an urge inherent in organic life to restore an earlier state of things* which the living entity has been obliged to abandon under the pressure of external disturbing forces; . . . it is a kind of organic elasticity, or, to put it another way, the expression of the inertia inherent in organic life."[27] Even death, apparently a renunciation of life, is, in this view, the fulfillment of a drive to return to a prior, inorganic state.

Four ideas remained constant in Freud's drive theories. First, the drives

25. Ibid., pp. 580-581.
26. For accounts of the history of instinct theory, see *An Autobiographical Study* (1925), *SE* 20:56-57; *Beyond the Pleasure Principle* (1920), *SE* 18:50-53, 60-61, n. 1. First, ego (self-preservative) and sexual (libidinal) drives were opposed; then ego libido and object libido were considered to be the two driving forces; finally, in 1920, the notions of Eros and death were proposed. In this last formulation, Eros subsumed all the previous possibilities.
27. *Beyond the Pleasure Principle* (1920), *SE* 18:36. But, even though Eros, too, seeks to restore earlier pleasure, Freud notes that we can attribute to the sexual instincts "an internal impulse towards 'progress' and towards higher development"; ibid., p. 40, n. 1. He then suggests that both higher development and involution might be "consequences of adaptation to the pressure of external forces" so that the instincts might simply function to retain "an obligatory modification" in the form of an "internal source of pleasure" (ibid., p. 41).

are "historically determined,"[28] that is, they have adapted to the external pressures of reality on the pleasure-seeking organism. Second, their aim is always satisfaction. Third, satisfaction is obtained by a return to an (economically and historically) prior state of affairs. Fourth, this return signifies an increase in pleasure and a decrease in energic stimulation: "the ultimate aim of mental activity, which may be described qualitatively as an endeavour to obtain pleasure and avoid unpleasure, emerges, looked at from the economic point of view, as the task of mastering the amounts of excitation (mass of stimuli) operating in the mental apparatus and of keeping down their accumulation which creates unpleasure."[29]

In short, the internal battle with the drives is a battle between fulfillment and renunciation. Freud's psychology of fantasy is explicit about this battle. He wrote: "the human ego is, as you know, slowly educated by the pressure of external necessity to appreciate reality and obey the reality principle; in the course of this process it is obliged to renounce, temporarily or permanently, a variety of the objects and aims at which its striving for pleasure, and not only for sexual pleasure, is directed." He continued:

> But men have always found it hard to renounce pleasure; they cannot bring themselves to do it without some kind of compensation. They have therefore retained a mental activity in which all these abandoned sources of pleasure and methods of achieving pleasure are granted a further existence—a form of existence in which they are left free from the claims of reality. . . . Every desire takes before long the form of picturing its own fulfilment; there is no doubt that dwelling upon imaginary wish-fulfilments brings satisfaction with it, although it does not interfere with a knowledge that what is concerned is not real. Thus in the activity of phantasy human beings continue to enjoy the freedom from external compulsion which they have long since renounced in reality. They have contrived to alternate between remaining an animal of pleasure and being once more a creature of reason. . . .[30]

Illusion, like fantasy, is compensatory, but, in contrast to fantasy, illusion refers to a situation wherein the knowledge of reality may be falsified. In general, religious illusion is a symptom of unfulfilled wishes: "a symptom, like a dream, represents something as fulfilled: a satisfaction in the infantile man-

28. "Two Encyclopaedia Articles" (1923), SE 18:259.
29. "The Paths to Symptom-Formation," Lecture 23 of *Introductory Lectures on Psycho-Analysis* (1916-1917), SE 16:375.
30. Ibid., pp. 371-372.

ner."[31] But it is a distorted fulfillment, so psychoanalytic interpretation must decode its meaning.

As Freud developed his conceptualization of the primary (unconscious and wishful) mental processes as opposed to the secondary (rational and critical) processes in terms of the pleasure and reality principles, and as he later related these processes and principles to his structural model of id, ego, and superego, the possible varieties and miscarriages of fulfillment and renunciation became more complex, but the ethic remained unchanged: secondary processes and mental activity according to the reality principle were constructed on renunciations of wishes. The creature of reason had to renounce animal pleasure.[32] In one of his latest works, in 1938, Freud presented concisely the relationships between pleasure and reality, primary and secondary processes, and the psychical structure and again suggested that an increase in the level of energy *within* the system was entailed in passing from the first to the second set of psychical events. He wrote:

> The one and only urge of . . . instincts is towards satisfaction. . . . But immediate and unheeding satisfaction of the instincts, such as the id demands, would often lead to perilous conflicts with the external world and to extinction. . . . The processes which are possible in and between the assumed psychical elements in the id (the *primary process*) differ widely from those which are familiar to us through conscious perception. . . . The id obeys the inexorable pleasure principle. But not the id alone. It seems that the activity of the other psychical agencies too is able only to modify the pleasure principle but not to nullify it. . . .[33]

Ego development is concomitant with the development of psychical processes which modify the pleasure-dominated primary processes:

31. Ibid., p. 366.
32. Even sublimation, the process which is an apparent exception to this statement insofar as satisfaction per se is not given up, entails renunciation of the "original" erotic aim and object. There are several complexities in Freud's theoretical writings that are not addressed in this chapter, important as they are for understanding the changes in theory over time, because they seem not to have significantly influenced his critical position, based in his "moral economy," in his writings on gender difference and religion. On complexities in the relationships among the principles of inertia, constancy and Nirvana, and pleasure and reality, see *Beyond the Pleasure Principle* (1920), *SE* 18:62-64. On complexities in the relationships between the economic point of view and functions of ego, id and superego, see *Inhibitions, Symptoms, and Anxiety* (1926), *SE* 20:77-174.
33. *An Outline of Psycho-Analysis* (1940), *SE* 23:198.

> [The ego's] psychological function consists in raising the passage [of events] in the id to a higher dynamic level (perhaps by transforming freely mobile energy into bound energy . . .); its constructive function consists in interpolating, between the demand made by an instinct and the action that satisfies it, the activity of thought which, after taking its bearings in the present and assessing earlier experiences, endeavours by means of experimental actions to calculate the consequences of the course of action proposed. In this way the ego comes to a decision on whether the attempt to obtain satisfaction is to be carried out or postponed or whether it may not be necessary for the demand by the instinct to be suppressed altogether as being dangerous. (Here we have the *reality principle*.) Just as the id is directed exclusively to obtaining pleasure, so the ego is governed by considerations of safety.[34]

Only the ego—and at that, only "part" of the ego—prudently obeys the reality principle. The superego often disregards it because of its ties with the internalized authorities of the cultural past; it has deep bonds with the death drive as well.

Freud's 1911 paper which formally introduces and contrasts the pleasure and reality principles begins with the observation that "neurotics turn away from reality because they find it unbearable."[35] In doing so, they provide clues to the understanding of normal development. Originally, Freud suggested:

> whatever was thought of (wished for) was simply presented in a hallucinatory manner. . . . It was only the non-occurrence of the expected satisfaction . . . that led to the abandonment of this attempt at satisfaction by means of hallucination. . . . A new principle of mental functioning was thus introduced; what was presented in the mind was no longer what was agreeable but what was real, even if it happened to be disagreeable.[36]

This new principle was the reality principle. In a note to this passage, Freud commented: "the pleasure principle can really come to an end only when a

34. Ibid., p. 199. Cf. the following passage in *The Interpretation of Dreams* (1900), SE 5:599: "All that I insist upon is the idea that the activity of the *first* ψ-system is directed towards securing the *free discharge* of the quantities of excitation, while the *second* system, by means of the cathexes emanating from it, succeeds in *inhibiting* this discharge and in transforming the cathexis into a quiescent one, no doubt with a simultaneous raising of its level."
35. "Formulations on the Two Principles of Mental Functioning" (1911), SE 12:218.
36. Ibid., p. 219.

child has achieved complete psychical detachment from its parents."[37] Later, he would suggest that such detachment issues from the dissolution of the boy's Oedipus complex, a relatively rare and fortunate event for boys and a barely possible one for girls.

In the 1911 essay, reality principle thinking, having renounced the pleasure principle, is credited with purposeful action to alter the conditions of satisfaction in reality and with thinking itself, "an experimental kind of acting."[38] Rationality is defined as thought processes that take place according to the reality principle. While the unconscious processes continue to "equate reality of thought with external actuality, and wishes with their fulfilment," the reality ego strives for what is useful and guards itself against damage.[39]

Narcissism and Object Love

Freud tied the pleasure ego to narcissism and to the narcissistic belief in "omnipotence of thoughts," which he ascribed to primitive processes in individuals and in the history of civilization. His view of the stages of the libido as it moves from narcissism to object love in a fashion parallel to the development from pleasure to reality principles became the basis of his critical contrast between religious and scientific world views. In Freud's 1911 "Formulations on the Two Principles of Mental Functioning," he commented that the advance from the pleasure ego to the reality ego is accompanied by changes in the sexual instincts, which "lead them from their original auto-erotism through various intermediate phases to object-love in the service of procreation."[40] Their development toward choice of heterosexual objects entails loss of pleasure both because the infantile body has potentialities for pleasure that are greater than genital pleasure and because civilization insists on restraining even genital pleasure to legitimate heterosexual expression in service of procreation and patrimony. The well-known Freudian stages in which pleasure is found in oral, anal, phallic and genital "zones" in the subject's own body have been discussed by Brown, who contrasts the infant's free and "polymorphously perverse" capacity for pleasure (a term used by Freud in the *Three Essays on the Theory of Sexuality*) with the tyranny of the much reduced adult, genital, capacity.[41] The sexual instinct

37. Ibid., p. 220, n. 4. Later, Freud doubted that the pleasure principle ever came "to an end."
38. Ibid., p. 221.   39. Ibid., pp. 223, 225.   40. Ibid., p. 223.
41. Norman O. Brown, *Life Against Death* (1970), pp. 23-29, 116-117.

"does not originally serve the purposes of reproduction at all, but has as its aim the gaining of particular kinds of pleasure," Freud explained. He referred to the original "autonomy" of the erotogenic zones and their later "subordination" under the primacy of the genitals. He then suggested three stages of civilization which conform to the stages of the libido, "a first one, in which the sexual instinct may be freely exercised without regard to the aims of reproduction; a second, in which all of the sexual instinct is suppressed except what serves the aims of reproduction; and a third, in which only *legitimate* reproduction is allowed as a sexual aim."[42] A true subordination of pleasure to the demands of cultural reality has occurred; pleasure is lost in development. This is so not only because of the advance to genitality but also because of the advance to socially approved object love.

The drives "represent an instigation to mental activity."[43] A drive is "the psychical representative of an endosomatic, continuously flowing source of stimulation. . . ."[44] As the sexual drives develop from primarily oral, to anal, to phallic, to genital expression, the objects which satisfy them also change; objects become progressively more external to the subject. From autoerotism, or self-satisfaction, develops primary narcissism, "an original libidinal cathexis of the ego." Freud came to believe that the libidinal drives were originally and permanently narcissistic to some degree and that the libido which later flows out onto objects is withdrawn from attachment to the subject's own ego, or part of its ego.[45] A regressive return to narcissism is always possible—this later narcissism is termed "secondary." Libidinal investment in "extraneous" objects takes place in relation to parents and later to objects whose prototypes are facets of the self (narcissistic object choice) or the parents (anaclitic object choice).[46] What Freud once called the "primitive objectless condition of narcissism"[47] is often contrasted first with oedipal (infantile) object choice and further with the reality orientation of extrafamilial object choice.

Freud drew on these contrasts to hypothesize analogous stages of civilization. Renunciation of narcissism became another way of describing men-

42. "'Civilized' Sexual Morality and Modern Nervous Illness" (1908), *SE* 9:188, 189.

43. *The Question of Lay Analysis: Conversations with an Impartial Person* (1926), *SE* 20:200.

44. *Three Essays on the Theory of Sexuality* (1905), *SE* 7:168.

45. "On Narcissism: An Introduction" (1914), *SE* 14:75. "Cathexis" refers to investment of psychical energy in an (internal or external) object. "Libido" means "the dynamic manifestation of sexuality"; "Two Encyclopaedia Articles" (1923), *SE* 18:255.

46. "On Narcissism" (1914), *SE* 14:87-88.

47. "The Unconscious" (1915), *SE* 14:197.

tal development through abandoning earlier pleasures. But the parallel between development from the pleasure principle to the reality principle, and from narcissism to object love, is more specific in Freud's thought than the fact that both developments entail abandoning pleasure under the pressure of reality. Under the dominance of the pleasure principle, both what is considered to be real and what is good (pleasurable) are perceived as part of the subject (internal) whereas under the dominance of the reality principle, what is external is regarded as real, whether it is pleasurable or painful. The pleasure ego introjects into itself what gives it pleasure and projects onto the outside world what is painful whereas the reality ego distinguishes between pleasure and reality regardless of the contrast between internal and external. In Freud's words, "what is bad, what is alien to the ego and what is external are, to begin with, identical." He continues:

> The . . . decision made by the function of judgement—as to the real existence of something of which there is a [mental] presentation (reality-testing)—is a concern of the definitive reality-ego, which develops out of the initial pleasure-ego. It is now no longer a question of whether what has been perceived . . . shall be taken into the ego or not, but of whether something which is in the ego as a presentation can be rediscovered in perception (reality) as well. It is, we see, once more a question of *external* and *internal*. What is unreal, merely a presentation and subjective, is only internal; what is real is also there *outside*. In this stage of development regard for the pleasure principle has been set aside. . . . In order to understand this step forward we must recollect that all presentations originate from perceptions and are repetitions of them. Thus originally the mere existence of a presentation was a guarantee of the reality of what was presented. The antithesis between subjective and objective does not exist from the first. . . . The first and immediate aim, therefore, of reality-testing is, not to *find* an object in real perception which corresponds to the one presented, but to *refind* such an object, to convince oneself that it is still there.[48]

Reality testing and the relation to progressively more external objects are developmentally inseparable. "It is evident that a precondition for the setting up of reality-testing is that objects shall have been lost which once brought real satisfaction," Freud explained.[49] In Mannoni's words:

48. "Negation" (1925), *SE* 19:237-238.
49. Ibid., p. 238.

for Freud it was not the presence of the object, however gratifying, that could provide a satisfactory solution (this would imply dependence on the pleasure principle), because that would lead to stagnation and retardation. It was the absence of the object, the only source of symbolic thought, that was the introduction to the reality principle—for that principle never implied that possession of the object was more real than its absence (which would mean adopting the pleasure principle!) but that the *reality to be controlled* was precisely the absence of the object.[50]

We can now see why Freud so frequently claimed that religious belief prolonged or reinstated the pleasure principle and that science alone came closest to conquering pleasure and replacing it with reality. In his view, religious belief maintained a conviction of the persistence of the pleasure-granting parental object whereas the scientific world view recognized the absence of parental figures, to which libidinal ties could be prolonged, in the natural universe. Religious belief was also diagnosed as narcissistic, in that external reality was constructed on the basis of inner wishes. Further, we can anticipate why it will be so important a differentiation between the sexes that femininity can recover lost father objects but that masculinity may not. For the father is the granter of feminine and religious fulfillment.

Freud's economic and genetic viewpoints reinforce each other by virtue of his critical emphasis on renunciation of pleasure in both points of view. The grounds on which he understands religion and science to be opponents are similarly both economic and genetic, with each strengthening the other. In Ricoeur's words, "resignation to the ineluctable is not reducible to a mere knowledge of necessity, i.e. to a purely intellectual extension of what we called perceptual reality-testing; resignation is an affective task, a work of correction applied to the very core of the libido, to the heart of narcissism. Consequently, the scientific world view must be incorporated into a history of desire."[51]

50. O[ctave] Mannoni, *Freud* (1974), p. 177.
51. Paul Ricoeur, *Freud and Philosophy* (1970), p. 332.

Chapter 5

Science and Civilization as Renunciation

There is a lake that one day ceased to permit itself to flow off; it formed a dam where it had hitherto flown off; and ever since this lake is rising higher and higher. Perhaps this very renunciation will also lend us the strength needed to bear this renunciation; perhaps man will rise ever higher as soon as he ceases to flow out *into a god.*
—NIETZSCHE, *The Gay Science*

What appears in a minority of human individuals as an untiring impulsion towards further perfection can easily be understood as a result of the instinctual repression upon which is based all that is most precious in human civilization. . . . The backward path that leads to complete satisfaction is as a rule obstructed by the resistances which maintain the repressions. So there is no alternative but to advance in the direction in which growth is still free—though with no prospect of bringing the process to a conclusion or of being able to reach the goal.
—FREUD, *Beyond the Pleasure Principle*

Science and Religion

Freud's most prolonged defense of the scientific world view is found in a late lecture, "The Question of a *Weltanschauung*" (1932), which contrasts its viewpoint to those of religion, relativism, and Marxist socialism. Science is presented as renunciatory, which establishes its superiority. In this context, Freud again called religion a wishful illusion, as he had some five years earlier in *The Future of an Illusion*. In the latter book, even Freud's definition of the religious attitude opposed it to scientific resignation and renunciation:

> Critics persist in describing as "deeply religious" anyone who admits
> to a sense of man's insignificance or impotence in the face of the uni-
> verse, although what constitutes the essence of the religious attitude is

not this feeling but only the next step after it, the reaction to it which seeks a remedy for it. The man who goes no further, but humbly acquiesces in the small part which human beings play in the great world—such a man is, on the contrary, irreligious in the truest sense of the word.[1]

The scientist begins with the presupposition "that there are no sources of knowledge of the universe other than the intellectual working-over of carefully scrutinized observations—in other words, what we call research—and alongside of it no knowledge derived from revelation, intuition or divination." Science, which includes investigation of human intellectual and emotional functions, reckons intuition and divination as "illusions, the fulfilments of wishful impulses."[2] Science studies these emotional demands but refuses to entertain their messages.

> We are ready to trace out the fulfilments of [wishes] which [men] have created for themselves in the products of art and in the systems of religion and philosophy; but we cannot nevertheless overlook the fact that it would be illegitimate and highly inexpedient to allow these demands to be transferred to the sphere of knowledge. For this would be to lay open the paths which lead to psychosis, whether to individual or group psychosis, and would withdraw valuable amounts of energy from endeavours which are directed towards reality in order, so far as possible, to find satisfaction in it for wishes and needs.[3]

The truth cannot be tolerant; science must be "relentlessly critical" when another form of investigation tries to take over any part of its sphere of research, which includes all of human activity. Art is by and large beneficent, as it seeks to be nothing more than an illusion; religion is a serious enemy as it claims to know the truth; philosophy, too, departs from science "by clinging to the illusion of being able to present a picture of the universe which is without gaps and is coherent. . . ."[4]

In Freud's view, the characteristics of scientific thinking are like those of normal thought activity about everyday matters. But science has developed further certain features of that normal activity: "it takes an interest in things even if they have no immediate, tangible use; it is concerned carefully to

---

1. *The Future of an Illusion* (1927), *SE* 21:32-33.
2. "The Question of a *Weltanschauung*," Lecture 35 of *New Introductory Lectures on Psycho-Analysis* (1933), *SE* 22:159.
3. Ibid., p. 160.   4. Ibid.

avoid individual factors and affective influences; it examines more strictly the trustworthiness of the sense-perceptions on which it bases its conclusions," and it arranges experiments and uses instruments to extend the range of perception. Its goal is to arrive at "correspondence with reality—that is to say, with what exists outside us and independently of us and, as experience has taught us, is decisive for the fulfilment or disappointment of our wishes."[5] Correspondence with the real external world is Freud's criterion of truth. The process of scientific investigation is "slow, hesitating, laborious," he concedes. He then parries the thrust: "No wonder the gentlemen in the other camp are dissatisfied. They are spoilt: revelation gave them an easier time" in the search for truth.[6]

Religion is accused of being satisfying in its wholeness and certainty. It "derives its strength from its readiness to fit in with our instinctual wishful impulses."[7] In contrast, science attempts to take into account our dependence on the real external world, which Freud considers to be its main strength. In the long run, truth will be known, but much patient renunciation is first required. "A *Weltanschauung* erected upon science has, apart from its emphasis on the real external world, mainly negative traits, such as submission to the truth and rejection of illusions," Freud emphasizes. He concludes with a warning: "any of our fellow-men . . . who calls for more than this for his momentary consolation, may look for it where he can find it."[8]

The hostility to science, to reason, and to psychoanalysis on the part of those who wish "an easier time" of it, who require more immediate pleasure of their world views, was a favorite theme of Freud's. "From the very beginning, when life takes us under its strict discipline, a resistance stirs within us against the relentlessness and monotony of the laws of thought and against the demands of reality-testing. Reason becomes the enemy which withholds from us so many possibilities of pleasure," he wrote.[9] Science "is not a revelation," and it "still lacks the attributes of definiteness, immutability and infallibility for which human thought so deeply longs."[10] There is no present compensation for these unfulfilled wishes; such compensation is always an illusion when the real, external world does not offer it. Science offers only truth as its reward, but its truth is incomplete and is little comfort: "Obscure, unfeeling and unloving powers determine men's fate; the system of

5. Ibid., p. 170.   6. Ibid., p. 174.   7. Ibid., p. 175.   8. Ibid., p. 182.
9. "Dreams and Occultism," Lecture 30 of *New Introductory Lectures on Psycho-Analysis* (1933), *SE* 22:33.
10. *The Question of Lay Analysis* (1926), *SE* 20:191.

rewards and punishments which religion ascribes to the government of the universe seems not to exist."[11]

Nor is relativism or Marxism spared the charge of resting on illusion. The illusion of relativism is that the external world is *not* real and inexorable. In Freud's view, relativism, like mysticism, ignores the criterion of truth as correspondence to reality.[12] Marxism, on the other hand, rests on an illusion about human goodness, when scientific psychoanalysis knows that the instincts are untameable and that aggression and hostility are ineradicable.[13] Freud grants psychoanalysis the honor of being the severest scientific criticism of religious illusions. The three satisfying functions of religion—instruction about the origin and meaning of the universe, consolation about ultimate happiness and justice, and the authoritative direction of its requirements and precepts—have been understood by means of a psychoanalytic *genetic* analysis.[14] According to such an analysis, the religious believer is prolonging childhood relationships with the father: the adult "harks back to the mnemic image of the father whom in his childhood he so greatly overvalued. He exalts the image into a deity and makes it into something contemporary and real."[15] The psychoanalytic criticism of religion, "the last contribution to the criticism of the religious *Weltanschauung*," shows how religion originated from childhood helplessness.[16] But the real world is "no nursery," so the scientific judgment of religion is that it is "an attempt to master the sensory world in which we are situated by means of the wishful world which we have developed within us as a result of biological and psychological necessities." Because the consolations of religion derive from psychical rather than material or external reality, they deserve "no trust."[17] This stage of dependence on psychical needs for the source of an interpretation of the world is, in the view of psychoanalysis, not a "permanent acquisition" but a stage in human collective evolution in its passage from childhood to maturity, from pleasure to reality principle functioning.

Again, pleasure, wish, and infantile narcissism are chastened by maturation which moves toward acknowledgment of harsh reality and orientation to the external. The religious father figure is the transitional object between collective psychical infancy and maturity. The "recovery" from childish attachments to the father is a chapter in the history of desire. To understand Freud's claims about the development of the scientific spirit of renunciatory detachment, we must understand his theory of libidinal renunciations in the

---

11. "The Question of a *Weltanschauung*" (1933), *SE* 22:167.
12. Ibid., pp. 175-176.   13. Ibid., pp. 177-181.   14. Ibid., pp. 161-162.
15. Ibid., p. 163.   16. Ibid., p. 167.   17. Ibid., p. 168.

life history of masculinity. But before looking specifically at masculine development, we should examine texts in which such a "recovery" is more fully discussed. In several stage-theories of cultural and intellectual development, Freud locates a "religious stage" among other prescientific modes, and again places science at the end of, and on top of, the evolution of civilization. In these discussions, Freud combines his genetic views of father-son dynamics with his moral economy to provide a double critique of the wish-fulfilling character of earlier modes.

Stages of Civilization and Patriarchal Origins

Freud suggested several different but conceptually related sets of stages of the cultural development of humankind. One of these which was set forth in 1908 has been mentioned above; according to it, satisfaction of the libido, first allowed in disregard of reproduction, was progressively subordinated until it served only legitimate procreation. In Freud's view, the concept of "legitimacy" entails paternal possession of both the mother and her offspring. A father is not merely a biological begetter but, as Freud wrote to Jung, "a father is one who possesses a mother sexually (and the children as property)." Without such possession, fatherhood would have no psychological meaning, in his view, because the infant does not understand physical paternity.[18] And we begin to notice that renunciation is tied to paternal predominance. Three later Freudian accounts of stages of civilization also rely on renunciation and two invoke the law-giving father. In all three, renunciation of narcissistic perceptions and pleasure-seeking wishes marks each higher developmental stage.

In *Totem and Taboo* (1913) Freud proposed a progression from an animistic phase through a religious to a scientific one in an argument which he summarized elsewhere:

> An investigation of primitive peoples shows mankind caught up, to begin with, in a childish belief in its own omnipotence. A whole number of mental structures can thus be understood as attempts to deny whatever might disturb this feeling of omnipotence and so to prevent emotional life from being affected by reality until the latter could be better controlled and used for purposes of satisfaction. The principle

18. Letter 314F of May 14, 1912, in William McGuire, ed., *The Freud/Jung Letters* (1974), p. 504.

of avoiding unpleasure dominates human actions until it is replaced by the better one of adaptation to the external world. *Pari passu* with men's progressive control over the world goes a development in their *Weltanschauung*, their view of the universe. . . . They turn away more and more from their original belief in their own omnipotence, rising from an animistic phase through a religious to a scientific one. Myths, religion and morality find their place in this scheme as attempts to seek a compensation for the lack of satisfaction of human wishes.[19]

Two years earlier Freud had suggested one such compensation offered by religion. In his essay on the two principles of mental functioning, he suggested that the "endopsychic impression" made by the substitution of the pleasure principle by the reality principle in the history of civilization "has been so powerful that it is reflected in a special religious myth. The doctrine of reward in the after-life for the—voluntary or enforced—renunciation of earthly pleasures is nothing other than a mythical projection of this revolution in the mind." Because they offer future compensation, religions have been able to "effect absolute renunciation of pleasure in this life," but they have not thereby achieved a conquest of the pleasure principle. Rather, "*science . . .* comes nearest to succeeding in that conquest."[20]

A progression is outlined in *Totem and Taboo*: religion is more under the sway of the pleasure principle than is science, but less so than is animism. The animistic technique for controlling reality is magic. For Freud, magic derives from belief in the omnipotence of thoughts, the overvaluation of mental processes as compared with reality.[21] When human civilization is in the animistic (or mythological) stage, it sees a direct correspondence between its wishes and external events: "If I wish it to rain, I have only to do something that looks like rain or is reminiscent of rain." In the two later stages, by contrast, "instead of this rain-magic, processions will be made to a temple and prayers for rain will be addressed to the deity living in it. Finally, this religious technique will in its turn be given up and attempts will be made to produce effects in the atmosphere which will lead to rain."[22] When in the animistic stage people ascribe omnipotence to themselves, they do so because their thinking is not yet independent of sexuality. As is the case in narcissism, "the process of thinking is still to a great extent sexualized." The wishes which derive from libido hold sway over constructions about causa-

19. "The Claims of Psycho-Analysis to Scientific Interest" (1913), *SE* 13:186.
20. "Formulations on the Two Principles of Mental Functioning" (1911), *SE* 12:223.
21. *Totem and Taboo* (1913), *SE* 13:85.   22. Ibid., p. 81.

tion in the external world; subject and object are not clearly distinguished. In the religious stage, people transfer omnipotence to the gods "but do not seriously abandon it themselves, for they reserve the power of influencing the gods in a variety of ways according to their wishes."[23] If animism is analogous to the narcissistic stage of libidinal development, when part of oneself is loved, the religious stage is comparable "to the stage of object-choice of which the characteristic is a child's attachment to his parents. . . ."[24] The later scientific view of the universe, however, "no longer affords any room for human omnipotence; men have acknowledged their smallness and submitted resignedly to death and to the other necessities of nature."[25] This third stage "would have an exact counterpart" in individual libidinal development "in the stage at which an individual has reached maturity, has renounced the pleasure principle, adjusted himself to reality and turned to the external world for the object of his desires."[26]

In this account, the first renunciation of primitives was giving spirits some of the omnipotence which formerly had been vested in their own thoughts. This first renunciation is described as an achievement in theorizing; "man's first theoretical achievement" was "the creation of spirits." Freud suggested that the experience of someone else's death "caused primitive man to reflect, and compelled him to hand over some of his omnipotence to the spirits and to sacrifice some of his freedom of action," so that these cultural products, the spirits, "would constitute a first acknowledgement of *Ananke* ('Necessity'), which opposes human narcissism."[27] Even animism, then, achieved a higher level of civilization than is sometimes realized. "If we take instinctual repression as a measure of the level of civilization that has been reached," Freud wrote, even animism contains the "fundamental idea of gaining greater strength by renouncing some instinctual satisfaction. . . ."[28]

After discussing the relationship of stages of civilization to narcissism and the pleasure principle, Freud explains totemism and taboo in terms of the Oedipus complex. Then he attributes the civilizing renunciations that were enforced by totemism, which is Freud's dawn of religion, to the male's father complex. These renunciations signified to Freud the two oedipal renunciations—of the son's death wish toward the father (the totem animal must not be eaten) and of his sexual desire for the mother (totemism re-

---

23. Ibid., pp. 89, 88.   24. Ibid., p. 90.   25. Ibid., p. 88.   26. Ibid., p. 90.
27. Ibid., p. 93. Throughout, I have transliterated Freud's Greek spellings of *Ananke* and *Logos* ("necessity" and "reason").
28. Ibid., pp. 97-98.

quires exogamy). Freud saw these taboos as reinstatements of the demands of the terrible primal father who had been killed but who in death was psychologically more potent than he had been in life.

A second stage-theory, set forth in 1917, also rests on the principle of the opposition of (unpleasurable) reality to human narcissism. This is Freud's account of the stages by which the development of science has opposed human narcissism, which he uses to explain opposition to psychoanalysis. The first narcissistic theory was the geocentric belief that man's "dwelling-place, the earth, was the stationary centre of the universe." The central position of the earth "appeared to fit in very well with his inclination to regard himself as lord of the world." The destruction of this "narcissistic illusion" came with the discoveries of Copernicus, who dealt the first, or "cosmological," blow to human narcissism. The second, biological, blow to human narcissism was dealt by Darwin. Prior to Darwin, man "denied the possession of reason" to "his fellow-creatures in the animal kingdom." To himself he attributed an immortal soul and made claims to a divine descent which permitted him to break the bond of community with the animal kingdom. In so doing, he clung to his belief in his unique importance, a belief which evolutionary science took from him.[29] The third blow was dealt by psychoanalysis; this was Freud's "psychological blow." Freud credits psychoanalysis with destroying the illusion that man "is supreme within his own mind."[30] Therefore, not only is science "the most complete renunciation of the pleasure principle of which our mental activity is capable,"[31] but psychoanalysis has brought the renunciation of narcissism to its highest pitch. Now, humanity not only is no longer the center of the universe or the lord of creation; it is not even able to dominate its own mind. It is unpleasant to learn "that the life of our sexual instincts cannot be wholly tamed, and that mental processes are in themselves unconscious and only reach the ego and come under its control through incomplete and untrustworthy perceptions. . . ."[32] Once again, education has taken place through unpleasure, and Freud considers his discoveries to be the most unwelcome news yet brought by science.

Surpassed narcissisms are of a kind. The subject constructs a world view on the basis of the assumption of its own centrality, predominance, superi-

29. "A Difficulty in the Path of Psycho-Analysis" (1917), SE 17:139-141.

30. Ibid., pp. 141-143; quoted phrase on p. 141.

31. "A Special Type of Choice of Object Made by Men (Contributions to the Psychology of Love I)" (1910), SE 11:165.

32. "A Difficulty in the Path of Psycho-Analysis" (1917), SE 17:143.

ority, and paradigmatic importance, that is, on the basis that what the subject wishes must be true. Narcissistic assumptions are pleasant and their destruction is painful, except that the new truth offers a new pleasure of a new superiority. Freud was alert to this new pleasure; in *Moses and Monotheism*, it is treated as the source of Jewish pride. In another discussion of the contrast between faith and science, he wrote that the fabrication of *Weltanschauungen*

> may be left to philosophers, who avowedly find it impossible to make their journey through life without a Baedeker of that kind to give them information on every subject. Let us humbly accept the contempt with which they look down on us from the vantage-ground of their superior needs. But since *we* cannot forgo our narcissistic pride either, we will draw comfort from the reflection that such "Handbooks to Life" soon grow out of date and that it is precisely our shortsighted, narrow and finicky work which obliges them to appear in new editions. . . .[33]

The irony of the phrase "superior needs" shows in microcosm Freud's judgment on all critics who accused his science of belittling religious or philosophical longings.

Ricoeur has suggested that in his last book, *Moses and Monotheism*, Freud renounced "the value that his narcissism could still rightfully claim, the value of belonging to the race that engendered Moses and imparted ethical monotheism to the world."[34] In Ricoeur's view, when Freud argued that Moses was an Egyptian and Yahweh the resurgence of the primal father, he made this renunciation. (I will suggest the opposite in Part 4.) But it is already clear from an appraisal of a third Freudian stage-theory of cultural development that one narcissism went unrenounced: the conviction of the superiority of maleness and, more specifically, of paternity and patriarchy over femaleness, maternity, and matriarchy. Paternal and masculine superiority is treated not as a narcissism but as a renunciation.

Freud never settled to his satisfaction the question of the historical placement of a matriarchal stage in relation to patriarchal forms of society. He was familiar with Bachofen's theory of an original stage of social organization based on mother right, but, as he wrote to Jung, "I myself, in all modesty, favour a different hypothesis in regard to the primordial period—

---

33. *Inhibitions, Symptoms, and Anxiety* (1926), SE 20:96.
34. Paul Ricoeur, *Freud and Philosophy* (1970), p. 244.

Darwin's."[35] Freud meant Darwin's view that the original human organization was a primal group dominated by a single, strong male, who was father to all the children because he possessed all the females.[36] Alternative theories were available to Freud, as his reference to Bachofen in his letter to Jung indicates. The patriarchal primal horde hypothesis was truly a matter of preference, but it was a preference which he based on his psychoanalytic investigations of oedipal dynamics, which testified to him about the cultural primacy of fathers.[37]

Freud's chronological reconstructions of goddesses and gods and patriarchies and matriarchies do not all square with each other. But, in general, his view was that an absolute primordial patriarchy was followed by the sons' parricidal rebellion, which allowed more authority to mothers and freedom to women for some time, until the sons joined together to reinstate some of the restrictions (on incest, parricide, and murder) that the father had placed on them.[38] These restrictions and their enforcement created another father-dominated civilization, but this time there were many fathers, all of whom were equal to one another (as brothers) but predominant over women and children. Freud's assessment of the significance of the reinstatement of this more limited patriarchy was that it represented a valuable renunciation and a cultural advance. In the original horde, only the father had complete libidinal freedom; in the new patriarchy, each father had limited freedom.

In 1909 he had commented that, as Lichtenberg says:

> "An astronomer knows whether the moon is inhabited or not with about as much certainty as he knows who was his father, but not with so much certainty as he knows who was his mother." A great advance was made in civilization when men decided to put their inferences upon a level with the testimony of their senses and to make the step from matriarchy to patriarchy.[39]

35. Letter 314F of May 14, 1912, in McGuire, ed., *The Freud/Jung Letters*, p. 504.
36. See *Totem and Taboo* (1913), *SE* 13:125, for Freud's citation of Darwin.
37. For a comparative discussion of the claims regarding original patriarchy and matriarchy in anthropological theories that were available to Freud, including those of Maine, Bachofen, McLennan, Lubbock, Morgan, and Spencer, all published between 1860 and 1890, see Elizabeth Fee, "The Sexual Politics of Victorian Social Anthropology," in *Clio's Consciousness Raised: New Perspectives on the History of Women*, ed. Mary S. Hartman and Lois Banner (New York: Harper, Colophon, 1974), pp. 86-102.
38. See Freud's letter of February 9, 1919, to Lou Andreas-Salomé, in Ernst Pfeiffer, ed., *Sigmund Freud and Lou Andreas-Salomé Letters* (1966), p. 90.
39. "Notes upon a Case of Obsessional Neurosis" (1909), *SE* 10:233, n. 1.

The contrast between sensual and inferential evidence as warrant for the contrast in value between matriarchy and patriarchy was again set forth in *Moses and Monotheism*, where Freud asserted that turning from the mother to the father "points in addition to a victory of intellectuality over sensuality— that is, an advance in civilization, since maternity is proved by the evidence of the senses while paternity is a hypothesis, based on an inference and a premiss." He added that siding with "a thought-process in preference to a sense perception has proved to be a momentous step."[40] In Freud's view, this step, which created civilization as we know it, was analogous to accepting scientific evidence about the organization of the universe, the origins of species, and the nature of mind; a view which is sensually evident but scientifically mistaken is replaced by an interpretation of data which would not have been made on the basis of wishful, sensual evidence alone. The oddity in this reasoning, of course, is that maternity is not scientifically mistaken. But Freud's evaluation of this step toward using thought as the criterion for discovering reality recalls his first model of the mental apparatus, in which the "sensory end" of the apparatus was prior and lower, and according to which the transformation of thought or activity into a sensory perception or image was a regression, while the transformation of perception or image into an activity or idea was a progressive step. Maternity is tied to sense, wish, and pleasure; paternity to intellect, reality, and renunciation.

Freud's double decision in favor of patriarchy as both original and therefore "essential," as well as later, better, and based on renunciation of illusory sensory evidence, allowed him to account for the power of emotional relationships to the father that return from the repressed, to approve of patriarchal stringency, to advocate overcoming of father complexes, and to consider matriarchy and maternity narcissistic. He inserted all this into his overarching moral economy, his theory of the development of mind from wish to reality. In Freud's view, paternity is the principle of origination under the dominance of the reality principle whereas maternity is the principle of origination in prior, wishful stages. The primitive, the feminine, the immediate, the sensual, and the illusory belonged together in his view.

In several contexts, then, Freud associates paternity, renunciation, and cultural and intellectual advances. In another of Freud's theories of origins, this time of the origin of the control of fire, he explicitly associates the culture-creating capacity for renunciation with men's renunciation of libido. This odd hypothesis about fire was put forward briefly in 1930 and at greater length in 1931. The control of fire was, in Freud's view, a "quite extraordi-

40. *Moses and Monotheism* (1939), *SE* 23:114.

nary and unexampled achievement" of human control over nature. In his first explanation of it, he suggested that

> primal man had the habit, when he came in contact with fire, of satisfying an infantile desire connected with it, by putting it out with a stream of his urine. The legends that we possess leave no doubt about the originally phallic view taken of tongues of flame as they shoot upwards. Putting out fire by micturating . . . was therefore a kind of sexual act with a male, an enjoyment of sexual potency in a homosexual competition.

The culture hero who acquired fire was "the first person to renounce this desire and spare the fire. . . . By damping down the fire of his own sexual excitation, he had tamed the natural force of fire. This great cultural conquest was thus the reward for his renunciation of instinct."[41] Women, who were anatomically unable to yield to this temptation, were therefore made the guardians of fire. But, one notes, women are also anatomically spared the possibility of becoming cultural heroes through the renunciation of libidinal desires.

A year later Freud again addressed the origin of control of fire, this time paying more explicit attention to the Prometheus myth. Prometheus "had renounced an instinct and had shown how beneficent, and at the same time how indispensable, such a renunciation was for the purposes of civilization." Why, then, did "the legend treat a deed that was thus a benefit to civilization as a crime deserving punishment?" Freud's answer is consistent with his views that all renunciations of instinct, of narcissism, and of wish are simultaneously unpleasurable and valuable: "if, through all its distortions, it [the legend] barely allows us to get a glimpse of the fact that the acquisition of control over fire presupposes an instinctual renunciation, at least it makes no secret of the resentment which the culture-hero could not fail to arouse in men driven by their instincts. And this is in accordance with what we know and expect."[42] The man who renounces is the prototypical rejected and revered hero.

Renunciatory Morality and Mental Health

Freud manages to explain whatever is civilized, heroic, intellectual, or scientific in terms of renunciation. Renunciation is also assimilated to paternity,

41. *Civilization and Its Discontents* (1930), *SE* 21:90, n. 1.
42. "The Acquisition and Control of Fire" (1932), *SE* 22:189.

masculinity, morality, and, in some instances, mental health. The renunciatory dynamic is an index of value, even if that value is merely descriptive. While Freud distinguished between morality and mental health (the most obvious instance is in *Civilization and Its Discontents*, where neurosis as domination by the irrationally moral superego is stressed), insofar as he understands health as renunciatory, it is also an achievement of morality. "Sanity . . . is the most profound moral option of our time," Renata Adler writes.[43] For Freud, while too much uninformed morality is neurotic, the renouncing culture hero might be preferable to the merely sane. At the same time, mental health, understood as an approach to the ideal of accuracy about the gulf between the demands of wish and of reality—the dominance of ego—has overtones of the heroic: it is based in sacrifice of wishes.

Individual morality is rooted in renunciation, which is simultaneously, as in the case of Prometheus, a "cultural achievement." It is often suggested that Freud identified himself with Moses and identified the significance of psychoanalysis with the significance of Moses' new world view. About Michelangelo's sculpture of Moses, Freud commented: "the giant frame with its tremendous physical power becomes only a concrete expression of the highest mental achievement that is possible in a man, that of struggling successfully against an inward passion for the sake of a cause to which he has devoted himself."[44] In contrast, discussing Dostoevsky's stormy mental life, Freud judged it to have fallen short of morality because "a moral man is one who reacts to temptation as soon as he feels it in his heart, without yielding to it. A man who alternately sins and then in his remorse erects high moral standards lays himself open to the reproach that he has made things too easy for himself. He has not achieved the essence of morality, renunciation. . . ."[45] A wry example of Freud's association of morality and renunciation in a clinical setting (where the equation is often more ambiguous than in a cultural setting) is found in Abraham Kardiner's memoir of his analysis with Freud. One of Kardiner's colleagues, an American who was in Vienna, had completed an analysis with Freud. The American was having an affair with a Viennese woman when his wife arrived unexpectedly from New York. This man, Kardiner comments, had always boasted about his sexual prowess. "However, when his wife arrived—after he was discharged by Freud—he discovered that he was impotent. After a few more trials, he went into a panic. 'What? Impotent *after* analysis?' His despair was beyond control, and he finally decided to write to Freud for an appointment. . . . He

43. Renata Adler, *Speedboat* (New York: Popular Library, 1978), p. 8.
44. "The Moses of Michelangelo" (1914), *SE* 13:233.
45. "Dostoevsky and Parricide" (1928), *SE* 21:177.

thought Freud would wring his hands and take him back into analysis. Instead, Freud did not utter a word during the entire interview, and when his hour was up, he rose, seized my friend's hand with the usual handshake, and said, 'Und jetz sehe ich dass Sie ein wirklich und anständiger Kerl sind' (Well, now I see that you are a really decent fellow!), and ushered him out."[46] For Freud, even uninformed, autonomic renunciation was an ironic criterion of decency; in this case, the unanticipated renunciation served to inform the man of his own morality.

Science is Freud's cure for culture; renunciation situates the individual in this cultural process. If resignation to the ineluctable (*Ananke*), reliance on *Logos*, and morality are achieved through informed renunciation, and if the scientific attitude relies on this affective achievement, is there any other path to psychical health? In Freud's view, there are "only two possibilities for remaining healthy when there is a persistent frustration of satisfaction in the real world." The first is to transform the psychical tension which arises from unfulfillment into activity which eventually "extorts a real satisfaction of the libido" from the external world. The second is "renouncing libidinal satisfaction, sublimating the dammed-up libido and turning it to the attainment of aims which are no longer erotic and which escape frustration."[47] Retreats from reality into wish fulfillment characterize illness, as do uninformed renunciations, that is, unconscious defenses against inadmissible instinctual desires. Neurotic symptoms express the imprisoning compromise between unacceptable fulfillment and uninformed, unwitting renunciation.[48]

Freud's view of health is of course consistent with his understanding of the highest function of the healthy ego, which is its capacity to decide "when it is more expedient to control one's passions and bow before reality, and when it is more expedient to side with them and take arms against the external world—such decisions make up the whole essence of worldly wisdom."[49] Clearly, if one is uninformed about one's passions, one can neither (consciously) renounce them nor act in order to change reality to accommodate them. Freud's patients were systematically uninformed about their passions; in various ways they retreated into illusions. Psychoanalytic therapy, which cures the transference to the prototypically paternal analyst as the microcosm of unrenounced desire, has as its purpose the education of the ego

46. Abraham Kardiner, *My Analysis with Freud* (1977), p. 74.

47. "Types of Onset of Neurosis" (1912), *SE* 12:232.

48. See, for example, "The Sense of Symptoms," Lecture 17 of *Introductory Lectures on Psycho-Analysis* (1916-1917), *SE* 16:269.

49. *The Question of Lay Analysis* (1926), *SE* 20:201.

to reality. Such education includes knowledge about the passions and the defenses (wishes and uninformed renunciations). Thus, in analytic treatment, "as far as his relations with the physician are concerned, the patient must be left with unfulfilled wishes in abundance. It is expedient to deny him precisely those satisfactions which he desires most intensely and expresses most importunately," Freud wrote.[50] Nor is the solution to urge the patient to "'live in a full life' sexually." Such advice is not a solution

> if only because we ourselves have declared that an obstinate conflict is taking place in him between a libidinal impulse and sexual repression, between a sensual and an ascetic trend. This conflict would not be solved by our helping one of these trends to victory over its opponent. We see, indeed, that in neurotics asceticism has the upper hand; and the consequence of this is precisely that the suppressed sexual tendency finds a way out in symptoms.[51]

The inadmissible sensual trend is cut off from the ego and withdraws beyond its control; it is like an outlaw, "excluded from the great organization of the ego,"[52] and it "proliferates in the dark."[53] The therapeutic aim is to expose this symptom-producing proliferation to the light of the ego: "We try to restore the ego, to free it from its restrictions, and to give it back the command over the id which it has lost owing to its early repressions."[54] In the case history of little Hans, Freud commented that the analysis did not undo the effects of repression, because the instincts which were suppressed remain suppressed after analysis. But "the same effect is produced in a different way. Analysis replaces the process of repression, which is an automatic and excessive one, by a temperate and purposeful control on the part of the highest agencies of the mind. In a word, *analysis replaces repression by condemnation*."[55] This curative process is, in Freud's view, a work of *culture* but not of *salvation*, for a work of culture relies on renunciation whereas a sense of salvation rests on illusory fulfillment, on consolation. Freud cryptically compared mystical with psychoanalytic knowledge to make the distinction:

50. "Lines of Advance in Psycho-Analytic Therapy" (1919), *SE* 17:164.
51. "Transference," Lecture 27 of *Introductory Lectures on Psycho-Analysis* (1916-1917), *SE* 16:432-433.
52. *Inhibitions, Symptoms, and Anxiety* (1926), *SE* 20:153.
53. "Repression" (1915), *SE* 14:149.
54. *The Question of Lay Analysis* (1926), *SE* 20:205.
55. *Analysis of a Phobia in a Five-Year-Old Boy* (1909), *SE* 10:145.

> It is easy to imagine . . . that certain mystical practices may succeed in upsetting the normal relations between the different regions of the mind, so that, for instance, perception may be able to grasp happenings in the depths of the ego and in the id which were otherwise inaccessible to it. It may safely be doubted, however, whether this road will lead us to the ultimate truths from which salvation is to be expected. Nevertheless it may be admitted that the therapeutic efforts of psychoanalysis have chosen a similar line of approach. . . . Where id was, there ego shall be. It is a work of culture—not unlike the draining of the Zuider Zee.[56]

The possibilities for health, then, are informed renunciation of instinct, sublimations of the erotic into the nonerotic, and realistic activity in the external world on behalf of the passions. These are of course not mutually exclusive; all are cultural achievements.

How, in Freud's genetic psychology, is achievement of capacity for renunciation and activity possible? Activity and renunciation, as well as sublimation, are attributes of masculinity, as we will find when we look at his discussions of masculine oedipal development for an answer. Because Freud's life work began in order to understand neuroses, healthy, world-transforming activity received less of his attention than did the processes of renunciation that led to the therapeutic result. One who could love and work to wrest gratification from the external world of nature and from the social world would need no therapy. In *Moses and Monotheism*, Freud imaginatively reconstructed a figure whose worldly activity resulted in culture-creating renunciations, but much of his prior focus was on the psychical conditions, most of which cluster around the Oedipus complex, which render the possibilities of health tenuous. Still, one can assemble, from two other sources, a composite portrait of the requirements for achieving "ideal" masculinity. The first is Freud's psychobiography of Leonardo da Vinci; the second is his discussions of oedipal theory. The next topic, then, is how the individual male may undergo libidinal development such that he surpasses narcissism, achieves object love and then detachment from parental objects, and gains freedom from religious authority and illusion.

56. "The Dissection of the Psychical Personality," Lecture 31 of *New Introductory Lectures on Psycho-Analysis* (1933), *SE* 22:79-80.

Chapter 6

Masculinity as Renunciation

Renunciation—is a piercing Virtue—
The letting go
A Presence—for an Expectation—
Not now—
The putting out of Eyes—
Just Sunrise—
Lest Day—
Day's Great Progenitor—
Outvie
Renunciation—is the Choosing
Against itself—
Itself to justify
Unto itself—
When larger function—
Make that appear—
Smaller—that Covered Vision—Here—
—EMILY DICKINSON

Paternal Etiology and the Genesis of Masculinity

Freud's description of Leonardo's greatness and his account of its origins alert us to the key to achieving healthy renunciation: overcoming the mental father complex. For Freud, Leonardo was the first modern natural scientist; Leonardo "dared to utter the bold assertion which contains within itself the justification for all independent research: '*He who appeals to authority when there is a difference of opinion works with his memory rather than with his reason.*'"[1] Leonardo taught that "authority should be looked down on and . . . imitation of the 'ancients' should be repudiated." Freud tried to translate this teaching into "concrete individual experience" by understanding the

1. *Leonardo da Vinci and a Memory of His Childhood* (1910), SE 11:122; quoted phrase attributed to W. Von Seidlitz, *Leonardo da Vinci: Der Wendepunkt der Renaissance*, 2 vols. (Berlin: n.p., 1909), 2:270.

references to the "ancients" and authority as coded references to Leonardo's father.[2] But according to Freud's analytic reconstruction, Leonardo did not know his father in his earliest years, and this fatherlessness helped make his independence of thought possible.[3] The object of his thought—nature—was to Freud where the independent truth-seeker properly looks. He wrote:

> When anyone has, like Leonardo, escaped being intimidated by his father during his earliest childhood, and has in his researches cast away the fetters of authority, it would be in the sharpest contradiction to our expectation if we found that he had remained a believer and had been unable to escape from dogmatic religion. Psycho-analysis has made us familiar with the intimate connection between the father-complex and belief in God; . . . Thus we recognize that the roots of the need for religion are in the parental complexes; the almightly and just God, and kindly Nature, appear to us as grand sublimations of father and mother, or rather as revivals and restorations of the young child's ideas of them.[4]

Leonardo was psychically free to sublimate his desire for his mother into scientific research into nature because he had experienced no paternal interference. Nature, of course, is viewed as "mother," and Freud respects her, but as the impersonal and inexorable goddess *Ananke*.

Leonardo achieved Freud's psychological, intellectual, and moral ideal:

> In the notes that show Leonardo engrossed in fathoming the great riddles of nature there is no lack of passages where he expresses his admiration for the Creator, . . . but there is nothing which indicates that he wished to maintain any personal relation with this divine power. The reflections in which he has recorded the deep wisdom of his last years of life breathe the resignation of the human being who subjects himself to *Ananke*, to the laws of nature, and who expects no alleviation from the goodness or grace of God. There is scarcely any doubt that Leonardo had prevailed over both dogmatic and personal religion, and had by his work of research removed himself far from the position from which the Christian believer surveys the world.[5]

2. *Leonardo da Vinci* (1910), *SE* 11:122.
3. David Stannard has cited evidence that Freud was probably wrong about the absence of Leonardo's father; *Shrinking History* (1980), p. 14, and has listed qualities that "Freud claimed to find characteristic of Leonardo" that were certainly characteristic of Freud; ibid., pp. 20-21.
4. *Leonardo da Vinci* (1910), *SE* 11:123.
5. Ibid., pp. 124-125.

Leonardo has emancipated himself from the father to explore the now impersonal natural laws; sublimation has desexualized the mother. Freud had already discussed how Leonardo's sublimation of instinct differs from the "irruption from the unconscious" that characterizes neurosis.[6] Sublimation, that mysterious process which transforms impulses with a sexual aim into impulses with a nonerotic aim, is a desexualization which occurs without the severe loss of energy or control that results from repression. Because sublimation masters and transforms sexuality, it is correlated with the progressive impersonality of the parental figures represented in the mind (the impersonal superego and nature as indifferent necessity) and with independence from figures of authority which derive from the paternal figure. Such an ideal is rarely achieved. Freud warned that "only very few civilized people are capable of existing without reliance on others or are even capable of coming to an independent opinion. You cannot exaggerate the intensity of people's inner lack of resolution and craving for authority. The extraordinary increase in neuroses since the power of religions has waned may give you a measure of it."[7]

To trace the processes by which the father complex threatens to make men submissive and those which lead to a fortunate independence, it is necessary to examine what I will call Freud's theory of paternal etiology. Freud's earliest theory of the etiology of psychoneurosis was that hysteria originated in actual seduction (usually by the father) in the child's infancy whereas obsession was traceable to the (somewhat older) child's active seduction of someone else. In the first case, a forgotten *passive* sexual experience was at the root of the disorder. In Freud's words, "It seems to me more and more that the essential point of hysteria is that it is a result of perversion on the part of the seducer; and that heredity is seduction by the father."[8] In the case of obsessional neurosis, infantile sexuality was *active* rather than passive. This distinction fit Freud's conviction, which he maintained even after he revised his etiological theory, that hysteria and femininity and obsession and masculinity were somehow internally linked.[9] This never meant, of course, that all hysterics were women or all obsessional neurotics men. During the period of his work when he viewed the actual events in children's sexual histories as pathogenic, Freud referred to his "theory of pater-

6. Ibid., pp. 79-80.
7. "The Future Prospects of Psycho-Analytic Therapy" (1910), SE 11:146.
8. Letter to Fliess of December 6, 1896, in Marie Bonaparte et al., eds., *The Origins of Psycho-Analysis* (1954), pp. 179-180.
9. See, for example, *Inhibitions, Symptoms, and Anxiety* (1926), SE 20:142-143.

nal aetiology."[10] Later, as is well known, Freud decided that the seductions often had not taken place and that although "infantile sexuality" was still the root of neurosis, the child's repressed fantasy and not a traumatic event was at fault. He explained that, after discovering this error, he had

> learned to explain a number of phantasies of seduction as attempts at fending off memories of the subject's *own* sexual activity (infantile masturbation). When this point had been clarified, the "traumatic" element in the sexual experiences of childhood lost its importance and what was left was the realization that infantile sexual activity (whether spontaneous or provoked) prescribes the direction that will be taken by later sexual life after maturity. . . . It was only after the introduction of this element of . . . phantasies that the texture of the neurosis and its relation to the patient's life became intelligible.[11]

Thereafter, the question for the clinician was no longer "what sexual experiences a particular individual had had in his childhood, but rather of his reaction to those experiences—of whether he had reacted to them by 'repression' or not."[12] Psychical reality, rather than historical reality, became the object of analytic inquiry.

As long as it is understood that the mental parent as an object of fantasy, rather than the historical parent as a perpetrator of trauma, is at issue, Freud's oedipal theory may still be read as a theory of paternal etiology. Although both parents are involved in the oedipal triangle, the ideas of "Oedipus complex" and "father complex" are inseparable whereas the idea of a "mother complex" arises relatively infrequently in Freud's writings. Once the father has threatened castration, in fantasy or in reality, and the boy has responded, his incestuous mother complex is no longer possible. When the focus of discussion is the juncture between childhood and culture, the father represents the cultural reality principle whereas the mother represents wishes which must be surpassed for the child to enter culture at all. She may return to the independent masculine psyche only as indifferent nature. In Freud's view of the instincts and civilization in contradiction, the principle of contradiction is paternal; the mother-child dyad is the the ground prior to the contradiction (which is instigated by culture and represented by the fa-

10. Letter to Fliess of April 28, 1897, in Bonaparte et al., eds., *The Origins of Psycho-Analysis*, p. 195.

11. "My Views on the Part Played by Sexuality in the Aetiology of the Neuroses" (1906), *SE* 7:274.

12. Ibid., p. 277.

ther), but the mother figure embodies in itself no principle of contradiction or opposition to instinct.

Marcuse has summarized the many levels of significance of the boy's Oedipus complex and has properly emphasized its patriarchal content:

> In the Oedipus situation, the primal situation recurs under circumstances which from the beginning assure the lasting triumph of the father. But they also assure the life of the son and his future ability to take the father's place. How did civilization achieve this compromise? The multitude of somatic, mental, and social processes which resulted in this achievement are practically identical with the contents of Freud's psychology. . . . The function of the father is gradually transferred from his individual person to his social position, to his image in the son (conscience), to God, to the various agencies and agents which teach the son to become a mature and restrained member of his society. . . . Within this framework of objective laws and institutions, the processes of puberty lead to the liberation from the father as a necessary and legitimate event. It is nothing short of a mental catastrophe— but it is nothing more. Then the son leaves the patriarchal family and sets out to become a father and boss himself.[13]

In order to understand how the Oedipus complex is a theory of paternal etiology, how its outcome in normal cases makes the son able to be an authoritative father himself, and how, in ideal cases, he becomes independent of each element in the series of paternal analogues, we must look at Freud's views of the sexual development of the preoedipal and the oedipal boy and of the boy in the midst of the castration complex and during its resolution. In examining these frequently criticized ideas, it is important not to conflate what Freud claims that femaleness and maleness come to mean in children's mental lives with Freud's personal views, even though his syntax does not always encourage the distinction. Unless this distinction is maintained, though, one loses sight of Freud's attempt to explain, not his own biases, but the structure and contents of unconscious processes. If we have only his biases, we have an asymmetrical theory. If we have, also, insights into everyone's unconscious, we have, also, a theory of gender asymmetry.

Freud claimed that before the oedipal stage set in, component sexual drives had become organized around genital activity and sensation. This preoedipal (phallic) organization followed the oral and the anal stages of libidinal organization. The mental formations of earlier stages might be regressed to from later stages. In addition, stages overlap and intermingle. About the oral stage, Freud wrote:

> The first organ to emerge as an erotogenic zone and to make libidinal demands on the mind is, from the time of birth onwards, the mouth. To begin with, all psychical activity is concentrated on providing satisfaction for the needs of that zone. Primarily, of course, this satisfaction serves the purpose of self-preservation by means of nourishment; but physiology should not be confused with psychology. The baby's obstinate persistence in sucking gives evidence at an early stage of a need for satisfaction which . . . strives to obtain pleasure independently of nourishment and for that reason may and should be termed *sexual*.[14]

Note his warning that physiology not be confused with psychology; it is not the mouth per se nor its biological functions which psychoanalysis discovers but rather the libidinal demands they make on the mind.

While the sadism of biting is present in the oral stage, the second, anal stage is the one in which aggressiveness and urges toward mastery predominate. In the oral phase, sex distinction does not exist in the child's mind; the predominant distinction is between subject and object, or self and other, wherein the other who provides satisfaction is first viewed as part of oneself (the pleasure principle) until its absence and the resultant frustration teach the child to distinguish between internal and external, self and other, real and illusory. In the anal phase, too,

> the contrast between "masculine" and "feminine" plays no part . . . as yet. Its place is taken by the contrast between "active" and "passive," which may be described as a precursor of the sexual polarity and which later on is soldered to that polarity. What appears to us as masculine in the activities of this phase, when we look at it from the point of view of the genital phase, turns out to be an expression of an instinct for mastery which easily passes over into cruelty. Trends with a passive aim are attached to the erotogenic zone of the anal orifice, which is very important at this period.[15]

In both these stages, autoerotic and object-directed libidinal strivings exist, but it is only in the third, phallic, phase that, with his choice of his mother as

14. *An Outline of Psycho-Analysis* (1940), SE 23:153-154.
15. "The Development of the Libido and the Sexual Organizations," Lecture 21 of *Introductory Lectures on Psycho-Analysis* (1916-1917), SE 16:327.

an object for his phallic strivings, the Freudian boy prepares for oedipal conflict. In the phallic stage, "a genital organization of a sort is established; but only the male genitals play a part in it, and the female ones remain undiscovered."[16] The boy's phallic stage is "a forerunner of the final form taken by sexual life and already much resembles it."[17] (This statement is true only of boys.) For both boys and girls in the phallic stage, "the contrast between the sexes is not stated in terms of 'male' or 'female' but of 'possessing a penis' or 'castrated.'"[18] Such statement, of course, takes place in dreams, fantasies, and play. Phallic children of both sexes are interested in the presence and absence of the penis. "Stress falls entirely on the male organ, all the child's interest is directed towards the question of whether it is present or not."[19] While, for the boy, the phallic stage prefigures much of his adult sexual life in that his libido is concentrated in the organ which will be his adult sexual organ, the fact that only the phallus "comes into account" for members of both sexes caused Freud to emphasize the difference between this stage and the adult organization. "This consists in the fact that, for both sexes, only one genital, namely the male one, comes into account. What is present, therefore, is not a primacy of the genitals [the mature sexual organization] but a primacy of the *phallus*."[20] The boy in this stage assumes at first that all human creatures have an organ like his own because it is so important to him. Freud explains:

> This part of the body, which is easily excitable, prone to changes and so rich in sensations, occupies the boy's interest to a high degree and is constantly setting new tasks to his instinct for research. . . . The driving force which this male portion of the body will develop later at puberty expresses itself at this period of life mainly as an urge to investigate, as sexual curiosity. Many of the acts of exhibitionism and aggression which children commit, and which in later years would be judged without hesitation to be expressions of lust, prove in analysis to be experiments undertaken in the service of sexual research.[21]

16. *An Autobiographical Study* (1925), SE 20:37.
17. *An Outline of Psycho-Analysis* (1940), SE 23:154.
18. *An Autobiographical Study* (1925), SE 20:37.
19. *The Question of Lay Analysis* (1926), SE 20:212. The discovery that both boys and girls experienced the stage of phallic primacy caused Freud to realize that the two oedipal complexes were not analogous.
20. "The Infantile Genital Organization" (1923), SE 19:142.
21. Ibid., pp. 142-143.

This research leads to the boy's discovery that his "premiss of the universal presence of the penis" is in error. If he is already oedipally in love when he discovers that some human beings are not phallic but "castrated," this discovery (coupled with the threat of castration for masturbation, which he associates with his incestuous desires) produces "the greatest trauma of his life."[22] At first, the child disavows what he has seen in order not to be faced with the possibility that a penis can be absent, which means that his can be taken away. Because he assumes that lack of a penis results from castration, which he understands as punishment, he then is likely to assume that only "unworthy female persons" are castrated.[23] By the time the boy realizes that sex distinction is understandable in terms of a "male and female" polarity, superimposed on the polarity of phallic and castrated, he is well through the oedipal crisis. "It is not until development has reached its completion at puberty that the sexual polarity coincides with *male* and *female*. Maleness combines [the factors of] subject, activity, and possession of the penis. . . ." These are the oral, anal, and phallic alternatives, each superimposed on the last. In contrast, "femaleness takes over [those of] object and passivity."[24] As is clear in many other contexts, femaleness also continues to mean psychologically what it meant to the phallic boy—castration. The way in which femaleness gains the psychological meaning of being an object of phallic love is explained in Freud's notion of the boy's feminine oedipal attitude.

The Rise and Decline of Oedipus

For the boy, the transition from the phallic to the masculine oedipal phase is not strictly demarcated; he passes easily from the one into the other:

> When a boy (from age of two or three) has entered the phallic phase, . . . is feeling pleasurable sensations in his sexual organ and has learnt to procure these at will, . . . he becomes his mother's lover. He wishes to possess her physically in such ways as he has divined from his observations and intuitions about sexual life. . . . In a word, his early awakened masculinity seeks to take his father's place with her; his father has hitherto in any case been an envied model to the boy, owing to the physical strength he perceives in him and the authority with

22. *An Outline of Psycho-Analysis* (1940), SE 23:154, 155.
23. "The Infantile Genital Organization" (1923), SE 19:143-144.
24. Ibid., p. 145.

which he finds him clothed. His father now becomes a rival. . . . This
is the subject of the Oedipus complex. . . . Under the conditions of
our civilization it is invariably doomed to a frightening end.[25]

At first, the Oedipus complex was the core of Freud's theory of infantile
sexuality. "I have found love of the mother and jealousy of the father in my
own case too, and now believe it to be a general phenomenon of early childhood . . ." were the sweeping words in which Freud announced his discovery of the complex to Fliess.[26] Later he discovered preoedipal phases and the
many manifestations and crucial results of the castration complex. It gradually became apparent to him, though, that what was decisive about the Oedipus complex for male and for cultural development was not how the
complex came into being but rather the dynamics of its doom, how it
"came to a frightening end." In Freud's view, the threatening mental figure
of the father-as-castrator, whose threat was, essentially, to make the boy
feminine, interceded to force the child's mental life away from his incestuous desires and his rivalry with the stronger paternal authority.

The mental relation of the oedipal boy to femininity is not simply that
castration is the worst punishment he can imagine. The boy also experiences
a "feminine" oedipal attitude toward his father. His feminine attitude usually is not predominant, but it is present. The feminine oedipal position means
that instead of imagining himself replacing his father, who is perceived as
the active lover of his mother, the boy imagines himself as the passive object of his father's love. (For Freud, the father figure is always the active
partner.) The boy's fear of castration interferes with all his oedipal desires,
masculine and feminine, active and passive. The "positive," "masculine,"
oedipal attitude is the one in which his mother is his love object; his active,
phallic desires are directed toward her. "He could put himself in his father's
place in a masculine fashion and have intercourse with his mother as his father did, in which case he would soon have felt the latter as a hindrance, . . ." Freud writes.[27] The father is a hindrance because he is
considered the actual possessor of the mother; he has authority over her and
over the child. "Respect for this [incest] barrier is essentially a cultural demand made by society," and the father is the enforcer of this cultural demand.[28]

25. *An Outline of Psycho-Analysis* (1940), *SE* 23:189.
26. Letter of November 15, 1897, in Bonaparte et al., eds., *The Origins of Psycho-Analysis*, p.
223.
27. "The Dissolution of the Oedipus Complex" (1924), *SE* 19:176.
28. *Three Essays on the Theory of Sexuality* (1905), *SE* 7:225.

The boy's masculine attitude toward the mother is, then, the "simple positive male Oedipus" situation. Because of the "triangular character of the Oedipus situation and the constitutional bisexuality of each individual," Oedipus complexes are often "complete," that is, masculine and feminine, positive and negative.[29] In the boy's negative Oedipus complex, "he might want to take the place of his mother and be loved by his father, in which case his mother would become superfluous."[30] If the child's perception of his mother were like his perception of his father, as physically strong, "clothed" with authority, and the rightful owner of his father, she would not be superfluous but would be the boy's rival in his feminine attitude toward his father. Such, however, is not the case, when legitimate sexual lives are organized patriarchally.

What Freud claims is the case is that the boy realizes that both his feminine and masculine desires would entail castration if they were realized. If the child desires to be like his father (identification) and take a masculine attitude toward his mother, he will be castrated as punishment. If he desires to have his father as a lover (object choice) and to take a feminine attitude toward him, he will be castrated as a precondition.[31] "The boy understands that he must also submit to castration if he wants to be loved by his father as a woman," Freud wrote.[32]

The boy's dilemma is severe—"the greatest trauma of his life." According to Freud, his alternatives are to submit psychically to the possibility of castration, which requires him to give up all his oedipal loves of his parents or if he cannot either repress or destroy the Oedipus complex and enter the latency period, to fall ill. The father complex, the libidinal relationship to the father which is ambivalent, is the crux of the oedipal instinctual situation, which must now be overcome. In loving his mother, his father is a hated rival; at the same time, in loving his father, his father is his lover. In Freud's words:

> both impulses, hatred of the father and being in love with the father, undergo repression. There is a certain psychological distinction in the fact that the hatred of the father is given up on account of fear of an *external* danger (castration), while the being in love with the father is

29. *The Ego and the Id* (1923), *SE* 19:32-33.
30. "The Dissolution of the Oedipus Complex" (1924), *SE* 19:176.
31. Ibid. Identification and object choice in relation to the masculine and feminine (active and passive) oedipal desires are discussed in *Group Psychology and the Analysis of the Ego* (1921), *SE* 18:105-106.
32. "Dostoevsky and Parricide" (1928), *SE* 21:184.

treated as an *internal* instinctual danger, though fundamentally it goes back to the same external danger [castration]. . . . Of the two factors which repress hatred of the father, the first, the direct fear of punishment and castration, may be called the normal one; its pathogenic intensification seems to come only with the addition of the second factor, the fear of the feminine attitude.[33]

The infantile forces which are at issue in the related Oedipus, father, and castration complexes are love and hatred, femininity and masculinity, activity and passivity, *all* of which are contradicted by the mental father, "the superior being," which "once threatened castration. . . ."[34] The boy's feminine oedipal attitude, in which he imagines himself in his mother's place, is a precursor of masochism. The child imagines that intercourse is painful for a woman and that it is an act of aggression as well as love (sadism) on the part of the man. "You will scarcely have failed to notice that sadism has a more intimate relation with masculinity and masochism with femininity, as though there were a secret kinship present," Freud wrote.[35] In the course of a discussion of the feminine attitude, wherein he commented that "among the observations made by psycho-analysis of the mental life of children there is scarcely one which sounds so repugnant and unbelievable to a normal adult as that of a boy's feminine attitude to his father, . . ." Freud compared a masculine attitude toward the father (God) with fear of castration and a feminine attitude toward him (Him) with "desire for castration."[36] Such a desire for what is at the same time considered the most painful punishment is masochism. Further, a masochistic—like a feminine—attitude cedes the role of active subject (masculinity) to the father figure while the role of passive object is taken over by oneself; thus femininity takes on the qualities of object, passivity, castration, and masochism.[37]

33. Ibid.

34. *The Ego and the Id* (1923), SE 19:57.

35. "Anxiety and Instinctual Life," Lecture 32 of *New Introductory Lectures on Psycho-Analysis* (1933), SE 22:104.

36. "A Seventeenth-Century Demonological Neurosis" (1923), SE 19:91, 92. See also "Psycho-Analytic Notes on an Autobiographical Account of a Case of Paranoia (Dementia Paranoides)" (1911), SE 12:55-56:

> In the final stage of Schreber's delusion a magnificent victory was scored by the infantile sexual urge; for voluptuousness became God-fearing, and God Himself (his father) never tired of demanding it from him. His father's most dreaded threat, castration, actually provided the material for his wishful phantasy (at first resisted but later accepted) of being transformed into a woman.

37. See "Instincts and Their Vicissitudes" (1915), SE 14:127. In the conversion of sadism into

The related facts—that the father is the castrator in the child's mental life and that the experience of castration anxiety is the greatest trauma of his still brief life—mean that the figure of the father colors all subsequent mental development. Although it is clear in his theoretical writings, it is even clearer in some of Freud's case histories that at issue is not only an individual experience of a particular father but the historical and social institution of fatherhood as authority itself. The mental correlation between this cultural father figure and the child's understanding of God is likewise emphasized in case studies. In Freud's account of the Wolfman's castration anxiety, he wrote:

> There is no doubt whatever that at this time his father was turning into the terrifying figure that threatened him with castration. The cruel God with whom he was then struggling—who made men sinful, only to punish them afterwards, who sacrificed his own son and the sons of men—this God threw back his character on to the patient's father. . . . At this point the boy had to fit into a phylogenetic pattern, and he did so, although his personal experiences may not have agreed with it. Although the threats or hints of castration which had come his way had emanated from women, . . . it was his father from whom in the end he came to fear castration. In this respect heredity triumphed over accidental experience; in man's prehistory it was unquestionably the father who practised castration as a punishment. . . .[38]

This explanation of the father as castrator because of primeval heritage was never abandoned; in 1932 Freud reasserted it:

> Above all, it is not a question of whether castration is really carried out; what is decisive is that the danger is one that threatens from outside and that the child believes in it. He has some ground for this, for people threaten him often enough with cutting off his penis during the phallic phase, at the time of his early masturbation, and hints at that punishment must regularly find a phylogenetic reinforcement in him. It is our suspicion that during the human family's primaeval period

---

masochism, the following happens: the "object is given up and is replaced by the subject's self," who becomes the object of the exercise of violence or power. "With the turning round upon the self the change from an active to a passive instinctual aim is also effected." The subject, activity, sadism, and masculinity are thereby psychologically associated with one another over against object, passivity, masochism, and femininity.

38. "From the History of an Infantile Neurosis" (1918), SE 17:86.

castration used actually to be carried out by a jealous and cruel father upon growing boys. . . .

"We are aware that here we are diverging widely from the general opinion," Freud added. However, "we must hold fast to the view that fear of castration is one of the commonest and strongest motives for repression and thus for the formation of neuroses."[39] In invoking the primal father, Freud was invoking the patriarchal structure of civilization; he was claiming that this structure is the engine of mental development. It makes renunciation necessary and makes neurotic and ideal masculinity possible.

Fear of castration forces the boy beyond the precultural mother-child dyad and into the mental world of his culture. The relative strength of his phallic narcissism as compared with his oedipal wishes accomplishes this task as soon as the threat of castration is experienced. Freud suggested several bases of the boy's extreme narcissistic cathexis of his penis. On one occasion, he suggested that "the high degree of narcissistic value which the penis possesses can appeal to the fact that that organ is a guarantee to its owner that he can be once more united to his mother—i.e., to a substitute for her—in the act of copulation."[40] Another time, he cited Sandor Ferenczi's explanation, which attributed this "extraordinarily high narcissistic cathexis" of the penis to its significance for propagating the species. In this case, Freud noted, "the catastrophe to the Oedipus complex (the abandonment of incest and the institution of conscience and morality) may be regarded as a victory of the race over the individual."[41] The organically valuable penis was preserved, at the psychological expense of the child, so that the species might continue.

Such a teleological view is unlikely to be the child's view, but these explanations are unnecessary, for Freud's accounts combine to produce a description of the boy's experience of his phallic nature as inseparable from psychical activity, subjectivity, sensuality, love, and his capacity for mastery and curiosity. It is central to his sense of self as a male child. In terms which are not Freud's, gender identity is the core of identity, and the healthy boy will give up his illicit attachments to his parents to preserve himself, once prohibitions have been made by the father and femininity is understood as punishment, as it is when the genders have asymmetrical cultural value.

39. "Anxiety and Instinctual Life," Lecture 32 of *New Introductory Lectures on Psycho-Analysis* (1933), *SE* 22:86-87.
40. *Inhibitions, Symptoms, and Anxiety* (1926), *SE* 20:139.
41. "Some Psychical Consequences of the Anatomical Distinction Between the Sexes" (1925), *SE* 19:257.

What come into conflict within the castration complex, then, are the boy's "narcissistic interest in that part of his body and the libidinal cathexis of his parental objects. In this conflict the first of these forces normally triumphs: the child's ego turns away from the Oedipus complex."[42] It does so by giving up the instinctual satisfaction of masturbation accompanied by fantasies about his parents; in normal cases, "the boy gives way to the threat [of castration] and obeys the prohibition either wholly or at least in part. . . . In other words, he gives up, in whole or in part, the satisfaction of the instinct. . . ."[43] A renunciation of instinct has taken place, and the boy begins to be socialized. In the normal case it is mostly masculine instinctual urges which are renounced—in order to preserve them. "There is an inherent contradiction about this state of affairs," Freud observed, "in which, precisely in the interests of masculinity (that is to say, from fear of castration), every activity belonging to masculinity is stopped."[44] Freud views the situation as tragically inevitable: later masculinity relies on the suppression of the earliest, infantile, masculinity. The boy's later cultural position rests on this early cultural achievement. Infantile masculinity inevitably involves the boy in mental submission to the castrating father; that is, it involves him in femininity. Failure to resolve the Oedipus complex in an "ideal manner," that is, one which is "correct both psychologically and socially," means remaining neurotically involved with the parents, which means, in Freud's words, that "the son remains all his life bowed beneath his father's authority and he is unable to transfer his libido to an outside sexual object."[45]

Throughout his texts, Freud is certain that the Oedipus complex is the "nucleus of the neuroses" so that it is "characteristic of a normal individual that he learns to master his Oedipus complex, whereas the neurotic subject remains involved in it."[46] But until he viewed the castration complex as the major force which destroyed the Oedipus complex, he made no systematic distinction between its repression and its destruction or dissolution; "mastery" was used in a general way. Finally, in a 1924 paper entitled "The Dissolution of the Oedipus Complex," Freud distinguished between normal and ideal resolutions of the complex. While working on this paper, he had written to Lou Andreas-Salomé that he hoped its title sounded "as tragic as the

42. "The Dissolution of the Oedipus Complex" (1924), SE 19:176.
43. "Splitting of the Ego in the Process of Defence" (1940), SE 23:277.
44. Inhibitions, Symptoms, and Anxiety (1926), SE 20:115.
45. "The Development of the Libido and the Sexual Organizations," Lecture 21 of Introductory Lectures on Psycho-Analysis (1916-1917), SE 16:337.
46. "Two Encyclopaedia Articles" (1923), SE 18:245-246.

title of Spengler's book" (*The Decline of the West*).[47] The tragedy is that "if the satisfaction of love in the field of the Oedipus complex is to cost the child his penis," such love cannot be satisfied. The love is given up; "the whole process has, on the one hand, preserved the genital organ—has averted the danger of its loss—and, on the other, has paralysed it—has removed its function. This process ushers in the latency period. . . ." What is tragic for the boy at the time is nonethelesss his only hope for future masculine health. Freud explained:

> the process we have described is more than a repression. It is equivalent, if it is ideally carried out, to a destruction and an abolition of the complex. We may plausibly assume that we have here come upon the borderline—never a very sharply drawn one—between the normal and the pathological. If the ego has in fact not achieved much more than a *repression* of the complex, the latter persists in an unconscious state in the id and will later manifest its pathogenic effect.[48]

This distinction was again drawn some years later: "in this desirable case, therefore, [the Oedipus complex is] not simply repressed but destroyed in the id."[49] If the civilizational precepts are not heeded so that the Oedipus complex is not destroyed, illness will result. Such precepts oppose *all* libidinal drives of the oedipal boy. While Freud was not opposed to culture per se, his sympathies here seem to lie with the so rudely civilized boy. In a later context he stressed the other side: "It is easy, as we can see, for a barbarian to be healthy; for a civilized man the task is hard. The desire for a powerful, uninhibited ego may seem to us intelligible; but, as we are taught by the times we live in, it is in the profoundest sense hostile to civilization."[50]

The dissolution of the Oedipus complex is the paradigmatic Freudian renunciation; if it is truly a dissolution, the way is prepared for the masculine and the psychological ideal of independence from parents (especially from ambivalent defiance of and submission to the father) and activity in the world. But the father's mental functions do not cease when the Oedipus

47. Letter of March 14, 1924, in Ernst Pfeiffer, ed., *Sigmund Freud and Lou Andreas-Salomé Letters* (1966), p. 133.

48. "The Dissolution of the Oedipus Complex" (1924), *SE* 19:176-177.

49. "Anxiety and Instinctual Life," Lecture 32 of *New Introductory Lectures on Psycho-Analysis* (1933), *SE* 22:92. See also *Inhibitions, Symptoms, and Anxiety* (1926), *SE* 20:142n, where Freud describes this as the "difference between mere repression and the real removal of an old wishful impulse."

50. *An Outline of Psycho-Analysis* (1940), *SE* 23:185. "The times" were Nazi times; the *Outline* was left unfinished in London when Freud died in 1939.

complex is overcome. An independent superego is created out of the earlier libidinal relationships with the father. The nucleus of the superego is the internalized father figure, so the superego replaces the superseded complexes. Only by understanding this continued, but transformed, mental presence of the paternal principle can we understand how the boy's resolution of the infantile complexes reproduces the paternal character of culture and the resultant dominance of masculinity over femininity.

Renunciation, Masculinity, and Culture

In the dilemma of the castration complex, the boy's ego was still too weak to master his instinctual desires on its own power. Freud's dramatization of the son's struggle continues:

> Clearly, the repression of the Oedipus complex was no easy task. The child's parents, and especially his father, were perceived as the obstacle to a realization of his Oedipus wishes; so his infantile ego fortified itself for the carrying out of the repression by erecting this same obstacle within itself. It borrowed strength to do this, so to speak, from the father, and this loan was an extraordinarily momentous act. The superego retains the character of the father, while the more powerful the Oedipus complex was and the more rapidly it succumbed to repression (under the influence of authority, religious teaching, schooling and reading), the stricter will be the domination of the super-ego over the ego later on. . . .[51]

As one might guess from the term "repression," this passage was written before Freud distinguished firmly between repression and "dissolution." Indeed, the problem of an overly severe superego, which neurotically dominates id and ego just as the father has dominated mother and child, may have made it useful for Freud to posit "dissolution" in order to account for nonneurotic, psychically independent, masculine development. His view was that mental health depends on the superego's "normal" development, that is, on its "having become sufficiently impersonal." And this is what has not taken place in neurotics, "whose Oedipus complex has not passed through the correct process of transformation. Their super-ego still confronts their ego as a strict father confronts a child; and their morality oper-

51. *The Ego and the Id* (1923), *SE* 19:34-35.

ates in a primitive fashion in that the ego gets itself punished by the super-ego."[52] If the superego replaces the father and other authorities to dominate the son, he has not overcome the father complex but has merely internalized it. If, however, the Oedipus complex could be destroyed in the id and if the superego which replaces the complex could become gradually emancipated from its particular paternal origins, the Freudian ideal, the primacy of the independent intelligence which submits itself only to impersonal *Ananke*, would be possible. The progressive depersonalization of the superego, which is also its desexualization, is discussed in the contexts of Freud's analyses of anxiety, where he describes the mental forces which make men afraid and thereby dominate them.

The dangers that threaten occur in stages. As the major determinant of anxiety, the danger of psychical helplessness fits the stage of the ego's early immaturity; "the danger of loss of an object (or loss of love) fits the lack of self-sufficiency in the first years of childhood; the danger of being castrated fits the phallic phase; and finally fear of the super-ego, which assumes a special position, fits the period of latency."[53] Castration anxiety develops into "moral anxiety—social anxiety"; this is the fear of the superego.[54] Fear of the superego is thus a transformation of fear of the father, but it, too, develops further. The superego is first built around the father image, but this personal figure is gradually generalized because of "influences of teachers and authorities, self-chosen models and publicly recognized heroes. . . ." And

> the last figure in the series that began with the parents is the dark power of Destiny which only the fewest of us are able to look upon as impersonal. There is little to be said against the Dutch writer Multatuli when he replaces the *Moira* (Destiny) of the Greeks by the divine pair *"Logos"* ("Reason") and *"Ananke"* ("Necessity"); but all who transfer

52. *The Question of Lay Analysis* (1926), SE 20:223.
53. "Anxiety and Instinctual Life," Lecture 32 of *New Introductory Lectures on Psycho-Analysis* (1933), SE 22:88. In a similar context, Freud stated:

> it is precisely in women that the danger-situation of loss of object seems to have remained the most effective. All we need to do is to make a slight modification in our description of their determinant of anxiety, in the sense that it is no longer a matter of feeling the want of, or actually losing the object itself, but of losing the object's love. Since there is no doubt that hysteria has a strong affinity with femininity, just as obsessional neurosis has with masculinity, it appears probable that, as a determinant of anxiety, loss of love plays much the same part in hysteria as the threat of castration does in phobias and the fear of the super-ego in obsessional neurosis. (*Inhibitions, Symptoms, and Anxiety* [1926], SE 20:143.)

54. *Inhibitions, Symptoms, and Anxiety* (1926), SE 20:139.

the guidance of the world to Providence, to God, or to God and Nature, arouse a suspicion that they still look upon these ultimate and remotest powers as a parental couple, in a mythological sense, and believe themselves linked to them by libidinal ties.[55]

The man with a truly impersonal superego recognizes reason and necessity as his laws and recognizes, too, that these forces have no love for him. In many instances, however, the superego is not altogether impersonal; civilization persists in reinstating the authority of fathers in such a way that men's superegos are too harsh and the burden of neurotic guilt is too great; morality is uninformed, not reasoned, renunciation. This was the dynamic which Freud dwelt on in *Civilization and Its Discontents*, in which he applied the problem of uninformed renunciation in the individual to culture itself to suggest that culture, too, might become neurotic. Culture uses the father figure to create the superego; the superego is the "heir to the Oedipus complex" and it represents "the cultural past."[56] At the same time, the Oedipus—castration—father complexes derive from paternal culture.

The superego also represents aggression against the punishing father; it turns the child's aggression against the father (the death drive directed outward) back on the ego. "The tension between the harsh super-ego and the ego that is subjected to it, is called by us the sense of guilt; it expresses itself as a need for punishment." The superego is "like a garrison in a conquered city."[57] The conqueror is civilization, its soldiers are the father figures, and the conquered city is instinctual desire. Now conscience requires renunciation of instinct. "Originally, renunciation of instinct was the result of fear of an external authority," the father. But when the father figure is internal, in the form of the superego, fear of it is no longer quieted by renunciation. "Here, instinctual renunciation is not enough, for the wish persists and cannot be concealed from the super-ego." Instinctual renunciation now no longer has a "completely liberating effect." In fact, each renunciation of instinct "now becomes a dynamic source of conscience and every fresh renunciation increases the latter's severity and intolerance." This happens because "every piece of aggression whose satisfaction the subject gives up is taken over by the super-ego and increases the latter's aggressiveness (against the ego)."[58] Hence discontent is permanent and increasing in civilization. Only if

55. "The Economic Problem of Masochism" (1924), *SE* 19:168.
56. *An Outline of Psycho-Analysis* (1940), *SE* 23:205, 206.
57. *Civilization and Its Discontents* (1930), *SE* 21:123, 124.
58. Ibid., pp. 127-128.

the superego is impersonal, so that it no longer wields the paternal power of threatening castration for instinctual satisfaction and promising rewards for renunciations, can this dilemma be resolved. Otherwise, "the super-ego fulfills the same function of protecting and saving that was fulfilled in earlier days by the father and later by Providence or Destiny."[59] The impersonal superego is capable of informed renunciation of all the internal derivatives of the father complex. This is the final renunciation: it is resignation to the ineluctable as ineluctable, not as maternal, and, more crucial to Freud, not as paternal.

Freud's economic and genetic accounts of the development of the mental apparatus, of civilization by stages, and of masculinity, both normal and ideal, turn on his critical vision of renunciation of wish as the source of development, culture, science, morality, and independent intellect. Renunciation of illusion is the consistent critical principle in all these accounts; Freud criticizes those psychical modes which carry on a search for fulfillments which contradict the demands of reality, whether it be social or "material."

The paradigmatic renunciation, in Freud's view, is the son's renunciation of oedipal libido: "the realization dawns on us that such an early attempt at damming up the sexual instinct, so decided a partisanship by the young ego in favour of the external as opposed to the internal world, brought about by the prohibition of infantile sexuality, cannot be without its effect on the individual's later readiness for culture," he wrote.[60] As we have seen, Freud is specific about what forces the drives away from paths leading to their satisfaction: the castration and father complexes. The decision "in favour of the external world" is first made in favor of paternal precepts.

Renunciation explains mental, masculine, and cultural development. Analogously, renunciation is the principle by which the individual is cured of unwitting bondage to passions and by which culture is cured of unwitting bondage to religious illusion. When renunciation is the source of higher development toward reality and independence, the psychical modes achieved by renunciation criticize those psychical modes which have been renounced. Just as renunciation overcomes illusion, paternity overcomes maternity, masculinity overcomes femininity, reality overcomes wish, and science overcomes religion. In each case, the former term is the source of judgment on the latter; it is the criterion by which the latter term is diagnosed as regressive, narcissistic, wishful. It is simultaneously the case, how-

59. *The Ego and the Id* (1923), *SE* 19:58.
60. *An Outline of Psycho-Analysis* (1940), *SE* 23:201.

ever, that the continued psychical viability of wishes imperils the higher forms. And the possibility of excessive neurotic renunciation, urged by the overly strict superego which relocates but continues the struggles of the father complex, is a second reason that mental independence is tenuous. The psychoanalytic view of the psychological, cultural, and masculine ideal is not simply that it shall have renounced prior psychical positions but also that it shall have achieved affective and intellectual independence from all the versions of the parental figures. Short of such independence, the value of renunciation is ambiguous. The dissolution of the Oedipus complex and scientific resignation to *Logos* and *Ananke* are correlative.

So far, it is apparent that Freud visualized a progressive hierarchy of mental positions in individual and collective masculine development. Discussion of his accounts of the development of the mental position of femininity on the part of women, who also encounter the issues of castration, the father complex, and oedipal wishes, will complete the picture of this hierarchy.

PART THREE

Fulfillment and Femininity

Chapter 7

Sex and Gender in Freud

Most important of all, that slimy snake, the first betrayer of our peace and the father of restlessness, never ceases to watch and lie in wait beneath the heel of woman, whom he once poisoned. By "woman" we mean, of course, the carnal or sensual part of man. For this is our Eve, through whom the crafty serpent entices and lures our minds to deadly pleasures.
—ERASMUS, *Enchiridion Militis Christiani*

E[. . .], whom I met in Florence, is now here and will probably visit me soon to give me detailed impressions of Amsterdam. He seems to have taken up with some woman again. Such practice is a deterrent from theory.
—FREUD, letter to Jung of September 19, 1907

Femininity as Fulfillment

For Freud, masculinity and sacrificial excellences, femininity and fulfilling shortcomings, are related in subtle but pervasive ways. They are so related in the shadow of the father. The question of femininity arises in Freud's thought in three overlapping but distinguishable senses. The first sense has been discussed; this is the psychological phenomenon of a boy's (and man's) feminine attitude. This feminine attitude toward the father, desiring to be loved by him, is part of what must be overcome by renunciation of oedipal libido if masculine development is to achieve its ideal end. The second sense is as a quality of women, who function as libidinal objects for men; as such, femininity represents libidinal fulfillment, the temptations of the pleasure principle, and the psychical dangers of wish fulfillment to the male ascetic, culture hero, or theorist. In its third sense, femininity is the psychological attitude which is unquestioningly considered to be the appropriate outcome of female psychical development. Understood in this third sense, too, femininity is allied with fulfillment. In Freud's view, femininity in a woman allows her to experience gratification that is renounced in ideal masculine development because the feminine attitude retains a dependent and consoling libidinal tie to paternal figures. Taken in its first and third senses, the feminine attitude allows fulfillment to be experienced whereas in its second sense, a feminine woman is the object which provides fulfillment.

Many criticisms of Freud's view of femininity have assumed that Freud confounded a male's view of women with the subjective phenomenon of femininity, as experienced by women, "itself." Of course, as a construction of patriarchal culture, femininity *is* defined in relation to men. Even so, the Freudian mistrust of femininity is anchored more firmly in his theory than this asymmetrical perspective alone would necessitate, although the male viewpoint is certainly taken throughout his writings. First, gratification itself is mistrusted on economic and genetic grounds, so it cannot be a critically neutral step when Freud allies femininity and fulfillment in such varied ways. Nor was Freud altogether inaccurate, I think, in seeing feminine women as representing fulfillment to men. Second, his writings pose the further question of how women themselves, who achieve (or fail to achieve) psychical femininity, not only represent, but also *experience*, fulfillments which the successful development of masculinity precludes. Finally, the fact that in Freudian theory the boy's and the girl's femininity is, by definition, a passive libidinal relationship to *the father* defines the issue that is important when Freud examines mental relationships to gods. The issue is that, whether the experiencing subject is a man or a woman, the problem of the feminine attitude is a problem in relationship to men: "The feminine predicament, for *both* sexes, applies only in the relationship to men."[1] Specifically, it applies prototypically and is recapitulated in relationship to fathers and father figures.

When the three relationships between femininity and fulfillment are understood (that is, that the boy's femininity means that he receives gratification from the father, that the "masculine" man looks to the "feminine" woman for gratification, and that the "feminine" woman receives gratifica-

---

1. Juliet Mitchell, *Psychoanalysis and Feminism* (1974), p. 52. There is at least one apparent exception to this generalization in Freud's texts. In "'A Child Is Being Beaten': A Contribution to the Study of the Origin of Sexual Perversions" (1919), Freud reports a boy's conscious fantasy of being beaten by the mother. This is taking a feminine attitude toward the mother, in his terms. He comments: "the remarkable thing about his later conscious phantasy is that it has for its content a feminine attitude without a homosexual object-choice"; *SE* 17:199. But Freud's reconstruction of the original, unconscious fantasy is that it expresses a feminine attitude toward the *father*, ibid., p. 198. This reconstruction leaves Freud's correlation of femininity and passive attachment to a father figure undisturbed.

tion from a father figure), it is clear that, in all three cases, some form of renunciation is judged not to have taken place. The pleasure principle has not
been completely submitted to reality; the oedipal attachments have not
been abolished. But, to reiterate, the problem of the theoretic relationships
between femininity and fulfillment is not resolved by observing that, for the
most part in our and Freud's society, women are defined in terms of ties to
and ties of men. Freud's discussions of males' and females' feminine attitudes reveal that, in his view, the father figure is by definition the active, loving (and threatening) subject and the feminine attitude (in either sex) is the
attitude of the passive object so that the paternal figure at the center of the
system defines both femininity "itself" as a psychical attitude and the specific fulfillments which are associated with it. These fulfillments are offered by
the father figure to the feminine object.

Once it is clear that femininity is allied with fulfillment in these ways, it is
no surprise to discover that, in terms of the polar concepts discussed in
Chapter 4, Freud usually located the psychical qualities of the feminine
woman closer to wish than to reality, to narcissism than to object love, to
pleasure than to reality, to fulfillment than to renunciation, than those of
men. Freud considered the feminine woman to be more likely to choose objects on a narcissistic than an anaclitic basis and to be more libidinally tied
to her parents than a man. For example, he wrote:

> A comparison of the male and female sexes then shows that there are
> fundamental differences between them in respect of their type of ob-
> ject-choice, although these differences are of course not universal.
> Complete object-love of the attachment type is, properly speaking,
> characteristic of the male. . . . A different course is followed in the
> type of female most frequently met with, which is probably the purest
> and truest one. . . . Strictly speaking, it is only themselves that such
> women love with an intensity comparable to that of the man's love for
> them. Nor does their need lie in the direction of loving, but of being
> loved. . . .[2]

2. "On Narcissism: An Introduction" (1914), SE 14:88-89. There is a point in this paper which
would seem to necessitate either narcissistic or homosexual object choice on the part of
women insofar as mature object choice recapitulates earliest loves and insofar as women
nurse children. Freud writes: "We say that a human being has originally two sexual objects—
himself and the woman who nurses him—and in doing so we are postulating a primary narcissism in everyone"; ibid., p. 88. Insofar as self and mother are similar for girls (and here one
needs to know if "him" is specific or, like "human being" [Mensch] in the same sentence, ge-
neric), that is, insofar as both are female and choice is on the basis of this characteristic, a

In the early *Three Essays*, Freud observed that at every developmental stage through which all ought to pass, a certain number were held back, "so there are some who have never got over their parents' authority and have withdrawn their affection from them either very incompletely or not at all. They are mostly girls, who, to the delight of their parents, have persisted in all their childish love far beyond puberty."[3] Women represent sensuality and tend to be deficient in intellect. Freud explains this deficiency with reference to the customary upbringing of girls:

> [It] forbids their concerning themselves intellectually with sexual problems though they nevertheless feel extremely curious about them, and frightens them by condemning such curiosity as unwomanly and a sign of a sinful disposition. In this way they are scared away from *any* form of thinking, and knowledge loses its value for them. The prohibition of thought extends beyond the sexual field, . . . like the prohibition of thought about religion among men, or the prohibition of thought about loyalty among faithful subjects. I do not believe that women's "physiological feeble-mindedness" is to be explained by a biological opposition between intellectual work and sexual activity, as Moebius has asserted in a work which has been widely disputed. I think that the undoubted intellectual inferiority of so many women can rather be traced back to the inhibition of thought necessitated by sexual suppression.[4]

Women's *own* sensuality and intellect are suppressed together; then women take on the cultural function of representing sensuality to men. Women who are feminine are also characterized by passive rather than active libidinal aims and by being more often hysterical or masochistic than obsessive or sadistic. Compared with masculinity, femininity makes a person less capable of sublimation, less likely to develop an objective superego, and therefore less likely to develop the social and cultural interests and capacities which the superego makes possible. Instead, women are enemies of culture. Freud explains this in terms of their already representing the sensual:

woman would choose a woman in both cases, thus making the choice appear narcissistic even if it were anaclitic. In the same essay, the catalogue of prototypes for choice is soon expanded. The narcissistic types are: (a) what he himself is, (b) what he himself was, and (c) what he would like to be. The anaclitic types are: (a) the woman who feeds him and (b) the man who protects him and the succession of substitutes who take their place; ibid., p. 90. Here, then, anaclitic object choice of a man by a woman is allowed for.

3. *Three Essays on the Theory of Sexuality* (1905), *SE* 7:227.

4. " 'Civilized' Sexual Morality and Modern Nervous Illness" (1908), *SE* 9:198-199.

women soon come into opposition to civilization and display their re-
tarding and restraining influence. . . . Women represent the interests of
the family and of sexual life. The work of civilization has become increasingly the business of men, it confronts them with ever more difficult tasks and compels them to carry out instinctual sublimations of
which women are little capable. . . . What [quantities of libido a man]
employs for cultural aims he to a great extent withdraws from women
and sexual life. His constant associations with men, and his dependence on his relations with them, even estrange him from his duties as
a husband and father. Thus the woman finds herself forced into the
background by the claims of civilization and she adopts a hostile attitude towards it.[5]

In the situation in which "civilization behaves towards sexuality as a people
or a stratum of its population does which has subjected another one to its
exploitation,"[6] women are integral to the sensual substratum which must be
suppressed in order to get on with the business of the ascendant culture.
Once again, pleasure and reality are opposed, and femininity represents and
partakes in those psychological modes that masculinity must renounce.
When sexuality and civilization are in contradiction and civilization is a masculine achievement, femininity is also in contradiction to the cultural reality
principle.

The relationships between femininity and fulfillment in Freud's thought
will now be examined in the context of a discussion of his theory of gender
difference. As is usual in asymmetrical theory, the "general" oedipal theory
applies to men, the differential one to women. For Freud, gender—both
masculinity and femininity—develops because of the Oedipus, castration,
and father complexes. When Freud's papers on the psychology of women,
on femininity, and on female sexuality are read in relation to his oedipal theory of masculine development and in terms of the place of gender differentiation within his theory of culture, a theory of gender difference, which is
important to understanding his theory of religion, can be discerned in them.
In Freud's theory of gender, femininity achieves precisely what is criticized
when his critical principle is renunciation.

The following questions guide the rest of this part: why is a concept of
gender necessary? On what bases can a theory of gender difference be discovered in Freud's discussions of sex difference? What is the content of his

5. *Civilization and Its Discontents* (1930), *SE* 21:103-104.
6. Ibid., p. 104.

theory of gender difference? And how is Freud's theory of gender also a critique of femininity as a psychical attitude that receives fulfillments?

The Need for a Concept of Gender

Gender has two related meanings in everyday usage. One is grammatical; the other refers to sexual differentiation. Both meanings are classificatory. The *Oxford English Dictionary* defines gender, first, as a "kind, sort or class"; second, as "grammatical 'kinds' corresponding more or less to distinctions of sex (and absence of sex)"; and third, in a sense transferred from grammar, as a synonym of "sex." Two American dictionaries give the grammatical as the first meaning and "sex" as the second (*Webster's New World*, 1968; *Random House Unabridged*, 1967). An older one gives "sex" first and the grammatical meaning second (*Webster's Seventh New Collegiate*, 1963). The fourth edition of the *New Columbia Encyclopedia* (1975) discusses grammatical gender only but relates it to "natural gender" (femininity and masculinity).

The similarity between the two meanings is evident: in both cases classificatory systems have been generated that are somehow based in the "data" of biological sex difference. In both cases, however, the members of each resultant class may be only remotely related to actual maleness or femaleness. The relationship is, rather, often one of extrapolation, of symbolic equivalence, or of similarities embedded in tradition. For example, the femaleness of the German *Mädchen* ("girl") is not sufficient to establish the gender of the word as feminine (it is neuter); the maleness of Schreber does not render impossible Freud's analysis of his psychological femininity. Similarly, Freud analyzed "feminine masochism" on the basis of case histories of men. In this analysis, "feminine" referred to fantasies that "place the subject in a characteristically female situation; they signify, that is, being castrated, or copulated with, or giving birth to a baby."[7] As the authors of a recent discussion of grammatical gender point out, "when grammarians use the word gender they know they are referring to a convention that may overlap sex or may have nothing to do with it. When psychiatrists use the word gender they, too, assign it a specific meaning that can match sex, although it does

7. "The Economic Problem of Masochism" (1924), *SE* 19:162. On Schreber's femininity, see "Psycho-Analytic Notes on an Autobiographical Account of a Case of Paranoia" (1911), *SE* 12:32-34, and throughout.

not necessarily do so. At the risk of oversimplification, sex in both contexts is a biological given; gender is a social acquisition."[8]

I use the term gender to refer to mental femininity and masculinity in Freud's theories. Masculinity and femininity are psychical attitudes that have cultural roots and consequences. This use has precedent in much recent work. For example, John Money and Anke Ehrhardt consider a differential concept of "gender identity" to be necessary for contemporary psychosexual theory. They write that "in developmental psychosexual theory, it is no longer satisfactory to utilize only the concept of psychosexual development. Psychosexual (or gender-identity) differentiation is the preferential concept. . . ."[9] Money and Ehrhardt define gender identity as "the sameness, unity, and persistence of one's individuality as male, female, or ambivalent, in greater or lesser degree, especially as it is experienced in self-awareness and behavior. . . ."[10] Gender identity need not "differentiate in conformity with registered sex," when registration has been based on anatomical evidence.[11] To illustrate the possibility of dysjunction between sex and gender identity in development, Money and Ehrhardt compare the development of gender identity with the development of language:

> Postnatally, the programing of psychosexual differentiation is, by phyletic decree, a function of biographical history, especially social biography. There is a close parallel here with the programing of language development. The social-biography program is not written independently of the phyletic program, but in conjunction with it, though on occasions there may be dysjunction between the two.[12]

Freud's theory of the oedipal development of masculinity and femininity agrees with Money and Ehrhardt's observations: psychological gender is differentiated out of what Freud conceptualized as an original bisexuality; this differentiation is understood as the result of sex-typical biographies and their variants; and masculinity and femininity may be "inappropriately " differentiated.

Money and Ehrhardt's conceptualizations have influenced much recent research and reflection on sex and gender. So have those of Robert Stoller, who also distinguishes gender from biological sex. Stoller's definition of

8. Casey Miller and Kate Swift, *Words and Women* (1976), p. 51.
9. John Money and Anke Ehrhardt, *Man and Woman, Boy and Girl* (1972), p. 1.
10. Ibid., p. 4.   11. Ibid., p. 15.   12. Ibid., p. 2.

gender, as a psychological and/or cultural attribute of maleness or femaleness which need not necessarily accompany it, has been widely popularized. He has studied and (psychoanalytically) treated persons of ambiguous, neuter, mistakenly assigned, or otherwise anomalous biological sex as well as biologically normal persons with disturbances in gender identity. For Stoller's purposes, biological sex is defined as an "algebraic sum" of "chromosomes, external genitalia, internal genitalia, . . . gonads, hormonal states, and secondary sex characteristics," so that it is no longer an unambiguous either-or but is rather a position somewhere on one of two overlapping bell curves, one called male and the other female. Gender, on the other hand, "has psychological or cultural rather than biological connotation. If the proper terms for sex are 'male' and 'female,' the corresponding terms for gender are 'masculine' and feminine.'"[13]

Obviously, the contents of individuals' gender identities vary because they include fantasies, thoughts, behaviors, needs, affects, and so forth, which are related to but not necessarily resultant from or subsumed by biological sex distinction. In Stoller's experience, however, once a particular gender identity is achieved, it cannot be changed. He has found that unless a gender identity has from the beginning been ambivalent, once it is learned it is unshakable. (By placing this learning process within the first year or two of childhood, Stoller's theory differs from Freud's oedipal theory of gender differentiation.) In accordance with evidence for persistence of gender identity, some current medical practice treats gender as the determinant of biological sex and social role when the three are somehow misaligned: "biological sex can be and often is reconstructed to allow the individual to play his or her gender role without confusion and risk of social ridicule."[14]

There is, then, an influential and controversial contemporary viewpoint that gender is both distinguishable from, and less malleable than, anatomical or biological sex whereas the popular view seems to have been that gender naturally accompanies and elaborates biological distinctions. Gender,

13. Robert Stoller, *Sex and Gender*, vol. 1: *Development of Masculinity and Femininity* (1968), p. 9. See also Ray L. Birdwhistell, "Masculinity and Femininity as Display" (1970), p. 42, for the distinction among "*primary* sexual characteristics which relate to the physiology of the production of fertile ova or spermatozoa, . . . *secondary* sexual characteristics which are anatomical in nature, and the *tertiary* sexual characteristics which are patterned social-behavioral in form. These latter are learned and are situationally produced."

14. Ann Oakley, *Sex, Gender, and Society* (Harper & Row, Colophon Books, 1972), p. 165. See Janice G. Raymond, *The Transsexual Empire: The Making of a She-Male* (Boston: Beacon Press, 1979), for a radical feminist criticism of ideological presuppositions of transsexual surgery.

which, if it was conceptualized at all, was conceptualized as a dependent variable, is now considered independent by some. At the very least, both clinical and theoretical need has arisen for conceptual distinctions between male and female (sex), masculinity and femininity (gender), and man and woman (social beings). As will be seen, Freud made these distinctions; indeed, Stoller cites Freud in presenting his definitions.

A detailed set of definitions of concepts resulting from a distinction between sex and gender is provided by Reesa Vaughter in the course of an argument for the methodological necessity of treating gender as an independent variable in empirical research:

> sex is the biological status of a person as congruently male or female or as hermaphroditic. . . . The sex role consists of all "irreducible" and nonoptional attributes and behaviors typically characteristic of congruent male or female or of hermaphroditic persons. Sex role behaviors are defined biologically by the structure and function of the reproductive system. . . . Sex role performance may or may not indicate the biological capacity of the person. Sex role identity is the experiencing of oneself, with concomitant cognitive organization, as female, male, or hermaphroditic. Gender is the perceived or measured status of a female or male in regard to the degree of femininity and the degree of masculinity as pertaining to some attribute or behavior. Prescription of gender is based upon assigned sex. Gender status (feminine, masculine, androgynous) is defined by the female's or male's enactment of gender roles. Gender role consists of all optional and prescribed attributes, attitudes, and behaviors defined appropriate for and expected of females and males within the culture. The gender role definition exists independently of the person's experiencing of, or performing the role. . . . Gender role performance may or may not reflect the person's role capacities in any given situation. Gender role identity is the experiencing of oneself, with concomitant cognitive organization, as feminine, masculine, and androgynous to some degree or another. . . .[15]

15. Reesa M. Vaughter, "Review Essay" (1976), pp. 122-123, n. 14. Her essay provides an extensive bibliography and also discusses academic sources of the distinction between sex and gender, which I have not presented. These are cross-species and cultural comparisons of sex differences, studies of developmental changes in female and male behavior, and comparisons of sex differences in different ethnic and socioeconomic groups (p. 123). Responses to Freud's psychology of women, especially feminist responses, have also laid the groundwork for these distinctions by persistently keeping open the question of the part played by society

In short, "gender is a system that emerges out of assigned sex and sex identity; it is related to both but dependent on neither, with unique properties of its own."[16] Where sex is "irreducible" and "nonoptional," gender is "perceived," "prescribed," and "optional." Psychologists who undertake empirical studies must distinguish between sex and gender in order to avoid the methodological error of confounding sex differences and gender differences. If this error is not avoided, what is situationally determined (however profoundly it is determined) may be seen as naturally and inevitably developed, with the result that variants of expected gender differences will be preconceived of as deviations from normal sex differences rather than as gender variants. Eleanor Maccoby and Carol Jacklin, in a 1974 review of empirical psychological studies of sex differences, concluded that there are relatively few consistently discovered sex differences and that there is often as much or more variation in traits and capacities within the sexes than between them. However, they found that parents', teachers', researchers', and children's expectations of which differences would obtain were pervasive and relatively consistent. One reviewer described the theme of their study as: "we are prisoners of our own conceptions."[17]

The concept of gender is a way of naming this situation in which we are prisoners of our own conceptions and of specifying these conceptions, which are interpretations of the meaning of sexual distinction. "Gender" refers to the difference made (whether to a child, a psychologist, a parent, a society, a theory of human capacities, or a religion) by the fact that there are two sexes and the difference made by which sex someone is. In other words, gender refers to the interpretations of the meaning of sex differences that are characteristic of a given situation. Therefore, in asking what Freud's theory of gender differences was, I am asking what Freud found to be the *psychical* difference made by the fact of sex distinction for persons of both sexes, when psychoanalytic method was used to answer this question.

When he first tried to answer this question directly by conceptualizing which psychoanalytic "differences" would always correspond to sex differ-

---

in the formation of presumably sex-linked psychological traits. See, for example, Karen Horney, "The Flight from Womanhood" (1926); Clara M. Thompson, *On Women*, ed. Maurice R. Green (New York: Basic Books, 1964); Jean Baker Miller, ed., *Psychoanalysis and Women* (New York: Brunner/Mazel, 1973); and Jean Strouse, ed., *Women and Analysis* (1974).

16. Vaughter, "Review Essay," p. 123.

17. Eleanor E. Maccoby and Carol N. Jacklin, *The Psychology of Sex Differences* (1974), esp. pp. 347-374; quoted phrase from a review of this book by Susan Edmiston, *New York Times Book Review*, April 13, 1975, p. 3.

ence, Freud arrived at no satisfactory response. He anticipated that psychical activity and passivity should correlate with sex difference, but his frequent and inconclusive discussions of sex difference in relation to activity and passivity reveal the psychoanalytic inadequacy of his conventional anticipation. No exclusive association of activity and passivity with maleness and femaleness could be made because psychical bisexuality was a quality of *both* men and women. A second attempt to relate sex difference to another basic psychoanalytic concept also failed to meet the tests of clinical observation and theoretic coherence. Because the concept of repression was the cornerstone of psychoanalytic theory, Freud at first attempted to relate sex and repression by assuming either that (a) in a man, femininity was normally repressed whereas in a woman, masculinity was normally repressed, or that (b), in members of both sexes, femininity was repressed by masculinity.[18] But, in a 1919 paper, he argued against both these theories while attributing them, respectively, to Wilhelm Fliess and Alfred Adler. He represented Fliess's theory of the relation between sex and repression as follows:

> The dominant sex of the person, that which is the more strongly developed, has repressed the mental representation of the subordinated sex into the unconscious. Therefore the nucleus of the unconscious (that is to say, the repressed) is in each human being that side of him which belongs to the opposite sex. Such a theory as this can only have an intelligible meaning if we assume that a person's sex is to be determined by the formation of his genitals; for otherwise it would not be certain which is a person's stronger sex and we should run the risk of reaching from the results of our enquiry the very fact which has to serve as its point of departure.[19]

This theory confounded biological and psychical sex and was therefore circular, in Freud's view. The second theory, that of Adler, was described and argued against as follows:

> [It also] represents the struggle between the two sexes as being the decisive cause of repression. In other respects it comes into conflict with the former theory; moreover, it looks for support to sociological rather than biological sources. According to this theory of the "masculine protest," . . . every individual makes efforts not to remain on the inferior "feminine line [of development]" and struggles towards the "mas-

18. See Chap. 1, n. 49, for quotation of Freud's suggestions along these lines.
19. "'A Child Is Being Beaten'" (1919), SE 17:200-201.

culine line," from which satisfaction can alone be derived. . . . The repressing agency, therefore, would always be a masculine instinctual impulse, and the repressed would be a feminine one.[20]

In another context, Freud argued that Adler had "hopelessly mixed" the biological, social, and psychological meanings of masculinity and femininity.[21] He added:

> It is impossible, and is disproved by observation, that a child, whether male or female, should found the plan of its life on an original depreciation of the female sex and take the wish to be a real man as its "guiding line." Children have, to begin with, no idea of the significance of the distinction between the sexes; on the contrary, they start with the assumption that the same genital organ (the male one) is possessed by both sexes; they do not begin their sexual researches with the problem of the distinction between the sexes, while the *social* underestimation of women is completely foreign to them.[22]

In his 1919 paper, he tested both theories against evidence gained from his analysis of fantasies of a child being beaten, fantasies found in analysands of both sexes. He reconstructed three stages in these fantasies, which, when compared in terms of active or passive aim and sex of beater and beaten figure, were not patterned symmetrically when two males' and four females' fantasies were contrasted. The reasoning in this paper is complex, even for Freud, and need not be summarized here. But his conclusion was that "the motive forces of repression must not be sexualized." By "sexualized," he meant conceptualized as consistently feminine or masculine. Instead, "infantile sexuality, which is held under repression, acts as the chief motive force in the formation of symptoms; and the essential part of its content, the Oedipus complex, is the nuclear complex of the neuroses."[23] The psychical difference between the sexes had to be explained in terms of different oedipal dynamics and particularly in terms of different mental relationships to parents and to the paternal threat of castration rather than in terms of direct correlations between sex and the content of the repressed.

20. Ibid., p. 201.
21. *On the History of the Psycho-Analytic Movement* (1914), SE 14:55.
22. Ibid. As Strachey notes, the statement that "children do not begin their sexual researches with the problem of the distinction between the sexes" was corrected later in "Some Psychical Consequences of the Anatomical Distinction Between the Sexes" (1925), SE 19:248-258.
23. "'A Child Is Being Beaten'" (1919), SE 17:203-204.

Freud's specifically psychoanalytic formulation of the psychical significance of sex difference took form in the mid-1920s, when he corrected his previous assumption that the Oedipus complexes of boys and girls were symmetrically opposite. In Freudian terms, the different relationships between the castration and Oedipus complexes in boys and girls determined the possible masculine and feminine results of development. Thus, once again, psychical "paternal etiology" was drawn upon, this time to explain psychical gender difference. Even though it was not directly stated as such an answer, the answer to Freud's question of the psychoanalytic difference made by sex difference was his discovery that members of both sexes "repudiate" their own feminine attitudes (but that females are nonetheless expected to become feminine). With this answer, the idea that psychical sex, or gender, was a direct result of something biological, or that it was the psychical parallel to physiology, was left behind. Instead, Freud's reliance on the oedipal and castration crises to explain gender shows that he viewed gender as a developmental achievement. For him, gender is a complex psychical response to anatomical differences within the small society of the oedipal family, the family which is the "germ-cell of civilization."[24]

Nonetheless, as will be discussed below, Freud was impressed by the apparent inevitability of children's interpretations of anatomical sex distinction and of paternal predominance in the oedipal family. Therefore, he did in fact suggest that the "repudiation of femininity" was a psychical version of a "biological fact,"[25] a suggestion which was a departure from his frequent insistence that psychology must be distinguished both from biology and from sociology. This problem will be addressed after three prior issues are discussed. These are Freud's distinctions among biological, psychological, and sociological sex difference; his unsuccessful attempts to identify activity and passivity with sex distinction; and the content of his theory of gender as it emerged in his differential oedipal theories.

Freud's Need for a Theory of Gender

As is well known, Freud's use of the term "sexual" broadened its connotations. His theoretical emphasis on psychical reality was derived from his broader understanding of sexuality. For Freud, sexuality eventually included

24. *Civilization and Its Discontents* (1930), *SE* 21:114.
25. "Analysis Terminable and Interminable" (1937), *SE* 23:252.

not only what I here call gender but also an account of stages of development of gender differentiation. Because Freud wanted to expand the sphere of the sexual, he might have objected to gender as a distinct term. When he described "gender," he regarded it as a part of sexuality, which clearly it is. (In any case, the German word for "sex" is far more flexible in connotation than the English. *Geschlecht* may mean sex, genus, kind, species, race, family, stock, generation, and grammatical gender, which is not true of our words "sex" and "sexuality.") But gender is a part which is both crucial in the developmental sequence of psychical sexuality and an important result of that development.

In our day, as in Freud's, dictionary definitions of sexuality stress its biological and anatomical connotations, both as genital anatomy (maleness and femaleness) and as genital activity (copulation). To this understanding of sexuality Freud added the infantile and unconscious fantasies, longings, memories, and anxieties, which were related to sex, so that for Freud sexuality was a complex of phenomena that become related to one another over time rather than any single phenomenon. Further, Freud insisted on the oedipal direction of libidinal drives into characteristic "mental shapes assumed by the sexual life of children." By doing so, he retained the biological emphasis of the term "sexual" while he traced its psychical transformations and manifestations.[26] Freud assigned a similar borderline position—between the biological and the psychical—to his concepts of "instinct" and of "masculinity and femininity."[27]

In 1910, in an effort to distinguish the psychoanalytic understanding of sexuality from the popular one, and to dissociate his treatment technique from that of an unnamed physician who took into account only the "somatic factor," the need for orgasm, Freud wrote:

26. For an unambiguous statement of the priority of psychical sexual factors for psychoanalysis, see, for example, "The Resistances to Psycho-Analysis" (1925), *SE* 19:215-218. Freud's use of the phrase "mental shapes assumed by the sexual life of children" is in "Some Psychical Consequences of the Anatomical Distinction Between the Sexes" (1925), *SE* 19:249.

27. "The Claims of Psycho-Analysis to Scientific Interest" (1913), *SE* 13:182. Here is the passage:

> In spite of all our efforts to prevent biological terminology and considerations from dominating psycho-analytic work, we cannot avoid using them even in our descriptions of the phenomena that we study. We cannot help regarding the term "instinct" as a concept on the frontier between the spheres of psychology and biology. We speak, too, of "masculine" and "feminine" mental attributes and impulses, although, strictly speaking, the differences between the sexes can lay claim to no special psychical characterization.

psycho-analysis is commonly reproached with having extended the concept of what is sexual far beyond its usual range. . . . In psycho-analysis the concept of what is sexual comprises far more [than the need for coitus or analogous acts producing orgasm and the emission of the sexual substances]; it goes lower and also higher than its popular sense. . . . We reckon as belonging to "sexual life" all the activities of the tender feelings which have primitive sexual impulses as their source. . . . For this reason we prefer to speak of *psychosexuality*, thus laying stress on the point that the mental factor in sexual life should not be overlooked or underestimated. We use the word "sexuality" in the same comprehensive sense as that in which the German language uses the word *lieben* ["to love"].[28]

On the one hand, sexual phenomena that were commonly viewed as only biological were seen as also psychical; on the other, phenomena not previously considered sexual were so considered.

Roy Schafer has argued that for Freud, "psychosexuality means mental sexuality," that is, "a sexuality of meanings and personal relationships that have developed and been organized around real and imagined experiences and situations in a social world." He has further suggested that Freud himself tended to forget this in his psychology of women, where he "persevered with the biological, evolutionary model and value system."[29] Schafer's observation is true not only of several of Freud's discussions of the psychology of women but also of his many references to masculinity and femininity as biological factors, even when he had made it clear that they were psychoanalytically significant only as psychical ones.

In Schafer's view, Freud's category of "mental sexuality" includes masculinity and femininity (and much else as well). On occasion, however, Freud seems to have limited the term "mental sexuality" precisely to masculinity and femininity. In a statement which might be regarded as a cross-sectional description of the individual's sexual life, Freud wrote that the analysis of a homosexual makes clear that human sexuality is a complex combination of three sets of characteristics. These Freud called "physical sexual characters, mental sexual characters (masculine or feminine attitude)," and "kind of object-choice," and he noted that "up to a certain point" these three sets "vary independently of one another."[30] The set which Freud called physical sexual

28. "'Wild' Psycho-Analysis" (1910), *SE* 11:222-223.
29. Roy Schafer, "Problems in Freud's Psychology of Women" (1974), p. 472.
30. "The Psychogenesis of a Case of Homosexuality in a Woman" (1920), *SE* 18:170.

characters is what I call sex in the narrow sense; that called mental sexual characters is what I include in gender. "Kind of object-choice" is explained psychologically by the Oedipus complex. Object choice is also part of gender because, by definition, masculinity means an active attitude toward maternal love objects whereas femininity means a passive attitude to paternal love objects.

Although oedipally directed object choice is a more sociological notion because it involves the parental figures as individuals and as cultural representatives, object choice is central to the inner developmental sequence in the attainment of "mental sexuality," whether or not the latter includes more than gender differentiation.[31] Conversely, the oedipal child's "masculine and feminine attitudes" participate in the development and resolution of the oedipal crisis. But if psychical masculinity and femininity (gender) do have a measure of independence from the physical, then this potentiality for independence, as well as the frequent congruence between physical sex, psychical sex, and gender-appropriate object choice, must be explained psychoanalytically. This kind of explanation was first attempted in Freud's discussions of activity and passivity.

Freud considered psychological masculinity and femininity to be synonymous with preference for active and passive instinctual aims, respectively, and, by extrapolation, with an active or passive attitude toward the love object. This view was consistent with his bestowal of activity on the father, whether primal or contemporary. In a 1915 paper, he defined activity and passivity as one of the three sets of polar terms which govern mental life, the other two being subject and object (ego and external world) and pleasure and unpleasure. The active-passive polarity was named the biological one because of its then presumed relation to sex difference. An observation which pertained to the development of gender was included in this paper, when Freud noted that the active-passive antithesis coalesces later, in the oedipal phase, with the masculine-feminine antithesis, which, "until this has taken place, has no psychological meaning. The coupling of activity with masculinity and of passivity with femininity meets us, indeed, as a biological fact; but it is by no means so invariably complete and exclusive as we are inclined to assume."[32] In the same year, Freud clarified the problems inherent

31. Robert Stoller suggests that, to Freud, "sexuality" meant "both the development of the capacity for eroticism and the related, but still rather different quality, gender"; *Sex and Gender*, vol. 1: *The Development of Masculinity and Femininity* (1968), p. 52.
32. "Instincts and Their Vicissitudes" (1915), *SE* 14:134. In this essay, Freud pointed out that every instinct was "a piece of activity," so that a "passive instinct" is actually an (active) in-

in equating activity and masculinity and passivity and femininity. This clarification relied on distinctions among biological, psychical, and sociological factors.

> It is essential to understand clearly that the concepts of "masculine" and "feminine," whose meaning seems so unambiguous to ordinary people, are among the most confused that occur in science. It is possible to distinguish at least three uses. "Masculine" and "feminine" are used sometimes in the sense of activity and passivity, sometimes in a biological, and sometimes, again, in a sociological sense. The first of these three meanings is the essential one and the most serviceable in psycho-analysis. . . . The second, or biological, meaning of "masculine" and "feminine" is the one whose applicability can be determined most easily. . . . Activity and its concomitant phenomena (more powerful muscular development, aggressiveness, greater intensity of libido) are as a rule linked with biological masculinity; but they are not necessarily so, for there are animal species in which these qualities are on the contrary assigned to the female. The third, or sociological, meaning receives its connotation from the observation of actually existing masculine and feminine individuals. Such observation shows that in human beings pure masculinity or femininity is not to be found either in a psychological or a biological sense. Each individual on the contrary displays a mixture of the character-traits belonging to his own and to the opposite sex; and he shows a combination of activity and passivity whether or not these last character-traits tally with his biological ones.[33]

When masculinity and femininity are used properly in the psychological sense, they are applicable to the instinctual aim but not unambiguously to

stinct whose aim is passive. Therefore, by definition, "libido" was always masculine. He then distinguished the pressure, aim, object, and source as components of instincts. "The aim [*Ziel*] of an instinct is in every instance satisfaction, . . ." he wrote, "but although the ultimate aim of each instinct remains unchangeable, there may yet be different paths leading to the same ultimate aim; so that an instinct may be found to have various nearer or intermediate aims . . ." (p. 122). Active and passive aims would seem to be of this "nearer" sort although later in the same essay Freud wrote of active and passive aims without further comment (p. 127).

33. *Three Essays on the Theory of Sexuality* (1905), *SE* 7:219-220, n. 1, which was added in 1915. Here, activity and passivity are psychical. The German terms, *Männliche* and *Weibliche*, may be translated as "male, manly and masculine"; "female, womanly and feminine," respectively. This latitude in translation should be kept in mind in the discussion that follows.

the person. Not only could the two sets of terms—male, masculine, and man; female, feminine, and woman—be combined into eight possibilities, but in addition no individual is limited to either passive or active aims; instead, everyone is to some extent psychically bisexual. Freud continued, however, to employ "masculinity" and "femininity" in all three senses without always clarifying which sense(s) he intended, thereby encouraging confusion both within and about his science.

Activity and passivity were of great importance for instinct theory, which probably helps explain why Freud continued to attempt to link sex distinction with them.[34] Furthermore, when Freud was first concerned with the problem of psychological sex distinction, in the last years of the nineteenth century, writers on all sorts of topics associated femaleness with passivity and maleness with activity. It was a conventional and widespread association. The forced reasoning to which an equation of active and passive *behavior* with *men* and *women* could lead is illustrated by a passage from Havelock Ellis' *Man and Woman: A Study of Human Secondary Sexual Characters.* In an attempt to explain why, throughout Europe at that time, more men than women committed suicide by hanging themselves and more women drowned themselves, Ellis asserted:

> generally, men prefer to adopt *active* methods of suicide, which are at the same time usually more deliberate and more repulsive, [whereas] women prefer more *passive* methods, which are at the same time usually more decorous and require less resolute preparation. The only exception is in regard to the passive method of suicide by being run over by a train. About three men resort to this for one woman. The reason probably is that, though a passive method of self-destruction, it requires considerable resolution to face, and offends against women's sense of propriety and their intense horror of making a mess. . . .[35]

34. For discussions of these concepts as their significance surpasses the problem of sex distinction, see, for example, David Rapaport, "Some Metapsychological Considerations Concerning Activity and Passivity" (1953), in *The Collected Papers of David Rapaport*, ed. Merton M. Gill (New York and London: Basic Books, 1967), pp. 530-568; and Roy Schafer, "On the Theoretical and Technical Conceptualization of Activity and Passivity," *Psychoanalytic Quarterly* 37, no. 2 (1968):173-198. Neither of these articles does more than mention masculinity and femininity. For Freud, sex distinction continued to be a crucial if insoluble problem, but his systematizers have often treated his continued attentions to it with silence or as peripheral.

35. Havelock Ellis, *Man and Woman: A Study of Human Secondary Sexual Characters* (1914), p. 385.

Freud realized that activity and passivity were inadequate for a psychoanalytic understanding of the differences between the sexes, but he remained interested in discovering psychical differences in terms which were linked with the drives and thereby psychoanalytically basic. In 1929 or 1930, in a footnote to a passage in *Civilization and Its Discontents* about the fate of the sexual function in civilization, Freud wrote with somewhat less certainty than is found in his previously quoted passage:

> Sex is a biological fact which, although it is of extraordinary importance in mental life, is hard to grasp psychologically. We are accustomed to say that every human being displays both male and female instinctual impulses, needs and attributes; but though anatomy, it is true, can point out the characteristic of maleness and femaleness, psychology cannot. For psychology the contrast between the sexes fades away into one between activity and passivity, in which we far too readily identify activity with maleness and passivity with femaleness. . . . The theory of bisexuality is still surrounded by many obscurities and we cannot but feel it as a serious impediment in psycho-analysis that it has not yet found any link with the theory of the instincts.[36]

The theoretical situation remained what it had been in 1913, when Freud stated: "strictly speaking, the differences between the sexes can lay claim to no special psychical characterization. What we speak of in ordinary life as 'masculine' or 'feminine' reduces itself from the point of view of psychology to the qualities of 'activity' and 'passivity'—that is, to qualities determined not by the instincts themselves but by their aims."[37]

Throughout the 1920s and 1930s, Freud continued to make the apparently contradictory assertions that there were no essential psychological correlates to the distinction between the sexes but that the biological sexual distinctions must be of foundational importance for mental life. In 1920 he wrote that "psycho-analysis cannot elucidate the intrinsic nature of what in conventional or in biological phraseology is termed 'masculine' and 'feminine': it simply takes over the two concepts and makes them the foundation of its work."[38] In 1933, in a lecture written for a general audience (but never delivered), he stated that it was impossible directly to translate sex distinction into psychoanalytic concepts. "We are accustomed to employ 'masculine' and 'feminine' as mental qualities as well [as anatomical ones], and

36. *Civilization and Its Discontents* (1930), *SE* 21:105-106, n. 3.
37. "The Claims of Psycho-Analysis to Scientific Interest" (1913), *SE* 13:182.
38. "The Psychogenesis of a Case of Homosexuality in a Woman" (1920), *SE* 18:171.

have in the same way transferred the notion of bisexuality [from anatomy] to mental life," he explained. "Thus we speak of a person, whether male or female, as behaving in a masculine way in one connection and in a feminine way in another. But you will soon perceive that this is only giving way to anatomy or to convention. You cannot give the concepts of 'masculine' and 'feminine' *any* new connotation. The distinction is not a psychological one," he concluded.[39] In 1938, Freud called "the great enigma of the biological fact of the duality of the sexes . . . an ultimate fact for our knowledge, it defies every attempt to trace it back to something else." He admitted that "psycho-analysis has contributed nothing to clearing up this problem. . . . In mental life we only find reflections of this great antithesis; and their interpretation is made more difficult by the fact, long suspected, that no individual is limited to the modes of reaction of a single sex. . . ."[40] Once again, Freud considered sex distinction important for psychoanalysis, but he realized that activity and passivity were not necessarily correlative with either biological or social role. Freud's disagreements with Adler, who suggested that masculinity repressed femininity (the "masculine protest"), made clear that Freud could not accept a theory which reified masculine *versus* feminine psychical essences or forces. "In the last resort," Freud wrote, "we can only see that both in male and female individuals masculine as well as feminine instinctual impulses are found, and that each can equally well undergo repression. . . ."[41]

It seems then that Freud, by resisting attempts to identify a dynamic psychoanalytic factor with one sex or the other, by considering activity and passivity the only usable psychoanalytic definitions of masculinity and femininity, and by considering activity and passivity to be qualities of drives rather than of persons, developed an implicit theory of *gender* as distinguished from a psychology of either men and women or males and females. At the same time, he was certain that biological and social sex distinctions were somehow foundational to mental life. Therefore, if sex distinctions were to have psychoanalytic significance, that significance must reside in the differentiation of "appropriate" gender out of shared mental potentialities. But, as is apparent in the complexities of the preceding discussion, the

39. "Femininity," Lecture 33 of *New Introductory Lectures on Psycho-Analysis* (1933), *SE* 22:114.
40. *An Outline of Psycho-Analysis* (1940), *SE* 23:188.
41. "'A Child Is Being Beaten'" (1919), *SE* 17:202. Freud's reference here to masculine and feminine "instinctual impulses" (rather than aims) is one of many examples of his inconsistency in this area.

development of femininity was a far more profound puzzle to Freud than was the development of masculinity.

If we examine only Freud's discussions of activity and passivity, or of masculinity and femininity understood conventionally and descriptively, the question of the *relationships* among the psychical, biological, and sociological "sexual characters" cannot be addressed. Such an examination does show that Freud understood that these three sets were not necessarily congruent. The theories of bisexuality and of the instincts, as well as clinical observation, cooperated to prevent Freud from asserting that men were essentially or exclusively masculine or that women were essentially or exclusively feminine. Although Freud's theories do attribute positive valuation to the male and the masculine, they do not outline the misogynist's paradise which a necessary congruence among the three sets of terms in both cases would create.

Instead, Freud's view of the proper psychoanalytic question about the psychical meaning of sex difference is stated in the title of his paper, written in 1925, which first paid explicit attention to the different Oedipus complex of the girl: "Some Psychical Consequences of the Anatomical Distinction Between the Sexes." As he stated some years later, "psycho-analysis does not try to describe what a woman is—that would be a task it could scarcely perform—but sets about enquiring how she comes into being, how a woman develops out of a child with a bisexual disposition."[42] Oedipal theory had been addressed to the same question, asked about a man, from its inception. When, in his later differential oedipal accounts, he traced the relationships among (psychical) activity and passivity, (anatomical) maleness and femaleness, and (masculine and feminine) object choice, he was trying to account for the psychical development of gender rather than of boys and girls who were somehow already naturally masculine and feminine.

42. "Femininity," Lecture 33 of *New Introductory Lectures on Psycho-Analysis* (1933), *SE* 22:116.

Chapter 8

Femininity and the Father: Asymmetrical Genetics

You bring what has been taken by violence or is lame or sick, and this you bring as your offering! Shall I accept this from your hand? says the Lord. Cursed be the cheat who has a male in his flock, and vows it, and yet sacrifices to the Lord what is blemished. . . .
—MALACHI 1:13, 14

The Prehistory of Women

Because Freud considered the (male) Oedipus complex to be the nucleus of the neuroses, the basis of the (male) individual's appropriation of his cultural heritage and position, and the historical foundation of (patriarchal) civilization and religion, it is hardly surprising that this multifaceted acculturating crisis is also seen as the crisis of the confirmation of gender. The oedipal situation is the Freudian child's cultural initiation, and living in culture usually means living as a member of one or the other sex. Freud's view is that men and women live differently as cultural beings primarily because of their necessarily different mental positions vis-à-vis father figures.

After the inconclusive dualism of Freud's discussions of activity and passivity as masculinity and femininity, his descriptions of the oedipal development of gender strike the reader as dialectical insofar as in these descriptions biology, psychology, and society encounter one another. Biology and society are treated as givens (even though what is at issue is infantile interpretation of them); the "moving parts" in the system are the child's active and passive instinctual strivings. Biologically, the difference between the sexes is understood as "the lack of the penis," as Freud condensed it in one account.[1] The anatomical "given" for the preoedipal (phallic) child, which is penis possession versus the actuality or possibility of its absence

1. *The Ego and the Id* (1923), *SE* 19:31, n. 1.

(castration) is actually already a psychical "given." The psychical castration complex (a boy's fear of castration and a girl's "penis envy" because of its presumed accomplishment) redirects the mental activity of both boys and girls.

The second "given" is the child's view of the oedipal socius, which can be summed up as paternal authority and maternal submission. The child's perception of the father as physically strong and endowed with authority is correlated with the father's phallic state.[2] As Rieff has written, the Oedipus complex is first and foremost a question of the nature of authority.[3] Rieff explains:

> Stated briefly, the components of the Oedipus complex are, first, the sensual current (incestuous love for the mother), contradicted by, second, the relation to paternal authority; deference to that authority defines every successful resolution of the Oedipus complex. The child's sensual current is inhibited by such deference and thus it becomes a precondition of culture.[4]

The psychical "moving parts" are the child's activity and passivity, which, within the context of the biological and familial "givens," take on masculine and feminine content. Passivity is a wish to be loved by the father; activity is a wish to love, to make love to, the mother. Activity is also understood to be phallic or, in the girl, clitoral, which for Freud is phallic. Chronologically, both boy and girl children relate first passively to the mother and then actively to the mother in a stage which Freud named "phallic" for both cases.[5] "With their entry into the phallic phase the differences between the sexes are completely eclipsed by their agreements. We are now obliged to recognize that the little girl is a little man," Freud wrote.[6] The boy's phallic stage gives way to oedipal rivalry and becomes his Oedipus complex, but the girl's phallic stage is interrupted when she realizes that, unlike her father, she is "castrated." The figure of the phallic father intervenes to interrupt the masculine stage of attachment to the mother of both boys and girls. Juliet Mitchell provides diagrams which illustrate the asymmetry between the two

2. For example, see *An Outline of Psycho-Analysis* (1940), *SE* 23:189-190.

3. Philip Rieff, "Freud's Contribution to Political Philosophy" (1954), p. 104.

4. Philip Rieff, *Freud: The Mind of the Moralist* (1961), p. 176.

5. Freud found that for children of both sexes, before the castration complex, "only one genital, namely the male one, comes into account"; "The Infantile Genital Organization" (1923), *SE* 19:142.

6. "Femininity," Lecture 33 of *New Introductory Lectures on Psycho-Analysis* (1933), *SE* 22:118.

sexes' situations at this point. At first, Freud had assumed that there was a natural feminine attraction on the part of the girl to the father, symmetrical to the boy's oedipal desire for his mother, a situation shown in Figure 1. But when Freud learned that girls experience a long-term and complex preoedipal attachment to their mothers and that a phallic stage occurred in both sexes, it became clear that in both cases the father intervened in the mother-child dyad, a situation illustrated in Figure 2.[7] "It is only in the male child that we find the fateful combination of love for the one parent and simultaneous hatred for the other as a rival," Freud wrote.[8] The boy realizes that only the father can possess the mother, but the girl realizes that she, being like the mother, cannot possess her but rather must be possessed, in the passive mode, as she perceives her mother is. At this stage, the mother represents the girl's own limitation rather than her rival. The masculine attitude toward the mother, which prior to paternal intervention was held by both boy and girl, is submitted to the incest taboo in the case of a boy. In the case of a girl, it becomes psychologically impossible. Her problem is to become passive instead of active, feminine instead of masculine, and to change her love object from her mother to her father. "A girl has to change her erotogenic zone and her object—both of which a boy retains."[9] In Freud's words, "to the change in her own sex there must correspond a change in the sex of her object."[10]

The fundamental asymmetry in gender development is that when it is faced with the father, the masculinity achieved by a girl will "normally" be given up in favor of a feminine libidinal attachment to her father whereas the boy's masculine and feminine libido must be *renounced*.[11] What obliges the boy to "shatter" his Oedipus complex is his castration complex because the father's intervention threatens castration in his case. What obliges the girl to achieve her Oedipus complex, which is a feminine attitude of passive

7. Diagrams are in Juliet Mitchell's "On Freud and the Distinction Between the Sexes" (1974), p. 34.
8. "Female Sexuality" (1931), *SE* 21:229.
9. "Femininity," Lecture 33 of *New Introductory Lectures on Psycho-Analysis* (1933), *SE* 22:119.
10. "Female Sexuality" (1931), *SE* 21:228.
11. Current orthodox psychoanalytic theory states this asymmetrical situation even more strongly. See, for example, Humberto Nagera, *Female Sexuality and the Oedipus Complex* (1975), pp. 56-57; Nagera writes that both the boy and the girl develop "an active masculine phase," which, in the girl's case, is specific to her development and "phase-dominant." The boy, on the other hand, may or may not arrive at a "feminine-passive" position, and if he does so, it is a deviation in his development and not a "necessary, regular, and normal, phase-dominant stage of it."

Figure 1

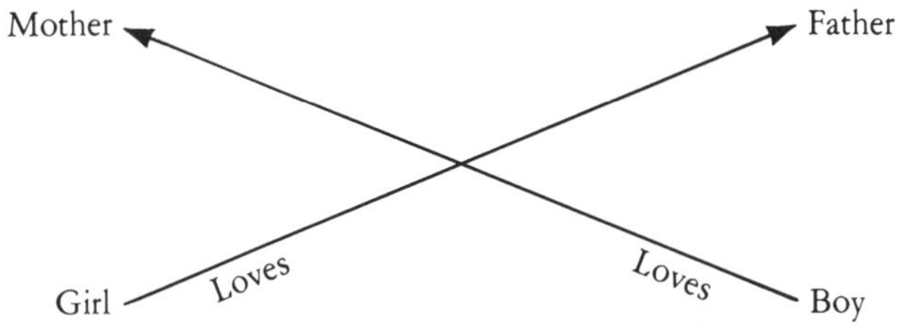

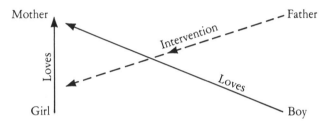

Figure 2

love with the father as subject, herself as object and the mother as rival, is her already accomplished "castration."

The results which Freud attributed to the different order of occurrence of the two complexes will be examined shortly. First, though, his account of the vicissitudes of activity and passivity should be discussed in greater detail to discern their effects in creating the masculine and feminine attitudes that result from the encounter with the idea of castration. In doing so, I will present only schematic accounts of the "normal" outcomes and disregard the many possible variants, such as identifications with the "wrong" parent or the girl's "masculinity complex."

Oedipus Comes to Stay

In 1924, Freud described the relationship between the Oedipus and castration complexes in the boy. In "ideal" cases, the boy's Oedipus complex was dissolved, abolished, or destroyed because of his impossible position vis-à-vis his own castration. To summarize briefly, when the boy discovers that some other people appear to be castrated, he has at that stage a "complete" Oedipus complex, which consists in two attitudes, a passive attitude whereby he wants to take his mother's place and be loved by his father and an active attitude whereby he wants to take his father's place and possess his mother. The boy ideally renounces both attitudes because he would be castrated, or become feminine, with the realization of either wish.[12] Therefore, in order to preserve his masculinity, the boy turns away from the Oedipus complex. In Freud's words:

> In his case it is the discovery of the possibility of castration, as proved by the sight of the female genitals, which forces on him the transformation of his Oedipus complex, and which leads to the creation of his super-ego and thus initiates all the processes that are designed to make the individual find a place in the cultural community. After the paternal agency has been internalized and become a super-ego, the next task is to detach the latter from the figures of whom it was originally the psychical representative.[13]

In the long run, "the dissolution of the Oedipus complex would consolidate the masculinity in a boy's character."[14] Psychically, masculinity has taken precedence over the threat of, and wishes for, femininity; activity and the phallus are preserved; future manhood and cultural activity are made possible.

Freud's explanation of the girl's development, which he outlined in 1925 and 1927, had to account for her achievement of femininity, with a paternal love object, when she began as a "little man," actively desiring a maternal love object. The explanation had to take into account the girl's preoedipal and phallic stages, in which her object is maternal. In Freud's view, the female castration complex, in the form of penis envy upon her discovery that "castration has already had its effect," requires her to adopt the normal feminine oedipal attitude. "The essential difference thus comes about that the girl accepts castration as an accomplished fact, whereas the boy fears the possibility of its occurrence."[15] A girl's feminine oedipal attitude means that her active libidinal trends have been replaced by passive ones. For her, this oedipal situation is not a developmental stage that she will necessarily overcome. The feminine oedipal complex itself is considered identical to the "normal female attitude." It is achieved with great difficulty and is unlikely to be dissolved quickly, if at all, because the girl can no longer be threatened by castration for her desires:

12. "The Dissolution of the Oedipus Complex" (1924), SE 19:176.
13. "Female Sexuality" (1931), SE 21:229.
14. The Ego and the Id (1923), SE 19:32.
15. "The Dissolution of the Oedipus Complex" (1924), SE 19:178.

in women the Oedipus complex is the end-result of a fairly lengthy de-velopment. It is not destroyed, but created, by the influence of castra-tion; it escapes the strongly hostile influences which, in the male, have a destructive effect on it, and indeed it is all too often not surmounted by the female at all. For this reason, too, the cultural consequences of its break-up are smaller and of less importance in her. We should prob-ably not be wrong in saying that it is this difference in the reciprocal relation between the Oedipus and the castration complex which gives its special stamp to the character of females as social beings.[16]

In Freud's formulation:

> In girls the Oedipus complex is a secondary formation. The operations of the castration complex precede it and prepare for it. As regards the Oedipus and castration complexes there is a fundamental contrast be-tween the two sexes. *Whereas in boys the Oedipus complex is destroyed by the castration complex, in girls it is made possible and led up to by the cas-tration complex.* This contradiction is cleared up if we reflect that the castration complex always operates in the sense implied by its subject-matter: it inhibits and limits masculinity and encourages femininity.[17]

Whereas in "ideal" cases, the boy escapes his femininity by dissolving the parental attachments of his Oedipus complex and replacing them with the internal superego, the girl establishes her femininity by entering her Oedipus complex. In this situation the father and later paternal figures are objects to which she is passively attached. The father figure remains external instead of being internalized and depersonalized. Because adult, normal femininity is psychically continuous with the feminine Oedipus complex, the girl's com-plex "escapes the fate which it meets with in boys: it may be slowly aban-doned or dealt with by repression, or its effects may persist far into women's normal mental life."[18] In Freud's view, the feminine situation is not com-pletely defined in terms of either a girl's identification with her mother or her "penis envy" (castration complex). The true feminine situation is rather a passive love relation to the father as progenitor. Freud wrote:

---

16. "Female Sexuality" (1931), *SE* 21:230.
17. "Some Psychical Consequences of the Anatomical Distinction Between the Sexes" (1925), *SE* 19:256.
18. Ibid., p. 257. Here Freud writes that in boys the complex is "literally smashed to pieces." It "exists no longer, even in the unconscious; the super-ego has become its heir" (in ideal cases).

The feminine situation is only established if the wish for a penis is replaced by one for a baby, if, that is, a baby takes the place of a penis in accordance with an ancient symbolic equivalence. It has not escaped us that the girl has wished for a baby earlier, in the undisturbed phallic phase: that, of course, was the meaning of her playing with dolls. But that play was not in fact an expression of her femininity; it served as an identification with her mother with the intention of substituting activity for passivity. *She* was playing the part of her mother and the doll was herself: . . . Not until the emergence of the wish for a penis does the doll-baby become a baby from the girl's father, and thereafter the aim of the most powerful feminine wish.[19]

In short, the boy shatters and moves beyond his oedipal relationships. By doing so, he preserves his active masculinity for later use. The girl embraces femininity then and for the future, losing what Freud referred to as "the prehistory of women," her masculinity.[20] "It does little harm to a woman if she remains in her feminine Oedipus attitude," Freud commented. "She will in that case choose her husband for his paternal characteristics and be ready to recognize his authority."[21] Normal femininity remains ever in the shadow of, and in need of love from, a paternal figure, a situation which, for Freud, makes feminine women lack the independent superego that has cultural value. Nor does Freud develop a concept of "ideal" femininity. In this asymmetrical situation, the ideal can only be masculine, just as the shared precultural phallic phase is masculine. In Freud's words:

In the absence of fear of castration the chief motive is lacking which leads boys to surmount the Oedipus complex. Girls remain in it for an indeterminate length of time; they demolish it late and, even so, incompletely. In these circumstances the formation of the super-ego must suffer; it cannot attain the strength and independence which give it its cultural significance, and feminists are not pleased when we point out to them the effects of this factor upon the average feminine character.[22]

19. "Femininity," Lecture 33 of *New Introductory Lectures on Psycho-Analysis* (1933), *SE* 22:128.
20. Ibid., p. 130.
21. *An Outline of Psycho-Analysis* (1940), *SE* 23:194.
22. "Femininity," Lecture 33 of *New Introductory Lectures on Psycho-Analysis* (1933), *SE* 22:129.

Femininity and attachment to the father are correlative; masculinity precludes attachment to the father. For Freud, there is "an antithesis between the attachment to the father and the masculinity complex; it is the general antithesis that exists between activity and passivity, masculinity and femininity."[23] The price of receiving fulfillments from father figures is femininity.

Asymmetry and the Critique of Femininity

The results of the different relationships between the castration and Oedipus complexes, then, define the asymmetrical psychical and cultural value of the genders in Freud's theories. Given paternal authority and the fact that only one sex possesses a sexual organ like the father's, the alternatives of being subject or object, phallic or "castrated," active or passive, masculine or feminine, cannot at any point in the developmental sequence be of equal but opposite value. "Psychological development does not follow the neat path of physiological evolution."[24] We are not surprised to learn, then, that in Freud's view the meaning of the castration complex is that the genders are of uneven value within the psychical lives of everyone. In his view, boys and girls, men and women, alike carry on, in their mental lives, a "repudiation of femininity."

Freud named this theme, the shared repudiation of femininity, in the context of a discussion of the most tenacious obstacle to the cure of members of both sexes. In the female, envy for the penis is the obstacle whereas in the male it is his "struggle against his passive or feminine attitude to another male." Both of these attitudes can be considered a repudiation of femininity: what has happened is that "something which both sexes have in common has been forced, by the difference between the sexes, into different forms of expression."[25] What they have in common is the castration complex. Freud admitted that Adler's term, the "masculine protest," adequately describes the man's attitude toward the castration complex; his masculinity, as it were, protests the possibility of femininity, or more specifically, of a feminine relation to another man, who is by definition a father figure if the feminine attitude is taken. But because both sexes have in common this objection to femininity, which is in both cases a passive relation to a paternal

23. "Female Sexuality" (1931), *SE* 21:243.
24. Juliet Mitchell, *Psychoanalysis and Feminism* (1974), p. 59.
25. "Analysis Terminable and Interminable" (1937), *SE* 23:250.

object, Freud suggested that the term "repudiation of femininity" best describes "this remarkable feature in the psychical life of human beings."[26] A recent discussion of this point in Freud's theory argues as follows:

> Nothing but powerful culturally imposed assumptions . . . can explain an error of logic in one of Freud's most profound late essays, "Analysis Terminable and Interminable." There he says that analysis as a therapy "is most difficult when trying to persuade a woman to abandon her wish for a penis or convince a man that passive attitudes towards another man are sometimes indispensable." Note the asymmetry in formulation: men need to be persuaded of the legitimacy of psychological bisexuality, while women have to abandon the idea of psychological bisexuality. . . . The phrase quoted shows that he did not really convince himself of the lack of parallel between the biological and the psychological spheres.[27]

On the contrary, I would suggest that the assertion that the castration complex lives on in both sexes in the form of the "repudiation of femininity" makes very clear that the lack of parallel between biology and psychology is located for Freud in the psychical function of the father figure as the (phallic) castrator. Given this figure, bisexuality cannot have the same mental meaning for both sexes. Therefore, for women, "castration" is inevitable but unacceptable whereas for men it is surmountable but continually threatening. Once again, paternal etiology is at work.

However, this was not Freud's own explicit interpretation of the phenomenon of the "repudiation of femininity." Instead, he suggested that the "repudiation of femininity can be nothing else than a biological fact, a part of the great riddle of sex."[28] This reference to biology directly raises the question of the interpretation one should place on the asymmetry between masculinity and femininity that pervades Freud's thought. To what extent did he understand masculinity and femininity as psychical genders that develop in a cultural context? To what extent did he, too, confound gender

26. Ibid.

27. Marie Jahoda, *Freud and the Dilemmas of Psychology* (1977), pp. 87-88. Quoted phrase in "Analysis Terminable and Interminable" (1937), *SE* 23:252, which reads:

> At no other point in one's analytic work does one suffer more from an oppressive feeling that all one's repeated efforts have been in vain, . . . than when one is trying to persuade a woman to abandon her wish for a penis on the ground of its being unrealizable or when one is seeking to convince a man that a passive attitude to men does not always signify castration and that it is indispensable in many relationships in life.

28. "Analysis Terminable and Interminable" (1937), *SE* 23:252.

difference and sex difference? On the basis of Freud's own statements, one cannot close this debate. A dispute among analysts was in progress during the years when Freud wrote his papers on the psychology of women.[29] Those analysts who opposed Freud's views agreed on one point: there must be some primary and essential psychologically feminine stage in girls that expressed the fact that from the beginning a girl was biologically female and not merely "not male" (castrated). Ernest Jones ended a paper with the question, "is a woman born or made?"[30] Jones thought a woman was born, but Freud seems to have found that both masculine men and feminine women were "made." Freud's criticism of his psychoanalytic critics is somewhat clarified in a recently published letter, which Freud wrote in 1935 to an analyst who took the other position in the debate. One passage reads:

> Your work fits into that of authors such as Horney, Jones, Rado, etc., who do not come to grips with the bisexuality of women and who, in particular, object to the phallic stage. . . . I object to all of you to the extent that you do not distinguish more clearly and cleanly between what is psychic and what is biological, that you try to establish a neat parallelism between the two and that you, motivated by such intent, unthinkingly construe psychic facts which are unprovable. . . . In addition, I would only like to emphasize that we must keep psychoanalysis separate from biology just as we have kept it separate from anatomy and physiology; at the present, sexual biology seems to lead us to two substances which attract each other. We deal only with one libido which behaves in a male [*männlich*, also translatable as "masculine"] way.[31]

On the evidence of this and other statements which present masculinity and femininity as positions of drive which are separable from biological sex, it is certainly possible to interpret Freud's analyses of these positions as a theory of the psychosocial differentiation of gender, as I have done here. This theory of gender is specifically based on analyses of the psychical results of development in a situation where the father is already preeminent. In this view, Freud's thought contains a theory of gender. Furthermore, this theory of gender amounts to a critique of femininity.

29. See n. 57 to Chap. 1, above.
30. Ernest Jones, "Early Female Sexuality" (1935), p. 495.
31. Letter to Dr. Carl Müller-Braunschweig of July 21, 1935, in Donald L. Burnham, "Freud and Female Sexuality: A Previously Unpublished Letter" (1971), p. 329. I owe knowledge of this reference to Mitchell, *Psychoanalysis and Feminism*, p. 131.

By delineating gender as a system which specifies psychosocial interpretations of bioanatomical sex difference, interpretations which are located both in psyches and in culture, it has been possible to find in Freud's writings a theory, not of natural and inevitable sex differences, but of the asymmetrical psychical development of genders. For Freud, the development of gender takes place in the oedipal socius, which is characterized by paternal authority and which thereby bestows asymmetrical value on, and requires asymmetrical developmental processes to achieve, masculinity and femininity. Freud found the meaning of sex difference to be the "repudiation" of femininity by members of both sexes. He suggests not just that he finds femininity inadequate but that everyone's unconscious does so as well. Freud's writings contain a critique of femininity which is more than simple bias, easily amenable to revision. This critique is anchored in his psychoanalytic account of individual and collective psychical development when paternal authority is presupposed. Not only is femininity submitted to a negative judgment, but it is also shown to be a humanly produced constraint when the logic of Freud's own theoretical arguments is given precedence over his statements about biological necessity or anatomical destiny. This Freudian critique holds that normal femininity necessarily achieves and retains an oedipal attitude toward father figures whereas ideal masculine development requires renunciation of oedipal attachments and internalization of the paternal carrier of culture, the superego, followed by depersonalization of the superego. Therefore, in relation to the father figure, femininity allows fulfillment whereas masculinity requires renunciation. The father complex is placed between biological sex and psychosocial gender. Freud's theory of gender contains a typology of psychical gender alternatives that are anchored in sex difference and that develop within civilization as he understood it: civilization begun and maintained by the father complex.

Having outlined this theory of gender, I will treat it as the basis for rereading some of Freud's writings about religion. Freud's theory of religion is inseparable from his theory of culture. If his theory of sexuality is inseparable from his theory of gender, which formulates the "encultured" psychical meanings of sex difference, then gender serves as both a formal and a substantive mediating term between these two parts of Freud's thought: the theory of sexuality and the theory of religion. Formally, gender mediates biology, psychology, and society as levels of psychoanalytic concern. Substantively, the content of Freud's theory of gender is shared by the theory of sexuality and the theory of religion. This content is a critique of the feminine psychical position in relation to the father figure. Further, Freud's understanding of the masculine and feminine positions has been characterized as a contrast between renunciation and retention of wishful illusion. For Freud, illusion can be traced to desire for paternal love and protection. I argue that echoes of these gender types are found in Freud's descriptions of the psychical origins and maintenance of religious belief and that they presuppose his differential oedipal developmental models.

If one takes seriously Freud's analyses of masculinity and femininity as central to an understanding of his theory of sexuality in culture, one must also take seriously Freud's insistence on the importance of the paternal character of God in his studies of religion in culture. The importance of what Rieff calls Freud's "religion of the fathers"[32] for a proper understanding of his psychology of religion is underscored when the critique of gender is treated as a principle of interpretation. If Freud implicitly drew upon his contrasting gender models when he turned his attention to religion, both Freud's criticism of religious belief as illusion and his respect for it as renunciation can be redescribed as analogous to his judgments of femininity and masculinity as they develop in a patricentric context.

In arguing for these relationships, I am guided by Freud's statement that "it is a good rule in the work of analysis to be content to explain what is actually before one and not to seek to explain what has *not* happened."[33] This statement appears in *Moses and Monotheism*, the book which might seem to adhere to it least. But if Freud posited historical events which may not have happened, it is, nonetheless, the case that paternal preeminence has occurred. If the historical claims in Freud's works on religion are considered to be reconstructions based on his analyses of psychical sexuality, then his works on religion are critiques of the psychological results of religious adherence. Freud's theory of gender is, I suggest, a source of his criteria for criticizing such psychical results. The theory of gender provides, then, not only a formal and a substantive mediating term between sexuality and religion but also a perspective on Freud's critical theory of religion.

32. Title of Chapter 8 of Rieff's *Freud: The Mind of the Moralist.*
33. *Moses and Monotheism* (1939), SE 23:93.

PART FOUR

Religion as Renunciation and Fulfillment

Chapter 9

Freud's Psychology of Religion

The psycho-analysis of individual human beings . . . teaches us with quite special insistence that the god of each of them is formed in the likeness of his father, that his personal relation to God depends on his relation to his father in the flesh and oscillates and changes along with that relation, and that at bottom God is nothing other than an exalted father. As in the case of totemism, psycho-analysis recommends us to have faith in the believers who call God their father, just as the totem was called the primal ancestor. If psycho-analysis deserves any attention, then—without prejudice to any other sources or meanings of the concept of God, upon which psycho-analysis can throw no light—the paternal element in that concept must be a most important one.
—FREUD, *Totem and Taboo*

Different Religious Psychologies

I will show that in *The Future of an Illusion* and *Moses and Monotheism*, Freud draws selectively on his economic concepts of fulfillment and renunciation of instinctual wishes and on his genetic concepts relating to the development and resolution of the Oedipus complex in order differently to evaluate the psychical consequences of two religious traditions. The different psychical effects, which he attributes, on the one hand, to acceptance of the religious ideas of "the final form taken by our present-day white Christian civilization"[1] and, on the other, to membership in the Mosaic tradition, anchor his attribution of different cultural value to Christianity and Judaism.

Belief in Christian ideas is seen as functioning to fulfill wishes for protection and as resulting in restriction of intellect. He describes the psychical and cultural results of the Mosaic tradition quite differently. The stringent instinctual renunciations that began and were continued within the Jewish

1. *The Future of an Illusion* (1927), *SE* 21:20.

tradition have, in Freud's view, strengthened spiritual and intellectual (*geistig*) faculties, thereby ushering in valuable psychological and cultural advances.[2] This distinction between economic "diagnoses" and their concomitant psychical and cultural value, whereby wish fulfillment is the foundation of restriction or regression and renunciation is the basis of advance, clearly relies on his critical principle of renunciation of wish. These different economic situations also correspond to different mental relationships to paternal figures. Different mental relationships to paternal authority were the bases of Freud's explanation of how varieties of masculinity and femininity develop and for his evaluation of them. Only the path of development that leads to masculinity is likely to lead to mental life according to the postpaternal reality principle; femininity achieves and retains wish-fulfilling relations to fathers.

In these two books on religion, Freud draws explicitly on his economic concepts of wish fulfillment and instinctual renunciation and on the criteria of psychical relationships to the father figure. He does not systematically employ categories of psychical femininity and masculinity vis-à-vis the father figure in his analyses of the two religions. He does compare developmental restriction of women's intellect with the restriction of intellect caused by religious adherence. He also emphasizes the masculine and paternal characteristics of Moses and the superiority of patriarchy for intellectual and spiritual advance. We are now in a position to reread to discover that these apparently tangential aspects of his argument point to deeper theoretical relationships between fulfillment, femininity and the psychical position of Christian believers as described in *The Future of an Illusion*, and between renunciation, masculinity, and the psychical position of the inheritors of Mosaic tradition in *Moses and Monotheism*. More precisely, the economic situation described in *The Future of an Illusion* is like the psychical structure of normal femininity. The psychical structure of Moses' heirs is like that of masculinity which is still under the sway of the father complex but which has differentiated itself from prior, wishful phases through renunciations. The form of deconverted conviction that corresponds to the psychical structure of "ideal masculinity" is like that of the postreligious scientist and scholar who is described in *The Future of an Illusion*. Although Freud contrasts the believer to the irreligious man in *The Future of an Illusion*, nowhere

2. Strachey notes at one point that he has translated *geistig* as "spiritual and intellectual"; *Moses and Monotheism* (1939), SE 23:19, n. 1. In *The Future of an Illusion*, Freud most often uses the words *Intellekt* and *Intelligenz* rather than *Geist*. I include the German term when the difference is important. Clearly, *Geist* has broader connotations than does *Intellekt*.

in *Moses and Monotheism* does he compare the psychical results of the Mosaic ethos with those of the scientific spirit; instead, one finds there a firm insistence on the superiority of the religion of renunciation over its polytheistic predecessors and its Christian descendant.

When, in a comparison of these two books, one supplements economic differentiae (wish fulfillment and renunciation) with gender-based genetic differentiae (masculinity and femininity), what emerges is a typological hierarchy of psychical positions that is based on an integration of the centrality of the father figure in Freud's theories with his consistent emphasis on the developmental advance which takes place from pleasure to reality principles through the agency of renunciation. By focusing on Freud's psychology of religion in these two books in terms of renunciation and fulfillment and in terms of the genders, we can see how Freud weaves together his patricentric, gender-asymmetric, and critical principles in his psychology of religion. This reading stresses Freud's account of the ultimately identical origins of all monotheistic beliefs in filial responses to the primal parricide[3] less than the *different* psychical attitudes toward the father figure that have grown out of this single postulated starting point. The original event cannot by itself explain the different individual and cultural values which Freud bestowed on the adherents of the two religious traditions. To explain this difference, we need to draw on his vision of gender-typical economics and genetics.

In emphasizing the different relationships to father figures which Freud discerns in the religious, I am treating these two books quite strictly and narrowly as psychoanalytic psychology of religion, even though both contain arguments and implications which escape its boundaries. In particular, much has been written about the covert autobiographical significance of *Moses and Monotheism*.[4] Freud wrote to Arnold Zweig, "The man [Moses]

3. This account never significantly varied. It is briefly discussed in *The Future of an Illusion* (1927) as the historical truth in religious ideas:

> Hence the religious explanation is right. God actually played a part in the genesis of that prohibition [against murder]; it was His influence, not any insight into social necessity, which created it. And the displacement of man's will on to God is fully justified. For men knew that they had disposed of their father by violence, and in their reaction to that impious deed, they determined to respect his will thenceforward. (*SE* 21:42)

The primal parricide is described at greater length in *Moses and Monotheism*, where the psychological power of the "historical truth" in religions is given greater emphasis. See *Moses and Monotheism* (1939), *SE* 23:81 for the description of the parricide.

4. See, for example, Ernest Jones, *The Life and Work of Sigmund Freud* (1953-1957), 3:367-369, and Marthe Robert, *From Oedipus to Moses* (1976), Chap. 5. Other discussions are noted above, Chap. 1, n. 48.

and what I wanted to make of him pursue me everywhere."[5] Freud's identification with Moses is not in question.[6] Nor is the historical context unimportant to an understanding of Freud's intense investment in his study of the man who he believed created the Jews. Freud worked on it between 1934 and 1938, when persecution of Jews in Europe had again increased alarmingly and when Freud was again forced to think about the psychology of Jews and of anti-Semites. In these years he knew his own death from cancer was imminent; he died in London in 1939, thirteen months after completing the last version of *Moses and Monotheism*. But *The Future of an Illusion*, with its argument for the psychological and cultural value of the "scientific spirit," the attitude of the "brain-worker" who discards religious illusions but retains an internalized, postparental morality, contains its autobiographical implications as well.[7] Jones mentions that Freud, in dismissing *The Future of an Illusion* in a letter to Ferenczi, referred to it as "inadequate as a self-confession."[8] Freud's view of his own character is evident in his descriptions of those whose only god is *Logos* and who, with the help of science, endure "the great necessities of Fate, against which there is no help," with resignation.[9]

Even so, when Freud wrote about religion, personal commitment was translated into the terms of his psychoanalytic theory. Even where he appears simply to be recounting history or to be putting forth a lay opinion, such accounts and opinions are rooted in psychoanalytic concerns. Freud examines religion in terms of its economic functions—its ways of balancing renunciations and fulfillments—and in terms of its genesis, a genesis with a paternal etiology.

5. Letter of December 16, 1934, in Ernst L. Freud, ed., *The Letters of Sigmund Freud and Arnold Zweig* (1970), p. 98.

6. See above, p. 81, for reference to Freud's earlier depiction of Michelangelo's Moses as "a concrete expression of the highest mental achievement that is possible in a man." See also Letter 125F to Jung of January 17, 1909, in William McGuire, ed., *The Freud/Jung Letters* (1974), pp. 196-197, where Freud wrote: "We are certainly getting ahead; if I am Moses, then you are Joshua and will take possession of the promised land of psychiatry, which I shall only be able to glimpse from afar."

7. See *The Future of an Illusion* (1927), SE 21:38-39. On p. 39, Freud writes: "Civilization has little to fear from educated people and brain-workers [*geistigen-Arbiters*]. In them the replacement of religious motives for civilized behaviour by other, secular motives would proceed unobtrusively; moreover, such people are to a large extent themselves vehicles of civilization." Such was Freud.

8. Jones, *The Life and Work of Sigmund Freud*, 3:138.

9. *The Future of an Illusion* (1927), SE 21:50.

The Psychological Reversal of Religion

In *Totem and Taboo*, in the context of his description of collective psychical transitions from animism (mythology) to concentration of power in the gods (religion) to recognition of the laws of external reality as impersonal (science), Freud commented that animism is a psychological theory.

> Animism came to primitive man naturally and as a matter of course. He knew what things were like in the world, namely just as he felt himself to be. We are thus prepared to find that primitive man transposed the structural conditions of his own mind into the external world; and we may attempt to reverse the process and put back into the human mind what animism teaches as to the nature of things.[10]

This is Freud at his most critical reach; here he employs psychoanalytic insight to continue the nineteenth-century criticism of religion as human production. For Freud, the data of the history of religions is data for psychology because religious theories are distorted projections of psychical states onto the world. Psychoanalytic studies of religion will, in his view, reverse the projective process and decode the distortions so that the beings and forces of the supernatural realm will be correctly understood as psychical. Withdrawal of projections from the natural world will free human minds to understand nature scientifically. Psychoanalytic psychology will criticize religious ideas about "external reality" in order that the way may be cleared for the replacement of religion by science. In *The Future of an Illusion*, while discussing early human strategies to defend against the "superior powers of nature" by humanizing it, Freud commented: "if everywhere in nature there are Beings around us of a kind that we know in our own society, then we can breathe freely, can feel at home in the uncanny and can deal by psychical means with our senseless anxiety." If these beings are like humans, "we can apply the same methods against these violent supermen outside that we employ in our own society; we can try to adjure them, to appease them, to bribe them, and, by so influencing them, we may rob them of a part of their power." He calls this strategy a "replacement . . . of natural science by psychology."[11]

With an adequate psychology, Freud believed that the religious move could be reversed: instead of replacing natural science with psychology in

10. *Totem and Taboo* (1913), *SE* 13:91.
11. *The Future of an Illusion* (1927), *SE* 21:17.

such a way that metaphysics results, psychology can analyze religious beliefs into their psychological components so that the natural world will be left to science, the psychical world will be left to the science of psychology, and religious explanations will no longer have a field of application. He had outlined this procedure as early as 1901, in the context of a discussion of the psychical bases of superstition. He wrote:

> *Because* the superstitious person knows nothing of the motivation of his own chance actions, and *because* the fact of this motivation presses for a place in his field of recognition, he is forced to allocate it, by displacement, to the external world. If such a connection exists, it can hardly be limited to this single application. In point of fact I believe that a large part of the mythological view of the world, which extends a long way into the most modern religions, *is nothing but psychology projected into the external world*. The obscure recognition (the endopsychic perception, as it were) of psychical factors and relations in the unconscious is mirrored—it is difficult to express it in other terms, and here the analogy with paranoia must come to our aid—in the construction of a *supernatural reality*, which is destined to be changed back once more by science into the *psychology of the unconscious*. One could venture to explain in this way the myths of paradise and the fall of man, of God, of good and evil, of immortality, and so on, and to transform *metaphysics* into *metapsychology*.[12]

In the two books discussed here, Freud exposes the psychological realities that he believes are transformed into beliefs in a paternal God. He then examines the psychological results of such transformation in terms of how they balance fulfillments and renunciations of wishes derived from the drives. In his hands, religious projections are resolved back into the various psychological situations of the father complex. It is no more important to an understanding of Freud's critique of religion to understand that he views God as a projection than it is to see how different relations to the projected father are of different mental values. The father complex and the Oedipus complex are, as we have seen, many-faceted affairs which have different psychical results. Just as individuals develop character types based on the vicissitudes of individual complexes, members of major religious communities are, in Freud's view, psychologically different. These different psychical configurations are best understood, I believe, in terms of his categories of

12. *The Psychopathology of Everyday Life* (1901), SE 6:258-259.

renunciation and masculinity, fulfillment and femininity, as they differentiate psychical relationships to fathers.

In *The Future of an Illusion*, Freud argued that the use of psychoanalysis as a method of research to study religion need not necessarily lead to the negative evaluation of it which he had therein expressed. Instead, he remarked, the negative attributes are attributes of the object of study. There, he claimed that

> psycho-analysis is a method of research, an impartial instrument, like the infinitesimal calculus, as it were. If a physicist were to discover with the latter's help that after a certain time the earth would be destroyed, we would nevertheless hesitate to attribute destructive tendencies to the calculus itself and therefore to proscribe it. Nothing that I have said here against the truth-value of religions needed the support of psycho-analysis; it had been said by others long before analysis came into existence. If the application of the psycho-analytic method makes it possible to find a new argument against the truths of religion, *tant pis* for religion; but defenders of religion will by the same right make use of psycho-analysis in order to give full value to the affective significance of religious doctrines.[13]

In the month of its first publication, Freud wrote to Pfister that the views he expressed in *The Future of an Illusion* were not part of analytic theory. "They are my personal views, which coincide with those of many non-analysts and pre-analysts, but there are certainly many excellent analysts who do not share them," he claimed. He explained that if he "drew on analysis for certain arguments—in reality, only one argument—that need deter no-one from using the non-partisan method of analysis for arguing the opposite view." Nonetheless, "if it were argued that that was not so easy, for the practice of analysis necessarily led to the abandonment of religion, the reply would be that that was no less true of any other science."[14] The negative evaluation of religion to which Freud refers in both contexts is probably the claim that objects of religious belief do not exist in "external reality." Neither in *The Future of an Illusion* nor in *Moses and Monotheism* does Freud display any temptation to waver on this point. However, when he wrote *Moses and Monotheism* some ten years later, he himself made use of psychoanalysis in order to "give full value to the affective significance" of adherence to the

13. *The Future of an Illusion* (1927), *SE* 21:36-37.
14. Letter of November 26, 1927, in Heinrich Meng and Ernst L. Freud, eds., *Psycho-Analysis and Faith* (1963), pp. 117-118.

Mosaic tradition. Given Freud's psychoanalytic doctrines about the psychical and cultural results of fulfillment and renunciation vis-à-vis wish and reality, his decision to emphasize renunciations and fulfillments in these different contexts necessarily reflected and then helped determine his evaluation not of the truth of religious belief but of the psychical value of religious belief for the past, present, and future of civilization.

Freud was fond of two methodological moves: drawing analogies and establishing dynamically differentiated dualities within his "intellectual scaffolding." In his studies of religion, the overarching analogy is between the individual and the collective father complex. This analogy allowed him a great deal of interpretive latitude because of the complicated nature of the Oedipus and father complexes, which makes possible so many different outcomes. Such different outcomes can in each case be understood in terms of the dualities of wish and reality, pleasure principle and reality principle, fulfillment and renunciation, femininity and masculinity. In *The Future of an Illusion*, Freud's guiding contrast is between wish fulfillment provided by the illusion of the father-God's loving existence and scientifically based resignation to reason and necessity, a resignation which issues from renunciation of childhood wishes. In *Moses and Monotheism*, he provides several related contrasts. Freud constructs counterpoints out of two Egyptian religions (those of Amun and Aten); two portions of the Jewish tradition, the Yahwistic and the original Mosaic portions; two modern religions, Christianity as a "son-religion" and Judaism as a "father-religion"; and, as an umbrella contrast for all of these, he contrasts "sensuous" polytheism and *geistig* monotheism more generally. Renunciation of the prior satisfactions that were provided by the first of each of these contrasting pairs explains, in each case, the *geistig* superiority of the second.

It is hardly remarkable that Freud was sufficiently aware of differences between religions to attribute different psychical attitudes to their adherents (although his sweeping usage often implies that whatever he says about one religion is true of religion in general). One might ask, though, why he singled out and treated as he did these particular traditions, contemporary central European Catholicism (which commentators agree is the implicit topic of *The Future of an Illusion*) and Mosaic monotheism, in two of his three books on religion. He emphasized the wish fulfillments offered by Catholicism when any historical survey would show that it had also imposed renunciations. Similarly, he emphasized the renunciations which Mosaic monotheism imposed when even in his own view Judaism had also fulfilled wishes.[15] It is evident that the basis of Freud's differentiation between the values of the two traditions is not *solely* within the religious forms which he took as objects of study. It is also within his selection of religious forms and within the theoretical models which he chose to draw upon in each case. It is likely that he selected traditions for study which seemed to him to fit the different evaluations which his psychoanalytic thought had already attached to fulfillments and renunciations, to femininity and masculinity. In showing no interest, for example, in the psychical results of the Reformation, many of which could be considered renunciatory and critical of "feminine" components of Catholicism even in Freud's own terms, he seems to have focused on two traditions of which he had direct experience and which served to exemplify the cultural results of the gender positions as he had already conceptualized them in terms of renunciation and fulfillment. Whatever else they are, Freud's studies of religion must be understood as applications of already available psychoanalytic concerns to topics that were also already important to him: the illusions of central European Catholicism and the stringent renunciatory ethic of Mosaic monotheism. A thorough discussion of Freud's reasons for choosing these psychoanalytic categories, with their already established critical weight, and these particular traditions would be speculative and biographically oriented in a way which would surpass the requirements of the present argument. For now, its purpose is to show *how* Freud constructed this critical differentiation between Christian and Jewish religious adherence on the basis of his psychoanalytic understanding of wish fulfillment and femininity, renunciation and masculinity.

15. Freud had earlier compared some Christian ritual actions with the self-imposed restrictions of obsessional neurotics; "Obsessive Actions and Religious Practices" (1907), *SE* 9:115-127. In a letter to Arnold Zweig, who was then living in Palestine, Freud commented that "Palestine has never produced anything but religions, sacred frenzies, presumptuous attempts to overcome the outer world of appearance by means of the inner world of wishful thinking. And we hail from there . . ."; letter of May 8, 1932, in Ernst L. Freud, ed., *The Letters of Sigmund Freud and Arnold Zweig* (1960), p. 40.

Chapter 10

Fulfillment Without Future:
The Future of an Illusion

*I am neither a self-tormentor nor am I cussed and, if I could, I should
gladly do as others do and bestow upon mankind a rosy future, and I should
find it much more beautiful and consoling if we could count on such a thing.
But this seems to me to be yet another instance of illusion (wish fulfilment) in
conflict with truth. The question is not what belief is more pleasing or more
comfortable or more advantageous to life, but of what may approximate more
closely to the puzzling reality that lies outside of us.*
—FREUD, *letter to Pfister of February 7, 1930*

Mental Wealth

The Future of an Illusion begins innocently enough. Freud wonders what the
future of civilization will be. Civilization means "all those respects in which
human life has raised itself above its animal status and differs from the lives
of beasts." It includes all the "knowledge and capacity that men have acquired in order to control the forces of nature and extract its wealth for the
satisfaction of human needs, and . . . all the regulations necessary in order to
adjust the relations of men to one another. . . ."[1] The imperfections of present "cultural forms" are indicated by the dissatisfactions of many participants in current civilization. People are hostile to it because it requires
sacrifices of everyone. In particular, incest, cannibalism, and the "lust for
killing" are desires which all must sacrifice.[2] Further, special, privations are
imposed upon the oppressed, those who are forced to work for others' gain,
and "it is understandable that the suppressed people should develop an intense hostility towards a culture whose existence they make possible by
their work, but in whose wealth they have too small a share." Those participants in civilization who have internalized what was originally external coer-

1. *The Future of an Illusion* (1927), *SE* 21:5-6.   2. Ibid., p. 10.

152

cion and whose superegos are thereby strengthened are described as "vehicles" of civilization, unlike the oppressed who are naturally its opponents. Neurotics, too, are unable to accept cultural demands (the demands of reality). In addition, many people obey cultural rules "only under the pressure of external prohibition." One such pressure is religious.[3]

Freud is not, however, going to offer a class analysis either of attitudes toward religious prohibitions or of attitudes toward civilization, nor will he suggest ways to redistribute material wealth. For him, the fact that civilization must rely on external coercion to extract the sacrifices which it demands is traceable to two human psychological characteristics: "that men are not spontaneously fond of work and that arguments are of no avail against their passions."[4] So Freud changes emphasis "from the material to the mental." The decisive question for the creation of a better civilization, one which will arouse less hostility, provide more happiness, and motivate more persons to become its "vehicles," is "whether and to what extent it is possible to lessen the burden of the instinctual sacrifices imposed on men, to reconcile men to those which must necessarily remain and to provide a compensation for them."[5]

What he names the "mental wealth" of civilization fulfills these functions. The question is whether it does so sufficiently and stably. "Mental assets" of civilization include measures of coercion, measures intended to reconcile, and measures intended to compensate.[6] They are the "moral level" of the participants in civilization, the ideals of a civilization, its artistic creations, and its religious ideas. The moral level is the "extent to which a civilization's precepts have been internalized," that is, the strength of the superego.[7] It is a mental asset insofar as its carriers are "vehicles" which carry civilization. A civilization's ideals are its "estimates of what achievements are the highest and the most to be striven after." In Freud's view, ideals are based on the earliest cultural achievements that are to be carried further. They provide, therefore, a narcissistic satisfaction to participants in the culture, who are proud of "what has already been successfully achieved." Art provides substitutive satisfactions "for the oldest and still most deeply felt cultural renunciations" and thereby, like ideals, reconciles those who enjoy it to the sacrifices they must make.[8] These criteria are apparently descriptive; Freud makes no claim for the absolute or universal value of this particular civilization's assets. But his inquiry is dedicated to stabilizing, not overthrowing, the civilization in which he participates.

3. Ibid., pp. 12, 11.   4. Ibid., p. 8.   5. Ibid., p. 7.
6. Ibid., p. 10.   7. Ibid., p. 12.   8. Ibid., pp. 13, 14.

In *The Future of an Illusion*, no further discussion takes place about how, in the future of civilization, ideals and artistic creations might strengthen it so that it could better fulfill its tasks of lightening the burden of instinctual sacrifices, reconciling, and compensating. In *Moses and Monotheism*, the function of the ideal for encouraging renunciations is emphasized. But *The Future of an Illusion* addresses the psychological status, value, and effects of religious ideas and the advantages that would accrue to "our present-day white Christian civilization" if its religious ideas were discarded as harmful illusions. A key point in Freud's argument is that these religious ideas, when accepted, are detrimental to the "moral level" of participants in Christian culture. They are also detrimental to their "intellectual level." They rob the culture of mental wealth. Christian religious belief is charged with encouraging dependence on a paternal figure, which, psychologically, means that external rather than internalized prohibitions are obeyed. Although religion has been the primary means of controlling the instincts, it has been an insufficient means. Freud comments that "it is doubtful whether men were in general happier at a time when religious doctrines held unrestricted sway; more moral they certainly were not. They have always known how to externalize the precepts of religion and thus to nullify their intentions. The priests, whose duty it was to ensure obedience to religion, met them halfway in this."[9] Like Dostoevsky, in Freud's view, one could disobey the prohibitions, do penance, obtain forgiveness, and disobey again. This situation encouraged wish-fulfilling adherence to demands of inner reality for pleasure rather than progressive renunciatory education to the demands of external reality. Because the "moral level" of religious believers is kept low, should they learn that science has demolished the claims of religious authority, they would no longer obey its prohibitions. In fact, his description of what "religious ideas" shall mean for this book presumes their imposition from without: "Religious ideas are teachings and assertions about facts and conditions of external (or internal) reality which tell one something one has not discovered for oneself and which lay claim to one's belief."[10]

Throughout his discussion Freud has in mind primarily the "moral level" of men. For example, he describes what would occur if religious prohibitions were lifted; in that case, he writes, "one may take any woman one pleases as a sexual object, . . . one may without hesitation kill one's rival for her love. . . ."[11] Yet the psychical situation that he describes, obedience to external paternal authority who is at the same time loving and loved, is the

9. Ibid., p. 37.   10. Ibid., p. 25.   11. Ibid., p. 15.

feminine position vis-à-vis the father, whether it is found in a man or a woman. The superego remains weak in such a relationship because postoedipal internalization and depersonalization of paternal precepts have not been completed.

The Father's Protection

Freud offhandedly announced the thesis of *The Future of an Illusion*, seventeen years before he wrote it, in a letter to Jung: "It has occurred to me that the ultimate basis of man's need for religion is *infantile helplessness*, which is so much greater in man than in animals. After infancy he cannot conceive of a world without parents and makes for himself a just God and a kindly nature, the two worst anthropomorphic falsifications he could have imagined. But all this is very banal," he concluded.[12] By the time he developed this thesis, in 1927, Freud had written "The Dissolution of the Oedipus Complex" (1924) and "Some Psychical Consequences of the Anatomical Distinction Between the Sexes" (1925), both of which addressed the problem of how mental development to a point beyond conceiving of the world upon a parental model might occur. This possibility was reserved for ideal masculine development whereas the outcome of normal feminine development (for women) was the continuation of the infantile position that *The Future of an Illusion* describes. As we have seen, the feminine relationship to the father is like an intellectual and moral tax.

Freud began to develop his thesis of infantile helplessness in the third chapter of *The Future of an Illusion*, which opens with the question, "In what does the peculiar value of religious ideas lie?" If the principal task of civilization is to defend against nature, which cruelly injures our natural narcissism in its inexorable indifference, the store of religious ideas provided by Christian civilization to its participants fulfills this task admirably from a psychological point of view. Again, Freud explains that religion humanizes nature so that natural forces may be mentally mastered by relating to them the way a helpless child relates to its powerful parents. This religious situation of helplessness, which is mastered by means of a psychological relationship with threatening powers, "has an infantile prototype, of which it is in fact only the continuation."

12. Letter 171F of January 2, 1910, in William McGuire, ed., *The Freud-Jung Letters* (1974), pp. 283-284.

For once before one has found oneself in a similar state of helplessness: as a small child, in relation to one's parents. One had reason to fear them, and especially one's father; and yet one was sure of his protection against the dangers one knew. Thus it was natural to assimilate the two situations. Here, too, wishing played its part. . . . A man makes the forces of nature not simply into persons with whom he can associate as he would with his equals—that would not do justice to the overpowering impression which those forces make on him—but he gives them the character of a father. He turns them into gods, following in this, as I have tried to show, not only an infantile prototype but a phylogenetic one.[13]

Whereas in his letter to Jung, Freud referred to the "parents" as protecting powers, in *The Future of an Illusion* and three years later in *Civilization and Its Discontents* he insisted that the father was the only parent capable of offering adequate protection against helplessness. In the former book, he suggested that we "transport ourselves into the mental life of a child" where "the mother, who satisfies the child's hunger, becomes its first love-object and certainly also its first protection against all the undefined dangers which threaten it in the external world—its first protection against anxiety, we may say." But, Freud continues, "In this function [of protection] the mother is soon replaced by the stronger father, who retains that position for the rest of childhood." The child's attitude toward the father is ambivalent; "it fears him no less than it longs for him and admires him." This childhood situation is continued into adulthood: "the growing individual finds that he is destined to remain a child for ever, that he can never do without protection against strange superior powers." So "he lends those powers the features belonging to the figure of his father; he creates for himself the gods whom he dreads, whom he seeks to propitiate, and whom he nevertheless entrusts with his own protection. Thus his longing for a father is a motive identical with his need for protection against the consequences of his human weakness," Freud explains.[14]

As is well known, Romain Rolland read *The Future of an Illusion* and doubted Freud's hypothesis that the longing for the father was the root of all religious feeling. For Rolland, the "oceanic feeling" of being part of something unbounded and limitless was this primal root. Freud's response to Rolland's objection provided his opening to *Civilization and Its Discon-*

13. *The Future of an Illusion* (1927), *SE* 21:17. "As I have tried to show" refers to *Totem and Taboo*, Freud notes.
14. Ibid., pp. 23-24.

tents. There, he bypassed the child's early attachment to the mother and underlined the father's centrality. Freud was not compelled by Rolland's claim. "After all," he wrote:

> a feeling can only be a source of energy if it is itself the expression of a strong need. The derivation of religious needs from the infant's helplessness and the longing for the father aroused by it seems to me incontrovertible, especially since the feeling is not simply prolonged from childhood days, but is permanently sustained by the fear of the superior power of Fate. *I cannot think of any need in childhood as strong as the need for a father's protection.*[15]

In denying psychological primacy to the oceanic feeling, Freud was in effect repeating his earlier claim that the psychically central mother was soon replaced by the "stronger father." Whatever else the oceanic feeling might be, it is surely, in Freudian terms, preoedipal. Freud's insistence on this point underlines both the tenacity with which he granted paternal authority a privileged place in mental life and the psychological importance he placed on the paternal character of the religious object.

Freud provided something of a historical outline of the stages of psychological response to helplessness in the history of religions. First, nature was humanized. Second, as natural laws were discovered, "the forces of nature lost their human traits." But human helplessness remained and with it the longing for the father and the gods. The gods retained their three tasks. They must "exorcize the terrors of nature," they must "reconcile men to the cruelty of Fate, particularly as it is shown in death," and they must "compensate them for the sufferings and privations which a civilized life in common has imposed on them." In the third stage, the emphasis within the divine functions changes. Nature and fate were suspected to be autonomous, so the gods' tasks became more specialized and their third function, attending to "morality," that is, compensating for sufferings imposed by civilization, gained in importance. In Freud's view, a further step in mental response to the experience of helplessness occurred when divine beings were concentrated into the figure of a single deity. This advance "laid open to view the father who had all along been hidden behind every divine figure as its nucleus. . . . Now that God was a single person, man's relations to him could recover the intimacy and intensity of the child's relation to his father," he wrote.[16]

15. *Civilization and Its Discontents* (1930), *SE* 21:72; emphases added.
16. *The Future of an Illusion* (1927), *SE* 21:17-19.

The remainder of Freud's argument in *The Future of an Illusion* centers on the dependent need for the father's love rather than on the other pole of the oedipal ambivalence: dread, rivalry, and the guilt they provoke. The father-god of the Christian believer that Freud describes in this book is a protector and a consoler, not a demander or a restrictor. Witness his summary of the "gist" of the religious "store of ideas," which protect against nature, fate, and injuries imposed by civilization:

> Life in this world serves a higher purpose; no doubt it is not easy to guess what that purpose is, but it certainly signifies a perfecting of man's nature. . . . Everything that happens in this world is an expression of the intentions of an intelligence superior to us, which in the end, though its ways and byways are difficult to follow, orders everything *for the best—that is, to make it enjoyable for us.* Over each one of us there watches a *benevolent Providence which is only seemingly stern* and which will not suffer us to become a plaything of the overmighty and pitiless forces of nature. Death itself is not extinction, . . . but the beginning of a new kind of existence which lies on the path of development to something higher. And, looking in the other direction, this view announces that the same moral laws which our civilizations have set up govern the whole universe as well, except that they are maintained by a supreme court of justice with incomparably more power and consistency. In the end all good is rewarded and all evil punished. . . . In this way *all the terrors, the sufferings and the hardships of life are destined to be obliterated.* . . . And the *superior wisdom* which directs this course of things, the *infinite goodness* that expresses itself in it, the *justice* that achieves its aim in it—these are the attributes of the divine beings who created us and the world as whole. . . .[17]

The appeal of such a set of ideas, Freud believes, can only be understood by understanding the paternal gratifications which they provide.

Freud's imaginary critic asks why his discussion of the origin of religion in the motives of the "son-father complex," which took place in *Totem and Taboo*, has now been transposed into terms of helplessness, of general human weakness. Freud responds that the unconscious, ambivalent collective father complex, on which he drew to explain the origins of totemism, was the "deeper motive" and that "helplessness and need for protection" was the "manifest motive" for the later adoption of a human god. Latent mo-

17. Ibid., pp. 18-19, emphases added.

tives always lie behind and below the manifest. Because the child's helplessness is continued in the adult's mental life, the childhood longing for the father is the "infantile contribution to the *manifest* motives," that is, to the motive of helplessness. The "defence against childish helplessness," that is, propitiation of the father, submission to him, and dependence upon him, "is what lends its characteristic features to the adult's reaction to the helplessness which *he* has to acknowledge—a reaction which is precisely the formation of religion," Freud explains.[18]

This book, then, is concerned with those motives for adults' relationships to a Christian paternal god that are apparent on the surface of the situation, motives which continue childhood helplessness and longing for the father. The childhood situation contributes to the manifest motives of the adult; behind both lies the latent motive for the formation of religion: the primal and continuing father complex.[19] The unconscious father complex contains incompatible emotional trends, but the adult believer singles out one component for conscious continuation: a dependent, obedient, and submissive attachment to an external paternal figure. All power is awarded to that figure except one's own power to influence it through childlike obedience. This conscious adult attitude can be seen as the psychological continuation of the feminine relationship of a son to the father within the now unconscious father complex (wishing for the father's love); it is also like the "normal" adult feminine relationship to men as loving and authoritative father figures.

When, as in *The Future of an Illusion*, Freud delivers a psychoanalytic verdict on the psychical results of the manifest need for paternal guarantees of security, his verdict is that as wishes are fulfilled, intellect and morality are restricted, just as he claims they are in women who take the "normal" femi-

---

18. Ibid., pp. 23, 24.

19. The origin of religion in the father complex as a male achievement was emphasized in 1923 in *The Ego and the Id*, wherein the ego ideal, which "answers to everything that is expected of the higher nature of man," is shown to be "a substitute for a longing for the father." Because of this substitutive function, the ego ideal "contains the germ from which all religions have evolved." Freud continues:

> Religion, morality, and a social sense—the chief elements in the higher side of man—were originally one and the same thing. . . . [T]hey were acquired phylogenetically out of the father-complex: religion and moral restraint through the process of mastering the Oedipus complex itself, and social feeling through the necessity for overcoming the rivalry that then remained between the members of the younger generation. The male sex seems to have taken the lead in all these moral acquisitions; and they seem to have been transmitted to women by cross-inheritance. (*SE* 19:37)

nine attitude toward paternal figures. Freud was elsewhere critical of the oedipal resolution, which, repeated in the religious sphere, made submission to an external god a guarantee of eternal solicitude. In such a situation, the superego is not an entirely internalized, let alone an impersonal, function. The external divine father takes the place of the impersonal superego in the psychical economy, with dire consequences for intellectual and moral independence. In 1927, in the brief paper entitled "A Religious Experience," Freud narrated and interpreted in oedipal terms an American doctor's rebellion against God and his subsequent conversion. Freud's view was that the man's

> ideas of "father" and "God" had not yet become widely separated; so that his desire to destroy his father could become conscious as doubt in the existence of God and could seek to justify itself in the eyes of reason as indignation about the ill-treatment of a mother-object. . . . The new impulse, which was displaced into the sphere of religion, was only a repetition of the Oedipus situation and consequently soon met with a similar fate. It succumbed to a powerful opposing current.[20]

The young man's childhood Oedipus complex, now unconscious, had been resolved by deference to the will of the father. In his adult conversion experience, "the outcome of the struggle was displayed once again in the sphere of religion and it was of a kind predetermined by the fate of the Oedipus complex: complete submission to the will of God the Father. The young man became a believer. . . ."[21] Because the ideas of father and God were not "widely separated," the adult's psychical position recapitulated that of the immediately postoedipal child: he submitted unconditionally to the will of the father.

Such a submission resolves the father complex in one possible manner. It is a resolution that is easily available and socially acceptable. "It is an enormous relief to the individual psyche if the conflicts of its childhood arising from the father-complex—conflicts which it has never wholly overcome—are removed from it and brought to a solution which is universally accepted," Freud commented. The child wishes for his father's "protection through love"; divine Providence, the will of a more powerful father, fulfills wishes for safety, justice, and a future life when safety and justice will be experienced.[22] The belief in divine Providence thus provides a remedy for life's ills. In *The Future of an Illusion*, Freud describes the "essence of the religious

20. "A Religious Experience" (1928), *SE* 21:171.   21. Ibid.
22. *The Future of an Illusion* (1927), *SE* 21:30.

attitude" as the persistence of the wish for such a remedy, rather than the renunciation of this wish as childlike.[23]

He gives the remedial religious ideas the psychological status of illusions
because they fulfill this wish and not because, as is often thought, these remedial ideas are *necessarily* false. In Freud's words, "illusions need not necessarily be false—that is to say, unrealizable or in contradiction to reality. For
instance, a middle-class girl may have the illusion that a prince will come
and marry her. This is possible, and a few such cases have occurred. That
the Messiah will come and found a golden age is much less likely." In short,
"an illusion is not the same thing as an error; nor is it necessarily an error."[24]
But the relative rarity of princes and Messiahs carries critical weight. Although the assessment of the "truth-value of religious doctrines does not lie
within the scope" of Freud's psychological inquiry, he admits that the "discovery" that religious doctrines are, "in their psychological nature, illusions
. . . also strongly influences our attitude" toward the question of whether
they should be accepted as truth. A prince would be nice for the promotion
of a bourgeois girl, and "it would be very nice if there were a God who created the world and was a benevolent Providence, and if there were a moral
order in the universe and an after-life; but it is a striking fact that all this is
exactly as we are bound to wish it to be," he warns.[25] The desirability of
these religious doctrines arouses analytic suspicion of them. The blatantly
childlike relationship to the protecting father that they contain, as Freud
presents them, forces his psychoanalytically based respect for the reality
principle to protest. Formally, he is not objecting to the probability that religious doctrines are false so much as he is objecting to the psychical and cultural consequences of widespread acceptance of wish-fulfilling falsehoods.
In a letter to Lou Andreas-Salomé, after wondering "why women give vent
to or appreciate humour so much more rarely than men," Freud mysterious-
ly continued, "You don't want to come to the aid of the Almighty either.
But my wrath [in *The Future of an Illusion*] was not so much directed against
him as against the gracious Providence and moral world-order for which he
is, to be sure, responsible. Nor do I pursue by any means all illusions, but
why should one cling precisely to the one which makes such mock of reason?"[26]

23. Ibid., p. 32. Paul Pruyser notes that *Abhilfe* ("remedy") is a word the root of which presupposes a call for help; *A Dynamic Psychology of Religion* (New York: Harper, 1968), paper
edition, p. 331.

24. *The Future of an Illusion* (1927), SE 21:31, 30.

25. Ibid., p. 33.

26. Letter of December 11, 1927, in Ernst Pfeiffer, ed., *Sigmund Freud and Lou Andreas-Salo-*

Consequences of Illusion

Religious doctrine "makes mock of reason" both manifestly, in that it is inaccessible to verification,[27] and, more profoundly, in that one psychical consequence of the wish fulfillment provided by illusion is restriction of the believer's intellect.[28] For Freud, intellect must develop from renunciation, not fulfillment of the promptings of the pleasure principle (unless intellectual activity is sublimated fulfillment, but this was not Freud's tack in *The Future of an Illusion*). Illusion, viewed economically, opposes psychological and cultural advance. Adherence to illusion retards the intellectual and moral "levels" of individuals and of the civilization in which they participate. Those under the sway of religious ideas have failed to dissolve the Oedipus complex in the ideal masculine way; for them, the pleasure principle rules, and they construct reality on the basis of libidinal ties to fathers. They fall short of adaptation to the reality principle, which ushers in the "primacy of the intellect," according to which external reality has no paternal quality. When the wish for the father's protection dominates interpretation of reality, the results for mental development are like the results of a feminine relationship to father figures.

Another context in which Freud associated Christian religious belief, personal relations with a protecting father-god, distance from the reality principle, and moral and intellectual inadequacy is his introduction to a psychobiography of Woodrow Wilson. Although it is unclear which portions of its text are Freud's work, the authenticity of the introduction is

---

mé Letters (1966), p. 172. Actually, Freud's associations of humor, sex difference, and the illusion of a benevolent Providence are not wholly mysterious. He is trying to relate two supposed characteristics of women: humorlessness and weak superegos. The reference is to a 1927 paper, which he entitled "Humour" and which was written concurrently with *The Future of an Illusion*. In it, Freud suggested that the superego, usually a "severe master," allows the "ego to obtain a small yield of pleasure" in humor. In this situation, "the super-ego is actually repudiating reality and serving an illusion." The intention which humor carries out is to say to the self or another: "'Look! here is the world, which seems so dangerous! It is nothing but a game for children—just worth making a jest about!'" In "Humour," the superego serves the same function as does Providence in *The Future of an Illusion*; it "speaks such kindly words of comfort to the intimidated ego. . . ." It "tries, by means of humour, to console the ego and protect it from suffering." These functions, Freud notes, do not "contradict its origin in the parental agency"; *SE* 21:166.

27. See *The Future of an Illusion* (1927), *SE* 21:25-29, for Freud's discussion of the "insusceptibility" of doctrine to rational verification.

28. Ibid., p. 48.

widely accepted on the basis of both external and internal evidence.[29] Because Freud's comments here are relatively unknown, I will quote at length. His judgment of Wilson's character is severe. "I do not know how to avoid the conclusion that a man who is capable of taking the illusions of religion so literally and is so sure of a special personal intimacy with the Almighty is unfitted for relations with ordinary children of men," Freud begins. Then, to explain this view, he presents the contrast between wish and reality.

> Through a long laborious evolution we have learned to set frontiers between our psychic inner world and an outer world of reality. The latter we can understand only as we observe it, study it and collect discoveries about it. In this labor it has not been easy for us to renounce explanations which fulfilled our wishes and confirmed our illusions. But this self-conquest has repaid us. It has led us to an undreamed-of mastery over nature.
>
> Recently we have begun to apply the same procedure to the content of our psychic inner world. Thereby even higher demands have been made upon our self-criticism and our respect for facts. In this field also we expect a like success. The wider and deeper becomes our knowledge of the inner life, the more will our power increase to hold in check and guide our original desires. Wilson, on the contrary, repeatedly declared that mere facts had no significance for him, that he esteemed highly nothing but human motives and opinions. As a result of this attitude it was natural for him in his thinking to ignore the facts of the real outer world, even to deny they existed if they conflicted with his hopes and wishes. He, therefore, lacked motive to reduce his ignorance by learning facts. Nothing mattered except noble intentions. As a result, when he crossed the ocean to bring to war-torn Europe a just and lasting peace, he put himself in the deplorable position of the benefactor who wishes to restore the eyesight of a patient but who does not know the construction of the eye and has neglected to learn the necessary methods of operation.
>
> This same habit of thought is probably responsible for the insincerity, unreliability and tendency to deny the truth which appear in Wilson's contacts with other men and are always so shocking in an

29. Freud and William C. Bullitt, *Thomas Woodrow Wilson* (1967). The introduction was probably written between 1930 and 1932. About its date and authenticity, see Erik H. Erikson, "A Questionable Cooperation: The Wilson Book," in his *Life History and the Historical Moment* (New York: Norton, 1975), pp. 82-95.

idealist. The compulsion to speak truth must indeed be solidified by ethics but it is founded upon respect for fact.

I must also express the belief that there was an intimate connection between Wilson's alienation from the world of reality and his religious convictions. Many bits of his public activity almost produce the impression of the method of Christian Science applied to politics. God is good, illness is evil. Illness contradicts the nature of God. Therefore, since God exists, illness does not exist. There is no illness. Who would expect a healer of this school to take an interest in symptomatology and diagnosis?[30]

When the correlates of religious illusion are so multifarious, we are hardly surprised when Freud argues in *The Future of an Illusion* that "civilization runs a greater risk if we maintain our present attitude to religion than if we give it up."[31]

For Freud, because religion restrains the drives by positing the existence of God and using His will and power as an external mode of control, civilization runs a risk of upheaval as more people learn about the results of critical studies of religion, "but without the change having taken place in them which scientific thinking brings about in people."[32] This change, of course, is "education to reality," which depends on renunciation of wishes in favor of the reality principle and dissolution of the Oedipus complex rather than a continued submission to or rebellion against paternal authority. Freud's pragmatic prescription strikes the reader as a brief and schematic response to his severe and more detailed diagnosis. It is that education to reality, which produces the "scientific spirit" (*wissenschaftliche Geist*), should replace religious training in the upbringing of all.[33] At present, civilization has "little to fear from educated people and brain-workers," who are its vehicles. The problem is to find a more reliable and rational way to control, reconcile, and console "the great mass of the uneducated and oppressed, who have every reason for being enemies of civilization."[34] Religion gains their obedience by fulfilling wishes arising out of the father complex, but stable control must transcend the father complex. In Rieff's words:

30. Introduction to *Thomas Woodrow Wilson*, pp. xi–xiii.
31. *The Future of an Illusion* (1927), SE 21:35.   32. Ibid., p. 39.
33. Ibid., pp. 38, 49. Octave Mannoni comments, "the science Freud was talking about was obviously not only positive science; it was all knowledge that aims only at truth, and psychoanalysis was part of it"; *Freud* (1974), p. 157.
34. *The Future of an Illusion* (1927), SE 21:39.

it was Freud's belief that now, after two thousand years of Christian culture, we are entering a new, scientific, phase of development, in which the instinctual renunciation he considered indispensable for man's communal existence has a chance of being maintained by rational means. As the chief instrument of culture, religion was an irrational means. . . . There is no more ambitious theme in the entire Freudian text; it announces that Christian culture is played out.[35]

The analyst judges that "the time has probably come, as it does in an analytic treatment, for replacing the effects of repression by the results of the rational operation of the intellect."[36]

Freud's critic asks why, since he has argued that "men are so little accessible to reasonable arguments and are so entirely governed by their instinctual wishes," he should now recommend depriving them of instinctual satisfaction and replacing it with arguments. Freud's response has led many commentators to observe that in *The Future of an Illusion* he most explicitly subscribed to the principles of the Enlightenment.[37] Freud argued that "it is true that men are like this; but have you asked yourself whether they *must* be like this, whether their innermost nature necessitates it? Can an anthropologist give the cranial index of a people whose custom it is to deform their children's heads by bandaging them round from their earliest years?"[38] His judgment that "man is a creature of weak intelligence who is ruled by his instinctual wishes" was purely descriptive, he states. His prescription is to bring up children with unbound heads, free from constraining inhibitions of thought about religion and sexuality; otherwise, his proposed new relation among religion, morality, and civilization will remain untested. Freud is blunt:

> When a man has once brought himself to accept uncritically all the absurdities that religious doctrines put before him and even to overlook the contradictions between them, we need not be greatly surprised at the weakness of his intellect [*Intelligenz*]. . . . How can we expect people who are under the dominance of prohibitions of thought to attain the psychological ideal, the primacy of the intelligence?

35. Philip Rieff, *Freud: The Mind of the Moralist* (1961), pp. 318-319.
36. *The Future of an Illusion* (1927), SE 21:44.
37. Ibid., p. 47. See, for example, H. Stuart Hughes, *Consciousness and Society* (Vintage ed., 1958), p. 140. Freud's friend Pfister had observed this in a letter of November 24, 1927, to Freud; see Heinrich Meng and Ernst L. Freud, eds., *Psycho-Analysis and Faith* (1963), p. 115.
38. *The Future of an Illusion* (1927), SE 21:47.

Here he compares the defect acquired by the religious to that acquired by the feminine:

> You know, too, that women in general are said to suffer from "physio-logical feeble-mindedness"—that is, from a lesser intelligence than men. The fact itself is disputable and its interpretation doubtful, but one argument in favour of this intellectual atrophy being of a secondary nature is that women labour under the harshness of a prohibition against turning their thoughts to what would most have interested them—namely, the problems of sexual life. So long as a person's early years are influenced not only by a sexual inhibition of thought but also by a religious inhibition and by a loyal inhibition derived from this, we cannot really tell what in fact he is like.[39]

We have seen that, for Freud, intellectual primacy is not only the psychological but also the masculine and the cultural ideal. It is an ideal that, for similar reasons, the believer and those who are psychologically feminine cannot achieve. We have also seen that its achievement relies not only on unfettered thought. Unfettered thought is inseparable from an affective achievement: replacement of the pleasure with the reality principle. This achievement is in turn inseparable from the masculine oedipal renunciations that, in ideal cases, comprise the dissolution of the Oedipus complex. Such a dissolution is, again, only a masculine possibility.

That Freud understands failure to achieve the psychological ideal as psychically equivalent to remaining involved in the father complex in a submissive way is clear when, in *The Future of an Illusion*, he describes the psychical orientation of those under the sway of religious ideas. Like children, they receive gratifications from the father. Freud urges stolid renunciation. He claims that it is possible for those into whom the "sweet—or bitter-sweet—poison" of religious dependence has not been instilled to do without the "consolation of the religious illusion." Such people, "sensibly" brought up, "will have to admit to themselves the full extent of their helplessness and their insignificance in the machinery of the universe; they can no longer be the centre of creation, no longer the object of tender care on the part of a beneficent Providence. They will be in the same position as a child who has left the parental house where he was so warm and comfortable." Freud calls going out into "hostile life" their "education to reality."[40] The adult who

39. Ibid., pp. 49, 48. Cf. the quotation on p. 110 above, wherein Freud makes the same point about the weakness of feminine intellect.
40. Ibid., p. 49.

lives under his father's or his Father's (God's) sway is still psychologically a child.

One is reminded of a paragraph which Freud had written a year earlier:

> The undesirable result of "spoiling" a small child is to magnify the importance of the danger of losing the object (the object being a protection against every situation of helplessness) in comparison with every other danger. It therefore encourages the individual to remain in the state of childhood, the period of life which is characterized by motor and psychical helplessness.[41]

In the same book, Freud had observed that "it is precisely in women that the danger-situation of loss of object seems to have remained the most effective."[42] Those who are not so spoiled, who can give up the protective parental object, will learn to use their resources and may "succeed in achieving a state of things in which life will become tolerable for everyone and civilization no longer oppressive to anyone." Scientific knowledge will give them some power, their energies which were concentrated on the other world will be released and directed toward solving the problems of this world, and, for the rest, they will learn to endure "the great necessities of Fate, against which there is no help, with resignation."[43] Resignation is the theme with which he concludes; it is acceptable to those who manfully renounce their childish wishes. "Our god *Logos* is perhaps not a very almighty one, and he may only be able to fulfill a small part of what his predecessors have promised. If we have to acknowledge this we shall accept it with resignation." Since "we are prepared to renounce a good part of our infantile wishes, we can bear it if a few of our expectations turn out to be illusions." It would truly be an illusion to "suppose that what science cannot give us we can get elsewhere."[44]

In *The Future of an Illusion*, then, Freud firmly portrays the religious attitude as pleasure-principle thinking for which "the outer world of appearance" is overcome by means of "the inner world of wishful thinking."[45] The wish in question is the wish for the father's love, protection, and consolation. The believer retains a submissive, feminine attitude toward the external father figure. The paternal figure is active, loving, and powerful; the believer

---

41. *Inhibitions, Symptoms, and Anxiety* (1926), SE 20:167.   42. Ibid., p. 143.
43. *The Future of an Illusion* (1927), SE 21:50.   44. Ibid., pp. 54, 56.
45. Letter of May 8, 1932, in Ernst L. Freud, ed., *The Letters of Sigmund Freud and Arnold Zweig* (1970), p. 40.

is in need of love, passive, and weak. The believer gains fulfillments and pays the price: mental and moral restriction.

At the further cost of obedience, the believer is rewarded by paternal protection and love. Freud judges the compensations for obedience to paternal authority to be unstable foundations for civilization because any undermining of authority may unleash fulfillment of more violent passions. As Rieff wrote, analysis "aims at a transformation of the passions, chiefly the passion of dependence itself."[46] The cure is a cure of *all* transference loves. Freud has elsewhere and at length described the psychical process in the life history of masculinity, by which renunciation of wishes provides a stable basis for the transcendence of irrational dependence on authorities, including gods. But, in *The Future of an Illusion*, Freud sets forth his recommendation for the "scientific spirit" without explaining how, from a psychoanalytical point of view, he believes this spirit relies upon and brings about inner psychical change; he merely refers once to "the change which scientific thinking brings about in people" and asserts the psychical and cultural superiority that results from its achievement. In order to understand Freud's view of the psychogenesis of this change, it has been necessary to examine his theory of masculine oedipal development, to contrast it with his theory of feminine development, and to set these within his moral economy. Only then can one understand the overdetermined psychological stakes in the illusion of the divine father and Freud's theoretical stakes in his demise.

Perhaps this lack of explanation, let alone argument, in *The Future of an Illusion* helps explain Freud's critical comments about it to two trusted fellow analysts who had been his pupils. He told Max Eitingon that it had very little value; he wrote to Sandor Ferenczi (in October 1927): "Now it already seems to me childish; fundamentally I think otherwise; I regard it as weak analytically and inadequate as a self-confession."[47] One cannot be sure what he meant by "fundamentally I think otherwise." Clearly the discussion was consistent with his long-standing views on the consequences of wish-fulfilling illusion. Possibly it was his optimism about a collective and enduring

46. Rieff, *Freud: The Mind of the Moralist* (1961), p. 186.

47. Quoted in Ernest Jones, *The Life and Work of Sigmund Freud* (1953-1957), 3:138. Clark quotes a more extreme self-critical reaction, which René Laforgue reported from a conversation with Freud soon after the book's publication: " 'This is my worst book!' . . . 'It isn't a book of Freud.' . . . 'It's the book of an old man.' . . . 'Besides, Freud is dead now, and, believe me, the genuine Freud was really a great man' "; Ronald W. Clark, *Freud: The Man and the Cause* (1980), p. 471. Clark considers this response to be largely the result of Freud's long and painful illness.

strengthening of intellect in the sensibly educated in which Freud himself could not believe. This confident hope *is* a departure from his more characteristic resignation to the shifting balance of rational and irrational powers.

The "analytic weakness" of the argument of *The Future of an Illusion* is obvious. Nowhere is his analytic distrust of fulfillment presented in a less careful or sophisticated manner. Freud had already provided several more adequate discussions of the economics of wish and renunciation and of oedipal dynamics as these related to reality and religion; he would provide more in the future. A reader of only *The Future of an Illusion* would be justified in taking at face value Freud's statement that the judgments on the value of religious ideas found therein were personal opinions, which did not necessarily implicate psychoanalytic theory, and this has been a frequent critical response to the book.[48] In fact, Freud's larger theory and his arguments against religious illusion are inseparable. The major alternative, from a Freudian viewpoint, would be to take the position which he believed that Jung advanced, that people are necessarily creatures who need illusion and that *therefore* illusion is good for them. This, however, was a viewpoint which Freud would not accept; for him, "the question is not what belief is . . . more advantageous to life." For Freud, the dissolution of the Oedipus complex was a real, if rare, possibility for masculine development, and its rarity was no argument against its value. In his theory and in his therapy, the critical view that renunciation of illusion was the source of intellectual, moral, and cultural advance was his overriding position. The superiority of the rare ideal both to normal or neurotic masculinity and to normal femininity was integral to his "moral economy." But only mental femininity, in man or woman, adopted the attitude to the paternal figure that is criticized in *The Future of an Illusion*. Christian fulfillment and feminine fulfillment are psychologically the same insofar as they are bestowed by the loving father.

48. Most recently, Hans Küng has written, "Freud's atheism was not grounded in his psychoanalysis, but preceded it." I believe that both options are true; see Küng's *Freud and the Problem of God* (1979), p. 75.

Chapter 11

Renunciations in the Past:
Moses' Monotheism

Though he disliked priests, and would not put his foot inside a church for anything, he believed in God. Were not the proclamations against tyrants addressed to the peoples in the name of God and liberty? "God for men— religions for women," he muttered sometimes.
—JOSEPH CONRAD, *Nostromo: A Tale of the Seaboard*

Polytheism and Monotheism

Schopenhauer's "Religion: A Dialogue" (written in 1851) contains the prediction that "perhaps the time is approaching which has so often been prophesied, when religion will take her departure from European humanity, like a nurse which the child has outgrown: the child will now be given over to the instructions of a tutor."[1] Girls and younger boys had nurses, but boys graduated to tutors as they grew older. Rieff has commented on the similarities between Schopenhauer's "Dialogue" and Freud's dialogue in *The Future of an Illusion*, as well as between Schopenhauer's and Freud's misogyny.[2] For Schopenhauer, the tutor is science and reason, just as it would have been for Freud had he employed this simile. But Freud not only invoked a tutor for the future but also uncovered one in the past: Mosaic monotheism. What he calls "sensuous polytheism" had been a nurse; monotheism, particularly Mosaic monotheism, was a tutor; Christianity, which in Freud's

1. Arthur Schopenhauer, "Religion: A Dialogue" (1951), pp. 26-27.
2. See Philip Rieff, *Freud: The Mind of the Moralist* (1961), p. 323. About Schopenhauer's "Dialogue," Rieff comments, "I should guess that Freud had read it, so closely does his own dialogue in *The Future of an Illusion* follow it"; on Schopenhauer's and Freud's misogyny, see Rieff, p. 200. Schopenhauer's essay "On Women" is also found in the same collection as the "Dialogue," *Arthur Schopenhauer: Essays* (1951), pp. 62-75. In it, Schopenhauer writes of women's lack of sense of justice, incapacity for objectivity, irrationality, and dependence on men.

view restored polytheistic characteristics, was a new nurse; science will be the last tutor. In *Moses and Monotheism*, polytheism, monotheism, and Christianity are examined.

As psychoanalytic theory of religion, *Moses and Monotheism* is richer than *The Future of an Illusion*. Freud saw *Moses and Monotheism* as a continuation of *Totem and Taboo*, filling the psychohistorical gap which he mentioned in *The Future of an Illusion* between the worship of the totemic animal and the worship of a "human" deity, both of which represent the primal father.[3] While, as we have seen, the argument in *The Future of an Illusion* rests largely on the economic contrast between wish and reality (but with little explanation of the psychoanalytic reasons for recommending the reality principle), the argument in *Moses and Monotheism* is based both in psychoanalytic genetic considerations (the return of the repressed) and economic considerations (instinctual renunciation).[4] *Moses and Monotheism* contains one of the most complete discussions of the process and consequences of instinctual renunciation to be found anywhere in Freud's work.

Freud's own preference for *Moses and Monotheism* was no secret. His letters contain many references to his investment in this work. To his autobiography he added, in 1935, that "in *The Future of an Illusion* I expressed an essentially negative valuation of religion. Later, I found a formula which did better justice to it: while granting that its power lies in the truth which it contains, I showed that that truth was not a material but a historical truth."[5] His notion of the historical truth of religion relies on genetic argument. The new appreciation of the affective value of religion relies on economic arguments about the results of renunciation for individuals and civilization. Freud's genetic argument will be examined after his discussions of intellectual advance and renunciation are presented. As we have seen, because oedipal genetics are inseparable from the achievements of renunciation and because the oedipal genetics that result in renunciation take place between fathers and sons, Freud is drawing in both arguments on a masculine model.

In Ricoeur's apt words, *Moses and Monotheism* contains "an impressive number of hazardous hypotheses."[6] The first is that Moses was an Egyptian, an official of noble birth who belonged to the monotheistic cult of Aten under Pharaoh Amenophis IV. The second hypothesis is the monotheism of

3. See *The Future of an Illusion* (1927), *SE* 21:23.
4. Paul Ricoeur makes a similar point. See his "Psychoanalysis and the Movement of Contemporary Culture" (1974), pp. 130-137.
5. "Postscript" to *An Autobiographical Study* (1925), *SE* 20:72.
6. Paul Ricoeur, *Freud and Philosophy* (1970), p. 245.

the Aten religion. The third is that the heroic Moses, who, after the Pharaoh's death and the reaction against monotheism in Egypt, led the Jews out and converted them, was murdered by his people, who were impatient with the stringent precepts of his beliefs. A fourth is that this Mosaic religion later merged with the Yahwistic religion. The latter boasted a second, Midianite, Moses. A fifth is that the Jewish prophets "engineered the return of the Mosaic god."[7] The return to Mosaic monotheism is explained as the return of the repressed; the trauma of Moses' murder had motivated the repression.

Historically, the hypotheses are probably insupportable.[8] They are, however, systematically useful to Freud to explain Jewish character as bearing the imprint of the original Mosaic character, to account for the strength of religious tradition as the compelling power of the repressed, and to assert the renunciatory superiority of Jewish monotheism. Qualities that correlate with wish and renunciation play a central role in Freud's reconstructions of Egyptian polytheism (the religion of the priests of Amun), Egyptian monotheism (the Aten religion), Jewish monotheism, ancient and modern, and Christianity, which Freud saw as similar in several respects to Egyptian polytheism. His hypotheses about historical continuity among these provided the context in which he could make psychoanalytic assertions about their different psychical values.

Freud underscored a "violent contrast" between the polytheistic Amun religion and that of Aten, which Moses allegedly introduced to the Jews. "In the Egyptian religion [of Amun] there is an almost innumerable host of deities of varying dignity and origin: . . . Magical and ceremonial acts, charms and amulets dominated the service of these gods as they did the daily life of the Egyptians." The Amun religion was an "unrestricted polytheism" with a wealth of clay images of the almost innumerable host of deities. It was, in this respect, "close to primitive phases" of development. Worship was still tied to immediate, sensual experience. In sharp contrast, the Aten religion rose to the "heights of sublime abstraction."[9] Amenophis IV (later

7. Ibid.

8. Ronald Clark quotes Ernest Jones's kind explanation of the historical and textual weaknesses in Freud's argument in his book: "[Freud] had a way of being very selective in his quotations, using only those he wanted to support a particular point and not reviewing the general literature as in his earlier years. This habit was connected with the small store of energy he had left and his conciseness. . . . There was little left of his strength when he was eighty-two"; *Freud: The Man and the Cause* (1980), p. 524.

9. *Moses and Monotheism* (1939), SE 23:18-19.

Akhenaten) "never denied his adherence to the sun cult of On . . . he praises
the sun as the creator and preserver of all living things with an ardour which
is not repeated till many centuries later in the Psalms in honour of the Jewish God Yahweh." He did not worship the sun as a "material object but as
the symbol of a divine being whose energy was manifested in its rays,"
Freud wrote.[10] Freud enumerated the respects in which the elite Aten and
the popular Amun religions were incompatible. Not only, in the Aten cult,
was "everything to do with myths, magic and sorcery" excluded. In addition, "the manner in which the sun-god was represented was no longer, as in
the past, by a small pyramid and a falcon, but—and this seems almost prosa-
ic—by a round disk with rays proceeding from it, which end in human
hands. In spite of all the exuberant art of the Amarna period, no other representation of the sun-god—no personal image of the Aten—has been found,
and it may confidently be said that none will be found," Freud predicts. Finally, there was in the Aten religion "complete silence about the god of the
dead, Osiris, and the kingdom of the dead. . . . The contrast to the popular
religion cannot be more clearly demonstrated," he concluded.[11] Later, Freud
again insisted that "with magnificent inflexibility" the monotheistic Pharaoh "resisted every temptation to magical thought, and he rejected the illusion, so dear to Egyptians in particular, of a life after death."[12]

Part of his argument for Moses being an Egyptian is Freud's description
of similarities between the Aten religion and ancient Judaism. He also mentions further refinements in ancient Judaism, allegedly introduced by Moses. The Jewish religion "is a rigid monotheism on the grand scale: there is
only one God, he is the sole God, omnipotent, unapproachable; his aspect
is more than human eyes can tolerate, no image must be made of him, even
his name may not be spoken."[13] Jewish religion "behaved in some respects
even more harshly than the Egyptian: for instance, in forbidding pictorial representations of any kind." Unlike the Aten religion, Judaism is without sun
worship; like it, it denies an afterlife.[14] Freud understands circumcision as
the continuation of an Egyptian practice imposed on the Jews by Moses.
Each of these characteristics of monotheism is interpreted psychoanalytically as a foundation for an advance in intellectuality (*Geistigkeit*) over more
primitive polytheism.

The stringency of Moses' precepts must be the Jews' motive for murdering him. "The Jewish people under Moses were just as little able to tolerate

10. Ibid., p. 22.   11. Ibid., p. 24.   12. Ibid., p. 59.
13. Ibid., p. 18.   14. Ibid., pp. 25-26.

such a highly spiritualized [*vergeistigte*] religion and find satisfaction of their needs in what it had to offer as had been the Egyptians of the Eighteenth Dynasty," who reverted to the Amun religion. "Those who had been dominated and kept in want rose and threw off the burden of the religion that had been imposed on them."[15] When Freud has the descendants of Moses' followers (and murderers) merge later with worshippers of Yahweh, the Mosaic tradition is again described as the more spiritualized, *vergeistigte*:

> The god Yahweh, to whom the Midianite Moses then presented a new people, was probably in no respect a prominent being. A coarse, narrow-minded, local god, violent and bloodthirsty, he had promised his followers to give them "a land flowing with milk and honey." . . . The Egyptian Moses had given to one portion of the people a more highly spiritualized notion of god, the idea of a single deity embracing the whole world, who was not less all-loving than all-powerful, who was averse to all ceremonial and magic and set before men as their highest aim a life in truth and justice. . . . The god Yahweh had arrived at undeserved honour when . . . he was credited with the deed of liberation which had been performed by Moses.[16]

Freud praises the prophets for instigating the gradual return of more spiritualized Mosaic precepts after unification of the two religions. There "arose from among the midst of the people an unending succession of men who were not linked to Moses in their origin but were enthralled by the great and mighty tradition which had grown up little by little in obscurity: and it was these men, the Prophets, who tirelessly preached the old Mosaic doctrine—that the deity disdained sacrifice and ceremonial and asked only for faith and a life in truth and justice." He gives with one hand and takes with the other when he comments that "it is honour enough to the Jewish people that they could preserve such a tradition and produce men who gave it a voice—even though the initiative to it came from outside, from a great foreigner."[17]

In Freud's judgment, the later god of the Jews became like the old Mosaic god in three important respects. He was acknowledged as the only god; monotheism was an idea that was the main content of the people's intellectual life which left them no interest for other things, especially ceremonial and magic; and the god desired only faith and ethical conduct, that is, a life of truth and justice.[18] Freud attributes these three qualities, exclusive univer-

15. Ibid., p. 47.   16. Ibid., p. 50.   17. Ibid., p. 51.   18. Ibid., p. 64.

sal monotheism, intellectual absorption with an unrepresented deity to the exclusion of magic and ceremonial, and the ethical emphasis of the religious teachings, to Moses' influence[19] and considers them the substance of Judaism's sublimity and greatness. Moses is a heroic great man with a sublime conception of god.

The Law-Giving Father

Freud's original title for his study of Moses was *Der Mann Moses, ein historischer Roman (The Man Moses, A Historical Novel)*. After one essay became two and then three, making the work also a psychoanalytic study of the origins and effects of monotheism, he changed its title to *Der Mann Moses und die monotheistische Religion: drei Abhandlungen (The Man Moses and the Monotheistic Religion: Three Essays)*. Both titles stress the masculinity and humanity of Moses in a way which the English title, *Moses and Monotheism*, does not.[20] This stress was not accidental. Freud endowed Moses with a personality, a history, and motivations. He made him a hero, who by definition must be a son who dares to defy and surpass the father, and a great man, who by definition has paternal characteristics. The sublime conception of God of which the Jewish tradition boasts is related to these sublime aspects of Moses' character because, in Freud's account, Moses created the Jews.[21]

Freud's story presents Moses as an energetic man, who, having lost political power and support for his religious convictions during the reaction after Akhenaten's death, was "at home with the plan of founding a new kingdom, of finding a new people to whom he would present for their worship the religion which Egypt had disdained." Freud admired Moses' action: "It was, we can see, a heroic attempt to combat destiny, to compensate in two directions for the losses in which Akhenaten's catastrophe had involved him."[22] This great foreigner, the Egyptian Moses, was heroic in Freud's view because he would not give up his monotheism. This view of Moses also appears in a passage in a letter to his son Ernst Freud: "It is typically Jewish not to renounce anything and to replace what has been lost. Moses . . . was the first to set an example."[23] Here, what Moses replaced was a lost renunciatory religion.

19. Ibid., p. 66.

20. See Marthe Robert, *From Oedipus to Moses* (1976), Chap. 5, p. 211, n. 24.

21. *Moses and Monotheism* (1939), *SE* 23:106.　　22. Ibid., p. 28.

23. Letter of January 17, 1938, in Ernst L. Freud, ed., *The Letters of Sigmund Freud* (1960), p. 440.

In Freud's romance, the Jews considered themselves chosen because the aristocratic Egyptian, Moses, had placed himself at "the head of a crowd of immigrant foreigners at a backward level of civilization."[24] Moses had "stooped to the Jews" and made them his people.[25] Freud draws on Otto Rank's study of hero birth myths in order to use the story of Moses' being drawn out of the water in his argument for his noble Egyptian origins. A hero has had the "courage to rebel against his father and has in the end victoriously overcome him." Moses is a hero whose origin myth reverses the usual pattern. "Whereas normally a hero, in the course of his life, rises above his humble beginnings, the heroic life of the man Moses began with his . . . descending to the level of the Children of Israel," Freud declares.[26]

The postulation of reversal is appropriate to Freud's argument about the psychical value of Judaism, which he traces to the Mosaic imprint on the less civilized Jews. Freud's Moses is an imposer of renunciations, and the impetus for renunciation must come from one who has himself achieved greater control of his own impulses. In *The Future of an Illusion*, Freud had discussed the necessity for discipline to be imposed on the "lazy and unintelligent" masses, who "have no love for instinctual renunciation." He explained there that only the influence of individuals who "set an example and whom masses recognize as their leaders" can induce them to "perform the work and undergo the renunciations on which the existence of civilization depends. All is well if these leaders are persons who possess superior insight into the necessities of life and who have risen to the height of mastering their own instinctual wishes."[27] Moses is portrayed as one of these rare successful leaders, as a man whose own superior capacity for renunciation was inseparable from the spiritual and intellectual elevation of his religious convictions. Such a man would necessarily be better bred than his followers. In Freud's view, superiority in renunciation accompanies superiority in psyche and intellect; hence, it fit to make Moses an Egyptian.

Moses is also a "great man." One of the questions addressed in *Moses and Monotheism* is how historical great men had their effect. Freud wished to show

> what the real nature of a tradition resides in, and what its special power rests on, how impossible it is to dispute the personal influence upon world-history of individual great men, what sacrilege one commits against the splendid diversity of human life if one recognizes only

24. *Moses and Monotheism* (1939), SE 23:18.   25. Ibid., p. 45.
26. Ibid., pp. 12, 15.   27. *The Future of an Illusion* (1927), SE 21:7-8.

those motives which arise from material needs, from what sources some ideas (and particularly religious ones) derive their power to subject both men and peoples to their yoke. . . ."[28]

So he inquires into the qualities of greatness. "Beauty, for instance, and muscular strength, however enviable they may be, constitute no claim to 'greatness.' It would seem," he concludes, "that the qualities have to be mental [*geistige*] ones—psychical and intellectual [*intellektuelle*] distinctions."[29]

The influence of the great man on others is twofold: they are moved by his personality and by the idea which he puts forward. That idea "may stress some ancient wishful image of the masses, or it may point out a new wishful aim to them, or it may cast its spell over them in some other way." Freud asserts the masses' need for an authority who is admired, even worshipped, and who rules, perhaps cruelly. "We have learnt from the psychology of individual men what the origin is of this need of the masses. It is a longing for the father felt by everyone from his childhood onwards, for the same father whom the hero of the legend boasts he has overcome," he explains. Now it is clear that the qualities of the great man are paternal qualities and "that the essence of great men for which we vainly searched lies in this conformity."[30] These paternal characteristics are decisiveness of thought, strength of will, energy of action, and, above all, autonomy and independence, "his divine unconcern which may grow into ruthlessness." An ambivalent attitude toward a great man is inevitable, for "one must admire him, one may trust him, but one cannot avoid being afraid of him too." Freud is now convinced that Moses, God, and the father are cast in the same mental mold. "There is no doubt that it was a mighty prototype of a father, which, in the person of Moses, stooped to the poor Jewish bondsmen to assure them that they were his dear children. And no less overwhelming must have been the effect upon them of the idea of an only, eternal, almighty God. . . ." It is likely, too, that Moses introduced into this idea of God some traits of his own personality, such as his "wrathful temper and his relentlessness," which characterize the paternal imposer of stringent restrictions.[31]

Had Freud wished to assert that belief in this god was an illusion, he could have done so at this point in his discussion of Moses, god, and the obsequious masses. But this is not his intent. Instead, he is interested in the sources, the "immense power," and the valuable mental effects of the be-

28. *Moses and Monotheism* (1939), *SE* 23:52-53.

29. Ibid., p. 108.   30. Ibid., p. 109.   31. Ibid., p. 110.

lief.[32] His procedure is to emphasize the restrictive, demanding paternal qualities of Moses and Moses' god and the intellectual advances which took place in the psychical economies of those who obeyed them and then to explain the tenacity and power of this sublime tradition in terms of the return of the repressed, which was a masculine oedipal resolution—complete with strong superego—writ large.

Moses is the hero, the son who overcame; he is the father; he is psychically effective like the primal father was because Moses, too, is the murdered father. The qualities of Moses and of his god are qualities worthy of the primal father, who "was lord and father of the entire horde and unrestricted in his power, which he exercised with violence." The primal father was jealous and cruel. But his parricidal sons not only hated and feared him but also honored him as a model.[33] Moses and his god are intractable lawgivers. In *Moses and Monotheism*, the firmly authoritative, and therefore psychically educative, qualities of Moses and his god overshadow the loving, protective, and consoling characteristics of fathers and god as they are portrayed in *The Future of an Illusion*. Followers of the Mosaic tradition do not passively submit to a comfortable dependence, which restricts their intellectual level; instead, they follow the masculine path of oedipal renunciation of instinct under the law of the father, and they achieve its economic correlates: advance in intellectuality, culture, and morality.

Consequences of Monotheism

Freud wished to show how monotheist religion "affected the Jewish people and how it was bound to leave a permanent imprint on their character." It did so "through its rejection of magic and mysticism, its invitation to advances in intellectuality [*Geistigkeit*] and its encouragement of sublimations." The people, "enraptured by the possession of the truth, overwhelmed by the consciousness of being chosen, came to have a high opinion of what is intellectual and to lay stress on what is moral." Even their "melancholy destinies and their disappointments in reality" served to intensify these trends.[34] Whereas Christian beliefs restricted intellectuality and morality, Mosaic beliefs advanced them. Judaism, in comparison with previous polytheisms, "brought the Jews a far grander conception of God, or, as we might put it more modestly, the conception of a grander God." One

32. Ibid., p. 123.   33. Ibid., pp. 81-82.   34. Ibid., pp. 85-86.

of the immediate psychical consequences of the grander god is pride, for the believer shares in his greatness and feels exalted.[35] A related source of pride is what Freud called the "advance in intellectuality" (*Der Forschritt in der Geistigkeit*).[36] Enhanced self-esteem, intellectual advance, and instinctual renunciations are of a psychical piece.

THE ADVANCE IN INTELLECTUALITY

Freud places strong emphasis on the psychical effects of the Mosaic prohibition against making an image of God, "the compulsion to worship a God whom one cannot see." The acceptance of this prohibition "meant that a sensory perception was given second place to what may be called an abstract idea—a triumph of intellectuality over sensuality or, strictly speaking, an instinctual renunciation. . . ." In order to convince the reader of the momentousness of this step, Freud describes three previous and analogous triumphs of intellect over sensuality in the history of civilization. First, the development of speech was so great an advance that the pride in its accomplishment is still expressed in the "belief in the 'omnipotence of thoughts,'" which is characteristic of children, neurotic adults, and primitive people. The development of speech "resulted in . . . an extraordinary advancement" of intellectual [*intellektuellen*] activities: "The new realm of intellectuality [*Geistigkeit*] was opened up, in which ideas, memories and inferences became decisive in contrast to the lower psychical activity which had direct perceptions by the sense-organs as its content."[37] The second analogous advance was when matriarchal social order was supplanted by patriarchal organization. This occurred, Freud wrote, under the influence of external factors and involved a "revolution in the juridical conditions that had so far prevailed." In addition,

> this turning from the mother to the father points . . . to a victory of intellectuality [*Geistigkeit*] over sensuality—that is, an advance in civilization, since maternity is proved by the evidence of the senses while paternity is a hypothesis, based on an inference and a premiss. Taking sides in this way with a thought-process in preference to a sense perception has proved to be a momentous step.[38]

35. Ibid., p. 112.   36. Ibid., pp. 111-116; the subtitle of Essay 3, Part 2, Section C.
37. Ibid., p. 113. See pp. 73-75 above for discussion of Freud's earlier conceptualizations of such advances.
38. Ibid., pp. 113-114. Although Freud discusses this change from matriarchy to patriarchy in

From the preceding quotations, it is again clear that Freud associates instinctual renunciation with advance in intellectuality, patriarchy, and advance in civilization. In the present context he also considers what might be
called the experiential origins of the religious sense to be an advance in intellect. This third analogous advance was the human recognition of "intellectual [*geistige*] forces," forces which cannot be grasped by the senses but
which produce undoubted and powerful effects. In the passage which discusses this discovery, Freud relies upon the "evidence of language," and, as
Strachey notes, *Geist* can be rendered "intellect," "spirit," and "soul," and
Seele can be rendered "soul," "spirit," and "mind."[39] The passage reads:

> it was the movement of the air that provided the prototype of intellec-
> tuality [*Geistigkeit*], for intellect [*Geist*] derives its name from a breath
> of wind—"*animus*," "*spiritus*," and the Hebrew "*ruach* (breath)." This
> too led to the discovery of the mind [*Seele* (soul)] as that of the intel-
> lectual [*geistigen*] principle in individual human beings. . . . Now, how-
> ever, the world of spirits [*Geisterreich*] lay open to men. They were
> prepared to attribute the soul [*Seele*] which they had discovered in
> themselves to everything in Nature. The whole world was animate [*be-
> seelt*]; and science, which came so much later, had plenty to do in di-
> vesting part of the world of its soul once more; indeed it has not
> completed that task even to-day.[40]

In chronological order, discovery of speech came first, discovery of *Geist*
second, the victory of the patriarchate third, and Moses' contribution, his
intellectual elevation of the idea of God through dematerializing it, fourth.
The next chronological step was Christian regression to a lower moral and
intellectual level. The triumph of the scientific spirit recommended in *The
Future of an Illusion* would be a fifth intellectual advance, analogous to Moses' achievement.

Just as the Mosaic prohibition against making images of God increased
the Jews' self-esteem because it raised their intellectual level, in Freud's view
"all such advances in intellectuality have as their consequence that the individual's self-esteem is increased, . . . so that he feels superior to other people

---

four different contexts in *Moses and Monotheism* (cf. pp. 45-46, n. 1; 83-84; 131), he evaluates
its psychological significance only in the passage quoted here. In general, the matriarchate
and the mother goddesses are associated with polytheism, but Freud is uncertain about the
chronology and causes of the change. See pp. 77-79 above for discussion of this issue.
39. Ibid., p. 114, n. 4.
40. Ibid., p. 114. Parenthetical terms provided by Strachey.

who have remained under the spell of sensuality."[41] With pride, Jews declare that "our God is the greatest and mightiest, although he is invisible like a gale of wind or like the soul."[42] Monotheists feel superior to polytheists, fathers to mothers, "spiritualists" (in the Freudian sense) to materialists, "brain-workers" to manual laborers in the Freudian schema of intellectual advance.

The Mosaic advance is credited with the continuing "inclination to intellectual interests" among Jews. Giving preeminence to the intellect has had great effects throughout some two thousand years in the life of the Jewish people, Freud comments in a passage which clearly alludes to Nazi ideology. Jewish emphasis on intellectual labors "has helped to check the brutality and the tendency to violence which are apt to appear where the development of muscular strength is the popular ideal. Harmony in the cultivation of intellectual and physical activity, such as was achieved by the Greek people, was denied to the Jews. In this dichotomy their decision was at least in favour of the worthier alternative [the alternative that was more significant culturally]."[43]

RENUNCIATION OF INSTINCT

The psychical and cultural worth of Judaism is next traced to its related specialization in instinctual renunciations. "The religion which began with the prohibition against making an image of God develops more and more in the course of centuries into a religion of instinctual renunciations," Freud observed. Renunciation grounds the ethical heights reached in the Jewish religion:

> It is not that it would demand sexual *abstinence*; it is content with a marked restriction of sexual freedom. God, however, becomes entirely removed from sexuality and elevated into the ideal of ethical perfection. But ethics is a limitation of instinct. The Prophets are never tired of asseverating that God requires nothing other from his people than a just and virtuous conduct of life—that is, abstention from every instinctual satisfaction which is still condemned by our morality to-day as well. And even the demand for belief in him seems to take a second place in comparison with the seriousness of these ethical requirements.[44]

41. Ibid., p. 115.   42. Ibid., p. 118.
43. Ibid., p. 115; the phrase in brackets appeared in the original version (see p. 115, n. 2).
44. Ibid., pp. 118-119.

To explain how renunciation creates pride, Freud discusses the relations between ego and superego, between superego and great man, and between religious precepts and the will of the oedipal father. In individual psychology, instinctual renunciation may bring a pleasure which is felt as pride, but not so long as it is undertaken only because of external prohibition. Renunciation because of external exigency causes psychical pain. But when renunciation is undertaken in obedience to internalized authority, the superego, "in addition to the inevitable unpleasurable consequences it also brings the ego a yield of pleasure—a substitutive satisfaction, as it were. The ego feels elevated; it is proud of the instinctual renunciation, as though it were a valuable achievement." When the "ego has brought the super-ego the sacrifice of an instinctual renunciation, it expects to be rewarded by receiving more love from it. The consciousness of deserving this love is felt by it as pride."[45] So renunciation brings a superior fulfillment because the authority who gives the reward of love is the internalized father. In a group, it could be the great man, who functions as the group ego ideal. Once the father enters the picture again, however, Freud finds it necessary to "interpolate" a genetic consideration in order to explain the deeper sources of this feeling of elevation that is consequent upon renunciation. In both individual and collective situations, the will of the murdered or rivaled father is carried out through renunciation. It is the "autocratic father" who decides "what is to be allowed and what forbidden." It is always a case of "instinctual renunciation under the pressure of the authority which replaces and prolongs the father."[46] But the distinction between external and internal prohibition is crucial; only if the will of the father is internalized does renunciation bring pride, a sense of elevation. Renunciations are undertaken for internal reasons, and each new renunciation strengthens the superego.

Freud also relates the concept of sacrality, or holiness, to the will of the father: "The father's will was not only something which one might not touch, which one had to hold in high respect, but also something one trembled before, because it demanded a painful instinctual renunciation."[47] Circumcision is interpreted analogously. When Moses introduced circumcision, he enhanced Jewish pride. "Those who have adopted circumcision are proud of it. They feel exalted by it, ennobled, as it were, and look down with contempt on the others, whom they regard as unclean."[48] Its deeper meaning as a symbolic submission to the will of the father, a submission (to castration), which demands a painful but prideful instinctual renunciation,

45. Ibid., p. 117.   46. Ibid., pp. 119-120.   47. Ibid., p. 122.   48. Ibid., pp. 29-30.

can now be understood, Freud believes.[49] Here submission is manifestly painful, not consoling. The pride that follows sacrifice is treated as a nobler fulfillment; indeed, nobility is its own reward.

Freud began his discussion of renunciation by emphasizing its function in making Judaism a highly ethical religion. Now that the genetic viewpoint has been introduced, he asserts that it can be seen that ethics and religion have the same roots. "What seems to us so grandiose about ethics, so mysterious and, in a mystical fashion, so self-evident, owes these characteristics to its connection with religion, its origin from the will of the father."[50] The psychical consequences of Judaism, then, are ethical, intellectual (spiritual), and cultural advances, which are traced to renunciations undertaken and maintained at the behest of the internalized paternal authority, who is Moses and, in the final analysis, the primal father. Freud's list of prior practices which provided psychical fulfillments whose renunciation Moses imposed is impressive: visual and tactile images of the deity, names of the deity, a multiplicity of deities, magic, ceremonial and sorcery, the assurance of an afterlife. All are understood as more sensual and pleasurable ways of constructing reality.

The Father Returns: Masculine Genetics

JUDAISM

In *Moses and Monotheism*, the genetic argument is the basis of Freud's assertion that the object of monotheistic religious belief is historically, but not materially, true. This assertion rests on two further "hazardous hypotheses." The first is of the inheritance of acquired (psychical) characteristics; the second is of the actual, historical murder of the primal father. Freud asserts that the "archaic heritage of human beings comprises not only dispositions but also subject-matter—memory-traces of the experience of earlier generations."[51] This hypothesis serves to bridge the gap between group and individual psychology, between a universal paternal etiology and the individual male's oedipal experience. With this hypothesis, the analogy which Freud has proposed between the processes of development of neurosis and development of religion, as collective neurosis, can be applied as a formula. The formula is "early trauma—defence—latency—outbreak of neurotic illness—partial return of the repressed."[52] Here, it is a male neurosis that is in ques-

49. Ibid., p. 122.   50. Ibid.   51. Ibid., p. 99.   52. Ibid., p. 80.

tion, for, as Freud had written several years before, "it is only in the male child that we find the fateful combination of love for the one parent and simultaneous hatred for the other as a rival."[53] This fateful combination may be repressed or destroyed (dissolved); if it is repressed, neurotic consequences are likely. The trauma, in the life of a neurotic male as well as in "the life of the human species," consists in events "of a sexually aggressive nature, which left behind them permanent consequences but were for the most part fended off and forgotten, and which after a long latency came into effect and created phenomena similar to symptoms in their structure and purpose."[54] The collective traumatic events were the murder and cannibalism of the primal father by the oppressed brothers of the horde. (Freud omits the primal rapes.) The murder expressed the brothers' hostility; the cannibalism did so as well, but in addition it served to "incorporate" the father's qualities and to lay the basis for identifications. The symptomlike consequences of the murder "are the phenomena of religion."[55]

If the "idea of a single god, as well as the rejection of magically effective ceremonial and the stress upon ethical demands made in his name, were in fact Mosaic doctrines," in which Freud "confesses" his belief,[56] then two problems remain: how to explain the delayed effect of these doctrines and their extraordinary power once they have had their effect. Freud accounts for their delayed effect by the related phenomena of latency and the gradual return of the repressed through the prophets, men in whose minds "the dark traces of the past lurked, . . . ready to break through into its more conscious regions."[57] The existence of the primal father, his murder, the sons' ambivalent emotions toward the father when it occurred, and their ambivalent responses to their "crime of liberation" are among the repressed memory traces, which can be inherited and therefore may return.[58]

In Freud's account, because the Jewish people had repeated the primal deed by murdering Moses, they were particularly susceptible to monotheism in general and to the gradual return of the Mosaic precepts in particular. "Fate had brought the great deed and misdeed of primaeval days, the killing of the father, closer to the Jewish people by causing them to repeat it on the

53. "Female Sexuality" (1931), SE 21:229.
54. Moses and Monotheism (1939), SE 23:80.
55. Ibid., pp. 81, 80.   56. Ibid., p. 66.
57. Ibid., p. 87. The quoted phrase was actually written about Paul, but Freud made the same point about the prophets, whose work of bringing the repressed to consciousness Paul carried on, in his account.
58. Quoted phrase from Freud, "Preface to Reik's Ritual: Psycho-Analytic Studies" (1919), SE 17:262.

person of Moses, an outstanding father-figure." It was a case of "acting-out" the repressed event rather than remembering it.[59] The former happens in neuroses; therapy works to replace acting-out with remembering. With such a double oedipal jeopardy in the Jewish past, the "tradition of a great [Mosaic] past . . . continued to work in the background," gradually gaining "more and more power over men's minds" and finally succeeding in "transforming the god Yahweh into the god of Moses and in calling back to life the religion of Moses which had been established and then abandoned long centuries earlier." Tradition is the repressed which returns, and the "religion of Moses only carried through its effect on the Jewish people as a tradition. . . ."[60] Freud explained:

> A tradition that was based only on communication could not lead to the compulsive character that attaches to religious phenomena. It would be listened to, judged, and perhaps dismissed, like any other piece of information from outside; it would never attain the privilege of being liberated from the constraint of logical thought. It must have undergone the fate of being repressed, the condition of lingering in the unconscious, before it is able to display such powerful effects on its return.[61]

What had held the Jews together through the centuries "was an ideal factor, the possession in common of certain intellectual [*intellektueller*] and emotional wealth."[62] This wealth had slowly returned from the repressed and reestablished the Mosaic religion; it enriched and ennobled the Jews' mental lives.

After he postulated the return of the repressed tradition as a collective neurosis, one factor remained unexplained, in Freud's view. "There is an element of grandeur about everything to do with the origin of a religion, certainly including the Jewish one, and this is not matched by the explanations we have hitherto given," he wrote.[63] Why should the compulsion to accept unquestioningly the monotheistic idea be overwhelming? Believers say it is overwhelming because it is true. But Freud dryly objects that the "pious argument rests on an optimistic and idealistic premiss. It has not been possible to demonstrate in other connections that the . . . human mind shows any special inclination for recognizing the truth. We have rather found, on the contrary, that our intellect very easily goes astray without any warning,

59. *Moses and Monotheism* (1939), SE 23:88-89.   60. Ibid., pp. 124, 127-128.
61. Ibid., p. 101.   62. Ibid., p. 123.   63. Ibid., p. 128.

and that nothing is more easily believed by us than what, without reference to the truth, comes to meet our wishful illusions."[64] Instead, Freud suggests that the element of truth in monotheism is historical. In the form in which it meets the believer it has been distorted, as is so often the case with repressed material. Freud's creed corrects the pious one:

> We too believe that the pious solution contains the truth—but the *historical* truth and not the *material* truth. And we assume the right to correct a certain distortion to which this truth has been subjected on its return. That is to say, we do not believe that there is a single great god to-day, but that in primaeval times there was a single person who was bound to appear huge at that time and who afterwards returned in men's memory elevated to divinity.[65]

An idea such as this "has a compulsive character: it *must* be believed." Freud classifies it as delusion insofar as it is distorted but as truth insofar as it brings a return of the past.[66]

When the repressed memory of the great father's existence returns to consciousness, the first emotional result is a rapture of devotion. "A child's emotional impulses are intensely and inexhaustibly deep to a degree quite other than those of an adult; only religious ecstasy can bring them back. A rapture of devotion to God was thus the first reaction to the return of the great father."[67] But, in time, the original ambivalent feelings toward the father must also have their effect. In reaction against hostility to the primal father (and to Moses), Freud locates the psychical source of ever more stringent Jewish ethics and an ever stronger superego. He writes: "There was no place in the framework of the religion of Moses for a direct expression of the murderous hatred of the father. All that could come to light was a mighty reaction against it—a sense of guilt on account of that hostility, a bad conscience for having sinned against God and for not ceasing to sin." When "things were going badly" for the people, they attributed it to punishment for more superficial trespasses against God's commands and felt guilt for these.

> [D]riven by the need to satisfy this sense of guilt, which was insatiable and came from sources so much deeper, they must make those commandments grow ever stricter, more meticulous and even more trivial. In a fresh rapture of moral asceticism they imposed more and more

64. Ibid., p. 129. 65. Ibid. 66. Ibid., p. 130. 67. Ibid., p. 134.

new instinctual renunciations on themselves and in that way reached—in doctrine and precept, at least—ethical heights which had remained inaccessible to the other peoples of antiquity.[68]

The religion of Moses became a renunciatory religion and leaped to ethical heights because it admitted the *existence* of the great father. But its knowledge of his murder had remained repressed so that Jewish guilt increased and, with it, ever sterner renunciations. The next step in the history of the return of the repressed was taken by Christianity, which, in Freud's account, allowed a distorted return of the repressed knowledge of parricide.

CHRISTIANITY

"The re-establishment of the primal father in his historic rights was a great step forward but it could not be the end," Freud commented.[69] Because the Jews could not admit they had killed the great father but instead reenacted it by killing Moses (and then could not admit the second murder, either), they "remained halted at the recognition of the great father." Paul, whom Freud considers the effective founder of Christianity, continued the process of the return of repressed primal history. Insofar as Christianity continued the return of the repressed, it was an advance: "in the history of religion—that is, as regards the return of the repressed," Christianity took a further developmental step.[70] In other respects, however, it was a regression.

Insofar as Christianity was an advance, it was so because it recognized, in distorted form, "other portions of the prehistoric tragedy" than just the *existence* of the great father. Freud interprets the concepts of original sin and redemption by the sacrifice of a victim as Paul's distorted recognition of the *murder* of the primal father. A stealthily increasing unconscious sense of guilt in antiquity, which Freud interprets as Jewish guilt, was resolved for those who became Christians, but only with a new distortion. The murder itself was not remembered, but there arose in its place a fantasy of its atonement.[71] In Freud's words, "it was after all a Jewish man, Saul of Tarsus, . . . in whose spirit [*Geist*] the realization first emerged: 'the reason we are so unhappy is that we have killed God the father.' And it is entirely understandable that he could only grasp this piece of truth in the delusional disguise of the glad tidings: 'we are freed from all guilt since one of us has sacrificed his life to absolve us.'" Freud decodes the delusion:

68. Ibid.   69. Ibid., p. 86.   70. Ibid., pp. 89, 88.   71. Ibid., p. 86.

In this formula the killing of God was of course not mentioned, but a crime that had to be atoned by the sacrifice of a victim could only have been a murder. And the intermediate step between the delusion and the historical truth was provided by the assurance that the victim of the sacrifice had been God's son. With the strength which it derived from the source of historical truth, this new faith overthrew every obstacle. The blissful sense of being chosen was replaced by the liberating sense of redemption. But the fact of the parricide, in returning to the memory of mankind, had to overcome greater resistances than the other fact, which had constituted the subject-matter of monotheism [the existence of the primal father]; it was also obliged to submit to a more powerful distortion. The unnameable crime was replaced by the hypothesis of what must be described as a shadowy "original sin."

Nonetheless, in Freud's view, Christianity could not escape "the fate of having to get rid of the father."[72] The "final outcome of the religious novelty," which was "ostensibly aimed at propitiating the father god," was his dethronement. Judaism had been a religion of the father; Christianity became the religion of the son. "The old God the Father fell back behind Christ; Christ, the Son, took his place, just as every son had hoped to do in primaeval times. Paul, who carried Judaism on, also destroyed it," Freud concluded.[73]

From a psychoanalytic point of view, the "redeemer" could be "none other than the most guilty person, the ringleader of the company of brothers who had overpowered their father." If historically there had been such a ringleader, Christ was "his successor and his reincarnation." If there had been no such leader, but a fantasy of one, "Christ was the heir to a wishful phantasy which remained unfulfilled," for Freud assumed that each son at least wished that he alone had done the heroic deed. In this fantasy of the single "ringleader" son, Freud discovers "the origin of the concept of a hero," the son who "rebels against his father and kills him in some shape or other."[74] While on the manifest level, Christ was an antihero, having let himself be killed *for* the father, on the latent level, Freud believes, he represented the hero who *was* the parricide. Christ was Paul's fulfiller of filial fantasy.

In 1921, in *Group Psychology and the Analysis of the Ego*, Freud had discussed heroism in its relationship to the primal deed. There, he contrasted individual to group psychology in a way which his later characterizations of a great man versus Christian believers recall. He asserted:

72. Ibid., pp. 135-136.   73. Ibid., pp. 87-88.   74. Ibid., p. 87.

from the first there were two kinds of psychologies, that of the individual members of the group and that of the father, chief, or leader. The members of the group were subject to ties just as we see them today, but the father of the primal horde was free. His intellectual acts were strong and independent even in isolation, and his will needed no reinforcement from others. . . . . He, at the very beginning of the history of mankind, was the "superman" whom Nietzsche only expected from the future.[75]

The father forced his sons into group psychology, and the first hero was the son who freed himself from it. In this account, the hero is the parricide and the poet; but his crime was psychical, not historical. Freud wrote then that "he who did this was the first epic poet; and the advance was achieved in his imagination. This poet disguised the truth with lies in accordance with his longing. He invented the heroic myth. The hero was a man who by himself had slain the father—the father who still appeared in the myth as a totemic monster."[76] In this context, Freud had also called his own version of cultural and religious origins his "scientific myth of the father of the primal horde."[77]

Why, by 1936, was he prepared to confirm the historicity of the primal father, the primal murder, and even perhaps the first hero? Maybe Freud's awareness of the undiminished and ambiguous psychical power of religion had by then increased. The political situation in Germany and in Austria testified to the irrational power of religious adherence even so long after the criticism of religion as human production had taken place. Freud's hopes for enlightened irreligious reform were dashed by events in the thirties. Perhaps he judged that the primal Oedipus complex *must* have achieved its aim historically and then become immensely powerful under repression because its symptoms were evidently still in full flower. Responses to the father complex had not weakened; perhaps the trauma had been too powerful, more powerful even than a fantasy. Certainly the collective complex showed few signs of having been dissolved in the ideal manner. And, further, as Freud thought had happened in many different contexts in the past, those who were, for him, most intellectually advanced because they continued to undertake the strictest Mosaic renunciations were turned on by the masses, who were at a lower mental and cultural level. For, in *Moses and Monotheism*,

75. *Group Psychology and the Analysis of the Ego* (1921), *SE* 18:123.
76. Ibid., p. 136.   77. Ibid., p. 135.

Freud presented Christianity as also a cultural regression from the heights achieved by Judaism.

> The Christian religion did not maintain the high level in things of the mind to which Judaism had soared. It was no longer strictly monotheist, it took over numerous symbolic rituals from surrounding peoples, it reestablished the great mother-goddess and found room to introduce many of the divine figures of polytheism only lightly veiled. . . . Above all, it did not, like the Aten religion and the Mosaic one which followed it, exclude the entry of superstitious, magical and mystical elements, which were to prove a severe inhibition upon the intellectual [geistige] development of the next two thousand years.

Therefore, Freud asserted, the "triumph of Christianity was a fresh victory for the priests of Amun over Akhenaten's god after an interval of fifteen hundred years and on a wider stage."[78] "It was as though Egypt was taking vengeance once more on the heirs of Akhenaten," he wrote.[79] It appeared that the masculine phylogenetic father complex was at work then in the triumph of Christianity and now, perhaps, in the triumph of Nazism. Those manly ones who renounce and those culture heroes who impose educative renunciations, Prometheus, Moses, the prophets, the Jews—and Freud—suffer the repeated fate of being sacrificed.

Moses and Monotheism, then, is a defense of the cultural value of Judaism. It can be grasped as such when one attends to the psychoanalytic categories that Freud employs to characterize and analyze it rather than to the two manifest offenses against it that he claimed to have committed: making the tradition psychoanalytically explicable and making Moses an Egyptian.

78. *Moses and Monotheism* (1939), *SE* 23:88.
79. Ibid., p. 136.

Chapter 12

Gender, Fathers, and God:
Conclusions

Indeed, no scientific theory about religion has ever been disinterested: the substitution of theory for belief is one of the highest achievements of secular scientific culture.
—RIEFF, *Freud: The Mind of the Moralist*

Gender and the Uses of God

William James decided after dogged psychological study that "the gods we stand by are the gods we need and can use, the gods whose demands on us are reinforcements of our demands on ourselves and on one another."[1] Freud's accounts of different uses of god in *The Future of an Illusion* and *Moses and Monotheism* are psychoanalytically specific. They reveal how he believes the father-god is mentally used to fulfill wishes and to induce renunciations. Christianity is treated primarily as a religion of fulfillments and Judaism primarily as a religion of renunciations. The fulfillments and renunciations in question flow between the believer and the father figure, who is at the center of belief. Freud assigns to these different psychical uses of god asymmetrical psychical and cultural value, and their uneven value repeats his evaluation of the results of typical masculine and feminine positions in relation to fathers. This repetition is traceable to the relationships he saw between fulfillment and femininity and fulfillment and Christianity, on the one hand, and between renunciation and masculinity and renunciation and the Mosaic tradition, on the other. These relationships run through his texts like a pattern through marble.

When Freud detects religion offering the believer a consoling, loving paternal God, he exposes it as the servant of wish fulfillment. The illusion of the existence and tender loving care of this sort of god is mentally like a

1. William James, *The Varieties of Religious Experience* (1958), p. 259.

feminine attitude toward fathers. Submission and its compensatory gratifications restrict intellect and morality. When intellectual and moral levels are thus lowered, culture is impoverished. As in the feminine situation, so in the religious: a personal relationship to the divine father as the loving progenitor is achieved and continued. For Freud, attachment to the father and femininity are correlative. Just as his theory of gender carries on an implicit critique of the feminine attitude (at the same time as femininity is considered normal for women in a patriarchal context), his indictment of standard Viennese Christian belief is based on the critical principle that renunciation of illusion means developing beyond attachment to the caring father. The psychical qualities of the Christian believer and the feminine or woman are the same: a weak superego, a poorly developed sense of morality, a restricted intellect, opposition to cultural advance, insufficient respect for reality, *Ananke*, and *Logos*. Compared with these qualities, those fostered by the religion of Moses were and are an advance, for renunciation signals the painful step beyond illusion. By emphasizing illusion in its quarrel with reality in *The Future of an Illusion*, Freud built his argument on a theoretical foundation that made its critical result a foregone conclusion: the renunciatory scientific spirit would be better—not salvific, but better.

The keynote of the psychical situation of Jewish believers is renunciation but not of all oedipal attitudes nor of a paternal construction of reality. The masculine resolution of the Oedipus complex that Freud portrays in *Moses and Monotheism* is one in which paternal restrictions have become internal. This resolution instigates intellectual and moral advance, but it betrays its paternal etiology. It surpasses polytheism in mental wealth, and from an economic point of view, it is superior to the later Christian regression. In choosing the theoretical foundation of renunciation for his analysis of Jewish monotheism, Freud made this conclusion, too, foregone. The psychical situation of Jewish believers is possible only within Freud's masculine developmental schema. Here, the father figure is not emphasized in his procreative or nurturant functions. Instead, he appears from outside and chooses his people, placing restrictions on them, which, when they are repudiated and then accepted, elevate his people to unprecedented intellectual, ethical, and spiritual heights. Heroes and great men strengthen the masculine developmental sequence on the larger historical stage, just as personal heroes and local great men strengthen it in a man's narrower life history. Asceticism holds sway; ethics are refined; sublimations multiply. Fulfillment is found only in the pride that comes from sacrificing wishes to the superego, the internal paternal agent. Guilt grows as renunciations multiply. This masculine dynamic is still guided by the repressed father complex. It has ushered in intellectual and cultural advances, which mark a progressive stage in the history of civilization; relative independence from prior, more wishful phases has been achieved. But this descriptively "normal" masculinity, with its father complex repressed but not dissolved, has a fluid border with the neurotic. The religion of renunciation is still a symptom of the universal masculine neurosis. Culturally, ethically, spiritually, and intellectually, sublime peaks are scaled, but these exalted positions are maintained for irrational reasons. The intellect, strong as it has become, does not yet have complete primacy. Nor does the reality principle alone hold sway, even though both are firmer in this stage than they were under polytheism or would be under Christianity.

Freud's hoped-for scientific stage is psychically possible given the possibility of ideal masculine development wherein oedipal attachments are somehow dissolved. An analytic cure may in principle achieve the same end: primacy of the intellect, dominance of the ego. Only reasoned renunciation of all father complex attachments would be a collective "cure." The gratifying release from ever-increasing guilt offered by Christianity (as Freud more thoughtfully analyzed it in *Moses and Monotheism*) is no cure, only a later—but regressive—historical step in the return of the repressed father complex. For resignation to *Logos* and *Ananke* to be achieved, the complex must stop its triumphant returns.

Freud's psychology of religion outlines a hierarchical typology of psychical positions toward the divine father, which correspond to his schema of gender attitudes toward the mental father, those of femininity, ordinary masculinity, and ideal masculinity. His psychologies of religion and of gender differentiation both rest on paternal etiology; they are theories of mental religiosity and sexuality within a patricentric and patriarchal mental world. Freud's patricentric, gender-asymmetrical, and critical principles are woven together in his psychology of religion. The message emerges that renunciation of illusion will mean renunciation of the feminine attitude to the divine father as well as renunciation of the normal masculine attitude to him, in favor of scientific resignation to a postpaternal universe.[2]

2. Unless, at the end, Freud chose Jewishness over science. But there is no evidence that he did, and, in any event, as long as his Jewishness was not religious, he had no trouble reconciling them. In his 1930 preface to the Hebrew translation of *Totem and Taboo*, Freud wrote that he hoped his readers would share his "conviction that unprejudiced science cannot remain a stranger to the spirit of the new Jewry"; *SE* 13:xv.

Integration and Summary

Let us step back briefly to place this reading of Freud's theory of religion within the context of the main points of the foregoing argument.

Freud's attention to sexuality in individual and cultural life is attention to mental sexuality, to the whence and whither of the "mental shapes assumed by the sexual life of children" in boys and girls, men and women, unbelievers and believers. Sexuality is what mind makes of its desiring organism. It is not unmediated biology. And gender asymmetry is a powerful formative component as well as a likely result of mental sexuality, as Freud presents it.

The kind of gender asymmetry which he both presupposes and accounts for relies on the concrete sociological and historical fact of paternal preeminence so that mentally, too, the paternal principle is privileged. In its preeminence, paternity is allied with reason, reality, and civilization and, therefore, with intellectual, ethical, and cultural value. In the Freudian rendition of gender asymmetry, masculinity, because of its special relationships to paternity, becomes normative, objective, universal, and more valuable than femininity; in short, it alone is potentially the human ideal. It expresses the victory of mind over sense. Femininity is no separate but equal or opposite but complementary principle. It is rather a deviation from the universal and the normative, a subjective falling-short from objectivity, having less psychical and cultural value than masculinity, if indeed it is not in contradiction to such value by representing sensual temptations to fall away from reason, reality, culture, and ethics. It lacks potential to realize the human ideal.

Freud's oedipal genetic theory explains mental assent to these asymmetrical meanings of gender difference by tracing mental dynamics to children's interpretations of paternal authority and maternal submission, with the result that everyone, consciously or unconsciously, repudiates his or her own mental femininity. Femininity is the passive love relationship to father figures, which infantile masculinity must renounce as a precondition for realizing itself as socialized masculinity. Within the already asymmetrically constituted oedipal family, masculinity is achieved, in part, through renunciation of feminine attachments, attachments that promise and threaten precisely the gratifications which a woman's achievement of femininity guarantees.

The guaranteed gratifications are surely a mixed blessing, though, because they also guarantee alienation from the "human" ideal. Ideal masculinity, the result of "complete" renunciation of parental attachments through the dissolution of the Oedipus complex, coincides with Freud's cultural and psychological ideals. For him, ideal masculinity, the cultural ideal, and the psychological ideal meet in the primacy of the intellect. Instinctual renunciation makes this intellectual dominion affectively possible, but because of gender asymmetry, that is, the preeminence of fathers, it is possible only within a rare masculine developmental process. The process is rare because the Oedipus and castration complexes are likely to be repressed and to return; it is masculine because in the girl an Oedipus complex is a haven rather than an illicit peril. Ideal masculinity has a paradigmatic renunciation in its history: the dissolution of the Oedipus complex. In contrast, femininity and fulfillment are allied both because normal femininity submissively receives fulfillment from father figures and because feminine women provide fulfillment to men. Feminine love objects restore, on a new level, gratifications provided by the mother. Hence, maternity can neither achieve nor instigate the renunciations which fathers achieve and enforce. Maternity is seen as prior to and hostile to culture, reason, reality, and morality.

In Freud's writings, the economic point of view asks questions about mental pleasure gained and gainsaid, about the reality and pleasure principles, about renunciations and fulfillments. I have called this body of Freudian thought his moral economy. An examination of the claims of the moral economy has clarified what was critically at stake when Freud treated Christian religious belief as wish-fulfilling illusion and adherence to the Mosaic tradition as a renunciatory process. According to the viewpoint of the moral economy, differentiation of renunciation from wish fulfillment takes place in a genetic process. Renunciation of wish is a developmental step toward thinking according to the reality principle, toward acculturated morality, and toward rationality, which is independent of a construction of reality on the model of libidinal relationships to parental figures. More specifically, Freud's oedipal genetic theory explains how renunciation and fulfillment are developmentally inseparable from different attitudes toward paternal figures. Different attitudes toward fathers define the genders, and gender difference is accounted for as having been established in relation to the mental father.

Freud traces not only gender-typical attitudes but also different religious psychologies to different relations to primal, familial, historical, and divine fathers. The psychological status and results of religious belief, whether these results are treated as progressive or regressive, are explained with reference to mental relationships to the fathers. Religious illusion is a fulfilled wish for gratification that is received from an external paternal figure; religious renunciation is obedience to the internalized will of the loved, murdered father. The feminine relationship to the father is like that of the naïve believer in the Christian father-god as it is portrayed in *The Future of an Illusion*. Not surprisingly, the mental and cultural results of illusion and of femininity receive similar criticisms in Freud's hands. Both are charged with restricting intellectual, moral, and cultural development, and for similar reasons: longing for the father is appeased rather than renounced.

For Freud, normal masculinity, which is not qualitatively distinguished from the neurotic, relies on accepting paternal restrictions of wish and internalizing paternal strength so that a strong superego results. External reality may still be construed as paternal, but the paternal principle now requires renunciations, and the inner heir to the Oedipus complex, the superego, demands that fulfillment of wishes be sacrificed. Component attitudes of the father complex are repressed, which means that they may return as symptoms, which, on the collective stage, are the phenomena of religion. This mental situation is like that of members of the Mosaic tradition. Renunciations for internal reasons are the source of intellectual, cultural, and ethical advances, but they are still dominated by paternally directed emotion.

In Freud's theory of gender difference, ideal masculinity is cured of the father complex. Its dissolution of the Oedipus complex and its gradually depersonalized superego mean it can look firmly at external reality as impersonal, "stripped of any paternal coefficient."[3] This postpaternal construction of reality coincides, for Freud, with the mental achievement of the *wissenschaftliche Geist*, which he recommends as the moral alternative to religion and which he hopes will result from the renunciation of religious illusion. The psychological, cultural, and masculine ideals meet here.

A hierarchy of religio-cultural attitudes, which recapitulate gender alternatives on the collective stage, is visible in Freud's thought. The unifying dynamic that explains development from lower to higher is renunciation of wish fulfillment. Freud's critical intention is an argument for renunciation of transferred ties to fathers, an argument which he carries on in many contexts. The postreligious "scientific" spirit is a mental and cultural advance, through the agency of renunciation, over Mosaic monotheism, which is in turn an advance beyond Christian illusion. This is the case in the same way that ideal masculinity is a mental and cultural advance beyond normal masculinity, which is in turn an advance beyond femininity. The theoretical bases of these parallel hierarchies pervade the Freudian texts and are not peculiar to his attentions to religion. These bases are economic, whereby re-

3. Paul Ricoeur, *Freud and Philosophy* (1970), p. 327.

nunciation of wish is the source of higher mental achievements, and genetic, whereby renunciation of wish is renunciation of oedipal relations to the mental father. Thus, at the highest level of the hierarchy, Freud places, not the father or God, but the masculine ideal.

I conclude, then, that the critical claims of Freud's psychoanalytic studies of religion are inseparable from his genetic and economic critique of wishes for fathers, which is in turn inseparable from the gender-asymmetric structure of his thought. Freud's psychology of religion as a complex critique of religious belief is better understood when it is read in terms of his critical touchstone of renunciation of illusion, which differentiates the genders. For Freud, renunciation is possible, necessary, and valuable because it occurs in the shadow of the preeminent father figure.

Religion is not approached sociologically, historically, phenomenologically, or, as goes without saying, theologically in the Freudian corpus. It is approached from his psychoanalytic point of view, which turns on the critical hypothesis about the dynamics of renunciation and fulfillment. This hypothesis is concretized in gender theory to explain how men and women psychosocially live their masculinity and femininity in a patricentric context. Freud's seemingly overly literal emphasis on the fatherhood of the monotheistic god should be read in relation to his psychoanalytic conclusions about the asymmetrical mental and cultural results of the genders' different relationships to fathers in order fully to comprehend what was critically at stake in Freud's studies of religion. Otherwise, it is not clear to what extent *Moses and Monotheism* was a covert defense of the psychological and cultural value of Judaism. Nor is it clear how thoroughgoing was the psychoanalytic base on which Freud built his attack on Christian illusion as an opponent of reason and culture.

Implications

This study has primarily intended to contribute to an understanding of the internal critical direction of Freud's psychology of religion by making the category of gender its principle of interpretation. At the same time, it has intended to show that we learn something new about Freudian criticism when we attend to his theory of gender rather than allowing it to remain an unexamined factor in an interpretation. A focus on the critical implications of Freud's theory of gender has established a context for understanding Freud's psychology of religion, and this context has placed in relief the "differential diagnoses" of belief that are found in *The Future of an Illusion* and *Moses and Monotheism*. This context has at the same time clarified the psychoanalytic bases for these diagnoses and the psychoanalytic reasons for Freud's different evaluations of what he diagnosed.

I have argued both that Freud's critique of religion is more fully comprehensible when it is read as continuous with the critical fabric of his economic and genetic points of view and, more specifically, that this fabric has father figures as its dominant design so that Freud diagnoses and evaluates patterns of mental life in terms of their relationship to these figures. I submit that what is interesting about Freud's theory of religion is not only that it is the theory of an atheist who treats gods as mental products. What is more interesting is how he distinguishes the functions of these gods—their uses—for those who produce them. Freud's accounts of their production never significantly changed, but his understanding of their uses became more differentiated over the years. His overarching topic was the intricacies of our mental ties to fathers as they direct how we live.

For Freud, they direct how we live as gender directs how we live. The critical design in Freud's texts is most starkly outlined in his critique of gender because there his judgments about the dynamics of renunciation and fulfillment and about consequences of mental relations to fathers are most explicitly joined. Freud's claim that culture is a renunciatory achievement depends on his claim that the father is the figure which requires renunciations. Because of patricentrality in psychoanalytic theory, renunciation will characterize masculinity and fulfillment, femininity. We can see that Freud's pejorative view of femininity is indeed a measure of the critical component of his thought rather than an incidental, disposable part of his texts. Freud's asymmetrical theory of the genders *and* his theory of gender asymmetry are trunk, not limb, within his theory. Masculinity and femininity are categories with critical weight; they are markers of relative value; they are types of psychical relationship to fathers that guide Freud's critique of religion as illusion and his appreciation of its interim enculturing function as renunciation.

When we look specifically at Freud's theory of gender, we find that masculinity and femininity are joined to value at its nexus in Freudian theory—at the point where oedipal ties to fathers are renounced or maintained. We have seen that in this one case, the situation which Simmel described has occurred: "the psychological superiority granted male behavior through the domination of man over woman, is transformed into a logical superiority; this state of affairs is given normative significance and claims a transsexual validity as the yardstick of truth and justice for both men and women."[4] It is useless to ask which comes first chronologically in Freud's thought: his respect for renunciation or for masculinity. Both are there in some form from the start, and when the masculine renunciatory dynamic is discovered in the Mosaic tradition and in the scientific attitude, belief in the value of masculinity, of renunciation, and of Judaism is transformed into a "scientific" theory. Here, I have only sketched this critical pattern because the texts do not provide bases to argue for cause and effect. But, in these texts, masculinity, renunciation, Moses' tradition, and the scientific spirit all become ways to discover truth, to distinguish more clearly between inner and outer reality.

Once the dynamics of renunciation and fulfillment are inseparable from gender—and gender is their instigation and their result—Freud's diagnoses of mental relationships to gods are not separable from gender either. In Freud's texts, gender psychology and religious psychology are inseparable parts of culture. Although he did not put it this way, his writings show how, from a psychoanalytic point of view, the problem of ambivalent ties to divine paternal objects is mentally related to ambivalent—masculine and feminine—ties to less than divine paternal figures. Religious psychology, viewed as a whole, is ambivalent. The religious person may submit in the feminine mode, as object, to the divine loving subject, achieving fulfillment at the price of autonomous reason and cultural advance. Or because the divine father is also feared and has been killed because he is hated, the religious person may follow the masculine model of progressive renunciation at the internalized altar of fathers, in which case the price of the resultant intellectual, moral, and cultural advance is accelerating guilt. Renunciation may be too costly, but so are the gratifications of illusion.

For Freud, this dilemma is the oedipal legacy of religion in patriarchal civilization. For him, religion is not only the symptomatic expression of struggles with paternal etiology; it is simultaneously the legitimate heir of the primal and reinstated patriarchy. Freud's rationalist doubts about the current value of the inheritance were firm, but he did not question its legitimacy; he opposed as utopian those who would take that step. His last word might be: what has been, is, however distorted it may now be.

There are several reasons for those who are interested in feminist questions to encounter Freud's writings. The first has been to delineate and criti-

4. Georg Simmel, "Das Relative und das Absolute im Geschlechter-Problem," trans. in Lewis A. Coser, "Georg Simmel's Neglected Contribution to the Sociology of Women," *Signs* 2, no. 4 (1977):872-873.

cize the misogyny in Freud's psychology of women. Numerous writers have done this, to the benefit of clinical theory. The second has been to see how Freud accounts for gender asymmetry analytically and to decide whether this account is useful. Juliet Mitchell has done so, and in examining this issue here I have drawn on her work. The third reason is to see how gender asymmetry is central to Freudian criticism, to understand how gender and value are intertwined in his theory. I have addressed this question here. I have wanted to show both that gender asymmetry is central to criticism in general and criticism of religion in particular in Freud's thought and that, in principle, the idea of gender can be a fruitful way to clarify the critical infrastructure of thought about religion. The next reason to encounter Freud may be to consider carefully the challenge of his claims that culture is renunciatory and that in renunciatory culture femininity represents fulfillment. One can, of course, dismiss these claims on the grounds that they represent Freud's personal achievement of turning belief into theory. But such a dismissal might be premature. The dilemma presented by Freud, that femininity represents fulfillment in renunciatory culture, might be a useful basis for asking further questions, within the context of feminist social theory, about how gender works in our moral economy and about how gender and uses of God are thereby intertwined.

Bibliography of Works Cited

Works by Freud

Chronological Listing of Books and Papers
Cited in the Standard Edition

The Standard Edition of the Complete Psychological Works of Sigmund Freud. Translated and edited by James Strachey in collaboration with Anna Freud, assisted by Alix Strachey and Alan Tyson. 24 vols. London: The Hogarth Press and the Institute of Psycho-Analysis, 1953-1974 (abbreviated as *SE* followed by volume and page numbers). The date given is that of first publication. When two dates appear, the form follows Strachey's in which the date of writing is given after the date of publication, if these differ.

With Josef Breuer. *Studies on Hysteria.* 1893-1895. *SE* 2:1-305.

Project for a Scientific Psychology. 1950 (1895). *SE* 1:295-391.

The Interpretation of Dreams. 1900. *SE* 4:1-338; *SE* 5:339-625.

The Psychopathology of Everyday Life. 1901. *SE* 6:1-279.

Three Essays on the Theory of Sexuality. 1905. *SE* 7:135-243.

"My Views on the Part Played by Sexuality in the Aetiology of the Neuroses." 1906 (1905). *SE* 7:271-279.

"Obsessive Actions and Religious Practices." 1907. *SE* 9:117-127.

"'Civilized' Sexual Morality and Modern Nervous Illness." 1908. *SE* 9:181-204.

"Analysis of a Phobia in a Five-Year-Old Boy." 1909. *SE* 10:5-149.

"Notes upon a Case of Obsessional Neurosis." 1909. *SE* 10:155-318.

Leonardo da Vinci and a Memory of His Childhood. 1910. *SE* 11:63-137.

"The Future Prospects of Psycho-Analytic Therapy." 1910. *SE* 11:141-151.

"A Special Type of Choice of Object Made by Men (Contributions to the Psychology of Love I)." 1910. *SE* 11:165-175.

"'Wild' Psycho-Analysis." 1910. *SE* 11:221-227.

"Psycho-Analytic Notes on an Autobiographical Account of a Case of Paranoia (Dementia Paranoides)." 1911. *SE* 12:9-82.

"Formulations on the Two Principles of Mental Functioning." 1911. *SE* 12:218-226.

"On the Universal Tendency to Debasement in the Sphere of Love (Contributions to the Psychology of Love II)." 1912. *SE* 11:179-190.

"Types of Onset of Neurosis." 1912. *SE* 12:231-238.

Totem and Taboo: Some Points of Agreement Between the Mental Lives of Savages and Neurotics. 1913 (1912-1913). *SE* 13:1-161.

"The Claims of Psycho-Analysis to Scientific Interest." 1913. *SE* 13:165-190.

"The Moses of Michelangelo." 1914. *SE* 13:211-238.

On the History of the Psycho-Analytic Movement. 1914. *SE* 14:7-66.

"On Narcissism: An Introduction." 1914. *SE* 14:73-102.

"Instincts and Their Vicissitudes." 1915. *SE* 14:117-140.

"Repression." 1915. *SE* 14:146-158.

"The Unconscious." 1915. *SE* 14:166-204.

Introductory Lectures on Psycho-Analysis. 1916-1917 (1915-1917). *SE* 15:15-239; *SE* 16:243-463.

"From the History of an Infantile Neurosis." 1918 (1914). *SE* 17:7-122.

"A Difficulty in the Path of Psycho-Analysis." 1917. *SE* 17:137-144.

"Lines of Advance in Psycho-Analytic Therapy." 1919 (1918). *SE* 17:159-168.

"'A Child Is Being Beaten': A Contribution to the Study of the Origin of Sexual Perversions." 1919. *SE* 17:179-204.

"Preface to Reik's *Ritual: Psycho-Analytic Studies.*" 1919. *SE* 17:259-263.

Beyond the Pleasure Principle. 1920. *SE* 18:7-64.

"The Psychogenesis of a Case of Homosexuality in a Woman." 1920. *SE* 18:147-172.

Group Psychology and the Analysis of the Ego. 1921. *SE* 18:69-143.

"Psycho-Analysis and Telepathy." 1941 (1921). *SE* 18:177-193.

"Dreams and Telepathy." 1922. *SE* 18:197-220.

"Two Encyclopaedia Articles." 1923 (1922). *SE* 18:235-259.

"A Seventeenth-Century Demonological Neurosis." 1923 (1922). *SE* 19:72-105.

The Ego and the Id. 1923. *SE* 19:12-66.

"The Infantile Genital Organization (An Interpolation into the Theory of Sexuality)." 1923. *SE* 19:141-145.

"A Short Account of Psycho-Analysis." 1924 (1923). *SE* 19:191-209.

"The Economic Problem of Masochism." 1924. *SE* 19:159-170.

"The Dissolution of the Oedipus Complex." 1924. *SE* 19:173-179.

"The Resistances to Psycho-Analysis." 1925 (1924). *SE* 19:213-222.

An Autobiographical Study. 1925 (1924). *SE* 20:7-74.

"Negation." 1925. *SE* 19:235-239.

"Some Psychical Consequences of the Anatomical Distinction Between the Sexes." 1925. *SE* 19:248-258.

Inhibitions, Symptoms, and Anxiety. 1926 (1925). *SE* 20:87-174.

The Question of Lay Analysis: Conversations with an Impartial Person. 1926. *SE* 20:183-258.

The Future of an Illusion. 1927. *SE* 21:5-56.

"Humour." 1927. *SE* 21:161-166.

"A Religious Experience." 1928 (1927). *SE* 21:169-172.

"Dostoevsky and Parricide." 1928 (1927). *SE* 21:177-196.

Civilization and Its Discontents. 1930 (1929). *SE* 21:64-145.

"Female Sexuality." 1931. *SE* 21:225-243.

"The Acquisition and Control of Fire." 1932 (1931). *SE* 22:187-193.

New Introductory Lectures on Psycho-Analysis. 1933 (1932). *SE* 22:5-182.

Moses and Monotheism: Three Essays. 1939 (1934-1938). *SE* 23:7-137.

"Analysis Terminable and Interminable." 1937. *SE* 23:216-253.

"Lou Andreas-Salomé." 1937. *SE* 23:297-298.

An Outline of Psycho-Analysis. 1940 (1938). *SE* 23:144-207.

"Splitting of the Ego in the Process of Defence." 1940 (1938). *SE* 23:275-278.

"Findings, Ideas, Problems." 1941 (1938). *SE* 23:299-300.

Other Primary Sources

Bonaparte, Marie, Anna Freud, and Ernst Kris, eds. *The Origins of Psycho-Analysis. Letters to Wilhelm Fliess, Drafts and Notes: 1887-1902.* Translated by Eric Mosbacher and James Strachey. New York: Basic Books, 1954.

Freud, Ernst L., ed. *The Letters of Sigmund Freud.* Selected by Ernst L. Freud. Translated by Tania and James Stern. New York: Basic Books, 1960; Harper & Row, Colophon Books, 1960.

————. *The Letters of Sigmund Freud and Arnold Zweig.* Translated by Elaine and William Robson-Scott. A Helen and Kurt Wolff Book. New York: Harcourt, Brace and World, 1970.

Freud, Sigmund. Introduction to *Thomas Woodrow Wilson, Twenty-Eighth President of the United States: A Psychological Study,* by Sigmund Freud and William C. Bullitt. Boston: Houghton Mifflin, 1967; Cambridge: Riverside Press, 1967.

————. Letter to Dr. Carl Müller-Braunschweig, July 21, 1935. In "Freud and Female Sexuality: A Previously Unpublished Letter," by Donald L. Burnham. *Psychiatry* 34, no. 3 (1971):328-329.

McGuire, William, ed. *The Freud/Jung Letters: The Correspondence Between Sigmund Freud and C. G. Jung.* Translated by Ralph Manheim and R. F. C. Hull. Bollingen Series 94. Princeton: Princeton University Press, 1974.

Meng, Heinrich, and Ernst L. Freud, eds. *Psycho-Analysis and Faith: The Letters of Sigmund Freud and Oskar Pfister.* Translated by Eric Mosbacher. International Psychoanalytical Library, no. 59. London: The Hogarth Press and the Institute of Psycho-Analysis, 1963.

Nunberg, Herman, and Ernst Federn, eds. *Minutes of the Vienna Psychoanalytic Society, Volume II: 1908-1910.* Translated by M. Nunberg. New York: International Universities Press, 1967.

Pfeiffer, Ernst, ed. *Sigmund Freud and Lou Andreas-Salomé Letters.* Translated by William and Elaine Robson-Scott. A Helen and Kurt Wolff Book. New York: Harcourt Brace Jovanovich, 1966.

Selected Secondary Sources

Berger, Peter L. "Towards a Sociological Understanding of Psychoanalysis." *Social Research* 32, no. 1 (1965):26-41.

Binswanger, Ludwig. "Freud's Conception of Man in Light of Anthropology." In *Being-in-the-World: Selected Papers of Ludwig Binswanger.* Translated with an introduction by Jacob Needleman. New York: Basic Books, 1963; Harper & Row, Torchbook edition, 1963. Pp. 149-181.

Birdwhistell, Ray L. "Masculinity and Femininity as Display." In *Kinesics and Context: Essays on Body Motion and Communication.* Conduct and Communication, edited by Erving Goffman and Dell Hymes, no. 2. Philadelphia: University of Pennsylvania Press, 1970. Pp. 39-46.

Boyers, Robert, ed. *Psychological Man.* New York: Harper & Row, Colophon Books, 1975.

Broverman, Inge K., Donald M. Broverman, Frank E. Clarkson, Paul S. Rosenkrantz, and Susan R. Vogel. "Sex-Role Stereotypes and Clinical Judgments of Mental Health." *Journal of Consulting and Clinical Psychology* 34, no. 1 (1970):1-7.

Brown, Norman O. *Life Against Death: The Psychoanalytical Meaning of History.* Middletown, Conn.: Wesleyan University Press, 1959; paper edition, 1970.

Chodorow, Nancy. *The Reproduction of Mothering: Psychoanalysis and the Sociology of Gender.* Berkeley, Los Angeles, and London: University of California Press, 1978.

Clark, Ronald W. *Freud: The Man and the Cause: A Biography.* New York: Random House, 1980.

Connerton, Paul. Introduction to *Critical Sociology: Selected Readings.* Edited by Paul Connerton. Penguin Modern Sociology Series. Tom Burns, general editor. Harmondsworth, Middlesex, Eng.: Penguin Books, 1976. Pp. 11-39.

Cuddihy, John Murray. *The Ordeal of Civility: Freud, Marx, Lévi-Strauss, and the Jewish Struggle with Modernity.* New York: Basic Books, 1974.

De Beauvoir, Simone. *The Second Sex.* Translated and edited by H.M. Parshley. New York: Alfred A. Knopf, 1953.

Ellis, Havelock. *Man and Woman: A Study of Human Secondary Sexual Characters.* 5th ed., revised. New York: Charles Scribner's Sons, 1914.

Ellman, Mary. *Thinking About Women.* New York: Harcourt Brace Jovanovich, Harvest Book, 1968.

Freud, Martin. *Glory Reflected: Sigmund Freud, Man and Father.* London: Angus & Robertson, 1957.

Fromm, Erich. *Psychoanalysis and Religion.* New Haven: Yale University Press, 1950.

————. *Sigmund Freud's Mission: An Analysis of His Personality and Influence.* New York: Harper & Row, Colophon Books, 1959.

Glock, Charles Y., and Phillip E. Hammond, eds. *Beyond the Classics? Essays in the Scientific Study of Religion.* New York: Harper & Row, Torchbook edition, 1973.

Heller, Judith Bernays. "Freud's Mother and Father: A Memoir." *Commentary* 21 (May 1956):418-421.

Homans, Peter. *Theology After Freud: An Interpretive Inquiry.* New York and Indianapolis: Bobbs-Merrill, 1970.

Horney, Karen. "The Flight from Womanhood: The Masculinity Complex in Women as Viewed by Men and Women." 1926. In *Feminine Psychology.* Edited and with an introduction by Harold Kelman. New York: Norton, 1967. Pp. 54-70.

Hughes, H. Stuart. *Consciousness and Society: The Reconstruction of European Social Thought, 1890-1930.* New York: Alfred A. Knopf and Random House, 1958; Vintage edition, 1958.

Jacoby, Russell. *Social Amnesia: A Critique of Conformist Psychology from Adler to Laing.* Boston: Beacon Press, 1975.

Jahoda, Marie. *Freud and the Dilemmas of Psychology.* New York: Basic Books, 1977.

James, William. *The Varieties of Religious Experience: A Study in Human Nature.* New York and London: Longmans, Green, 1902; New York: New American Library, Mentor Book, 1958.

Jones, Ernest. "Early Female Sexuality." 1935. In his *Papers on Psychoanalysis.* Boston: Beacon Press, 1961. Pp. 485-495.

————. *The Life and Work of Sigmund Freud.* 3 vols. New York: Basic Books, 1953-1957.

Jones, Jack. "Five Versions of 'Psychological Man': A Critical Analysis." In *Psychological Man*. Edited by Robert Boyers. New York: Harper & Row, Colophon Books, 1975. Pp. 57-84.

Kardiner, Abraham. *My Analysis with Freud: Reminiscences.* New York: Norton, 1977.

Klein, George S. "Freud's Two Theories of Sexuality." In *Psychology Versus Metapsychology: Psychoanalytic Essays in Memory of George S. Klein.* Edited by Merton M. Gill and Philip S. Holzman. *Psychological Issues* 9, no. 4, monograph 36. New York: International Universities Press, 1976. Pp. 72-120.

Klein, Viola. *The Feminine Character: History of an Ideology.* Introduction by Karl Mannheim. London: Routledge & Kegan Paul, 1946; reprint edition, Urbana: University of Illinois Press, 1971.

Küng, Hans. *Freud and the Problem of God.* Translated by Edward Quinn. New Haven: Yale University Press, 1979.

Lacan, Jacques. *The Four Fundamental Concepts of Psycho-Analysis.* Edited by Jacques-Alain Miller. Translated by Alan Sheridan. New York: Norton, 1978.

————. *The Language of the Self: The Function of Language in Psychoanalysis.* Translated with notes and commentary by Anthony Wilden. New York: Dell, Delta Book, 1968.

Laplanche, J., and J.-B. Pontalis. *The Language of Psycho-Analysis.* Translated by Donald Nicholson-Smith. Introduction by Daniel Lagache. New York: Norton, 1973.

Maccoby, Eleanor E., and Carol N. Jacklin. *The Psychology of Sex Differences.* Stanford: Stanford University Press, 1974.

Mannoni, O[ctave]. *Freud.* Translated by Renaud Bruce. New York: Random House, 1971; Vintage edition, 1974.

Marcuse, Herbert. *Eros and Civilization: A Philosophical Inquiry into Freud.* Boston: Beacon Press, 1962; New York: Random House, Vintage edition, 1962.

————. "Freedom and Freud's Theory of Instincts." In *Five Lectures: Psychoanalysis, Politics, and Utopia.* Translated by Jeremy J. Shapiro and Shierry M. Weber. Boston: Beacon Press, 1970. Pp. 1-43.

Miller, Casey, and Kate Swift. *Words and Women: New Language in New Times.* Garden City, N.Y.: Anchor Press/Doubleday, 1976.

Mitchell, Juliet. "On Freud and the Distinction Between the Sexes." In *Women and Analysis: Dialogues on Psychoanalytic Views of Femininity.* Edited by Jean Strouse. New York: Viking, Grossman, 1974. Pp. 27-36.

————. *Psychoanalysis and Feminism.* New York: Random House, Pantheon Book, 1974.

Money, John, and Anke A. Ehrhardt. *Man and Woman, Boy and Girl: The Differentiation and Dimorphism of Gender Identity from Conception to Maturity.* Baltimore and London: Johns Hopkins University Press, 1972.

Nagera, Humberto. *Female Sexuality and the Oedipus Complex.* New York: Jason Aronson, 1975.

Oakley, Ann. *Sex, Gender, and Society.* London: Maurice Temple Smith, 1972; reprint New York: Harper & Row, Colophon Books, 1972.

Pruyser, Paul W. "Sigmund Freud and His Legacy: Psychoanalytic Psychology of Religion." In *Beyond the Classics? Essays in the Scientific Study of Religion.* Edited by Charles Y. Glock and Phillip S. Hammond. New York: Harper & Row, Torchbook edition, 1973. Pp. 243-290.

Rainey, Reuben M. *Freud as Student of Religion: Perspectives on the Background and Development of His Thought.* AAR Dissertation Series 7. Missoula, Mont.: Scholars Press, 1975.

Ricoeur, Paul. *Freud and Philosophy: An Essay on Interpretation.* Translated by Denis Savage. New Haven: Yale University Press, 1970.

————. "Psychoanalysis and the Movement of Contemporary Culture." Translated by Willis Domingo. In *The Conflict of Interpretations: Essays in Hermeneutics.* Edited by Don Ihde. Evanston, Ill.: Northwestern University Press, 1974. Pp. 121-159.

Rieff, Philip. *Freud: The Mind of the Moralist.* New York: Viking Press, 1959; Garden City, N.Y.: Doubleday, Anchor edition, 1961; Chicago: University of Chicago Press, Phoenix edition, 1979.

————. "Freud's Contribution to Political Philosophy." Ph.D. dissertation, University of Chicago, 1954.

Robert, Marthe. *From Oedipus to Moses: Freud's Jewish Identity.* Translated by Ralph Manheim. Garden City, N.Y.: Anchor Press/Doubleday, 1976.

Robinson, Paul A. *The Freudian Left: Wilhelm Reich, Geza Róheim, Herbert Marcuse.* New York: Harper & Row, 1969.

Rosaldo, Michelle Zimbalist, and Louise Lamphere, eds. *Woman, Culture, and Society.* Stanford: Stanford University Press, 1974.

Sayers, Dorothy L. "The Human-Not-Quite-Human." In her *Unpopular Opinions.* London: Victor Gallanz, 1946. Pp. 116-127. Reprinted in *Are Women Human?* Introduction by Mary M. Shideler. Grand Rapids, Mich.: Eerdmans, 1971. Pp. 37-47.

Schafer, Roy. *A New Language for Psychoanalysis.* New Haven: Yale University Press, 1976.

————. "Problems in Freud's Psychology of Women." *Journal of the American Psychoanalytic Association* 22 (1974):459-485.

Schopenhauer, Arthur. "Religion: A Dialogue." 1851. In *Arthur Schopenhauer: Essays from the Parerga and Paralipomena.* Translated by T. Bailey Saunders. London: George Allen & Unwin, 1951. Pp. 5-39.

Schroyer, Trent. *The Critique of Domination: The Origins and Development of Critical Theory.* Boston: Beacon Press, 1973.

Simmel, Georg. "Das Relative und das Absolute im Geschlechter-Problem." In *Philosophische Kultur: Gesammelte Essais.* Philosophisch-soziologische Bücherei, Band 27, Leipzig: Verlag von Dr. Werner Klinkhardt, 1911. Pp. 67-100.

————. "Weibliche Kultur." In *Philosophische Kultur: Gesammelte Essais.* Philosophisch-soziologische Bücherei, Band 27. Leipzig: Verlag von Dr. Werner Klinkhardt, 1911. Pp. 278-319.

Stannard, David E. *Shrinking History: On Freud and the Failure of Psychohistory.* New York: Oxford University Press, 1980.

Stoller, Robert J. *Sex and Gender,* Volume 1: *The Development of Masculinity and Femininity.* New York: Jason Aronson, 1968.

Strouse, Jean, ed. *Women and Analysis: Dialogues on Psychoanalytic Views of Femininity.* New York: Viking, Grossman, 1974.

Sulloway, Frank J. *Freud: Biologist of the Mind: Beyond the Psychoanalytic Legend.* New York: Basic Books, 1979.

Trilling, Lionel. *Freud and the Crisis of Our Culture.* Boston: Beacon Press, 1955.

————. *Sincerity and Authenticity.* Cambridge: Harvard University Press, 1971.

Vaughter, Reesa M. "Review Essay: Psychology." *Signs* 2, no. 1 (1976):120-146.

Weinstein, Fred, and Gerald M. Platt. *The Wish to Be Free: Society, Psyche, and Value Change.* Berkeley and Los Angeles: University of California Press, 1969.

Wilden, Anthony. "Lacan and the Discourse of the Other." In *The Language of the Self: The Function of Language in Psychoanalysis* by Jacques Lacan. Translated with notes and commentary by Anthony Wilden. New York: Dell, Delta Book, 1968. Pp. 159-311.

Index

active-passive polarity, 23n, 90, 95, 117, 119, 124, 135
activity, 23n; and gender, 122-126; of instinctual aims, 20, 122-124; intrapsychic, 61; and masculinity, 20, 129; and sex distinction, 117, 119; in world, 82, 84, 99. *See also* passivity
Adler, Alfred, 23n, 117-118, 126
Akhenaten (Amenophis IV, Pharaoh), 171, 172-173, 175, 190
ambivalence, 51-52, 177; toward father, 156, 158, 184, 186; of religious psychology, 199
Amun (religion), 150, 172-173, 174, 190
anal stage, 65, 89-90
Ananke (Necessity), 21, 75, 82, 86, 101, 104, 192, 193. *See also* necessity
Andreas-Salomé, Lou, 36, 98, 161
animism, 73-75, 147
anti-Semitism, 146
anxiety, 101, 156
asceticism, 107, 186, 192; in neurotics, 83
Aten (religion), 150, 171-173, 190
atonement, 187
authority, 15, 168; paternal, 15, 16, 40, 48, 49, 86-87, 89, 92-93, 94, 96, 129, 135, 138, 144, 154, 159, 164, 182, 194; religious, 154; and superego, 64
autoerotism, 65

Bachofen, Johann Jacob, 77, 78
Binswanger, Ludwig, 43
bisexuality, 20, 94, 113, 117, 124, 136, 137; Freud's theory of, 125, 127
biology, distinguished from nature in psychoanalysis, 43. *See also* psychoanalysis and biology
Brown, Norman O., 10, 12, 41, 65

cannibalism, 152; of primal father, 184

castration: anxiety, 93, 97, 101; as punishment, 92, 93; threat of, 88, 96, 98, 118
castration complex, 56, 89, 93-97, 100, 102, 111, 132-133, 195; in girls, 119, 129; overcoming of, 56. *See also* penis, envy of
cathexis, 66n
Catholicism, 150, 151
censor, the, 57, 58
Christian believer(s), 86, 144, 158, 167-168, 192, 196
Christianity, 143, 150, 170-172, 187-193; beliefs of, 178, 192; Freud's evaluation of, 162-165, 191-192; Freud's psychology of, 4, 22, 158-164; as illusion, 2, 160-162, 195-197. *See also* civilization; illusion; religion
circumcision, 173, 182
civilization: assets of, 153-154; Christian, 143, 154, 155, 165; definition of, 13, 152; demands of, 48, 58; enemies of, 110-111, 164; future of, 152-154; hostility to, 152; level of, 75; as masculine, 111; patriarchal, 16, 18, 51, 97; as renunciation of instinct, 19, 58, 103, 158, 200; and sexuality in conflict, 58, 88, 111; stages of, 6, 56, 66, 73-80, 179; women's antagonism to, 20, 111. *See also* cultural achievements; cultural ideal; culture; society
Civilization and Its Discontents, Sigmund Freud, 13, 24, 43n, 81, 102, 156
conscience, 102
consciousness, as psychical quality, 44
constancy principle, 56, 56n
conversion (religious), 160
Copernicus, 76
critical principle, Freud's. *See* renunciation
criticism, 2, 26-29, 200; definitions of, 26, 28; and description in Freud, 13, 15, 16. *See also* femininity; gender; religion; renunciation